The Philosophy
of
Christian Education

by

PIERRE J. MARIQUE

Professor of History and Philosophy of Education
Fordham University

GREENWOOD PRESS, PUBLISHERS
WESTPORT, CONNECTICUT

Originally published in 1939
by Prentice-Hall, Inc., New York

First Greenwood Reprinting 1970

Library of Congress Catalogue Card Number 70-109781

SBN 8371-4271-7

Printed in the United States of America

To
The Right Reverend
MONSIGNOR JOHN F. BRADY, A.M., M.D., D.D.
Educator and Friend
This Book
Is Gratefully
Dedicated

Preface

THE TITLE itself serves notice that the philosophy of education herein outlined is emphatically antifaddist. The author wishes to set forth and stress those principles that have guided the best educational thought of the past and with the vigor of youth are facing the problems of the present.

Like the philosophy of life from which it springs and the system of education for which it provides inspiration and guidance, the philosophy of Christian education is first of all essentially religious, because it is religion (meaning here, of course, Christianity) that reveals to philosophy the true goal of life and, by the same token, of all education, together with its full significance for the individual and society. And through this revelation of the supreme end of human life, religion at once solves the problem of life values and educational aims because their one true norm is their relation to the supreme end of life.

The philosophy of Christian education is catholic, that is, universal in the widest, most comprehensive meaning of the term. It is not an educational philosophy devised for one age or nation or class or form of government. Its appeal is to all men, irrespective of the circumstances of time and country, of racial or political or social distinctions. It is today, in all essentials, what it was nineteen hundred years ago; it is today, in any one country, what it is in any other country.

The philosophy of Christian education is essentially religious and catholic; with all due consideration for political, or social, or economic changes, it is also essentially traditional, that is, closely related to history, particularly the history of education.

The chief objectives of this book are:

(a) To explain the essentials of education in the light of the Christian philosophy of life.

(b) To show that the Christian conception of education is at once comprehensive, liberal, and democratic.

(c) To use the Christian philosophy of education as the true norm in passing judgment on any philosophy of education.

Every essential phase of education is taken in. More specifically:

Chapter I is concerned with the nature and scope of the philosophy of education, its relation to the science and history of education and the characteristic features of the Christian philosophy of education. Chapter II is concerned with a brief critical examination of a few non-Christian philosophies and their educational consequences. The purpose is here two-fold: to illustrate the close relation between any given philosophy and its corresponding system of education; to show the antagonism to Christian education of non-Christian philosophies. The exposition of the Christian philosophy of education is then taken up, first from the viewpoint of society, second from that of the individual, the latter viewpoint leading to the following subdivisions: physical, intellectual, aesthetic, moral, and religious education. To this examination from the individual viewpoint, there is prefixed a chapter on educational aims and ideals. The survey of the philosophy of Christian education closes with a brief consideration of teacher training, and educational agencies. All through the book, the teachings of accepted Catholic philosophy are the guiding posts; now and then, in order to avoid possible misunderstandings, they are briefly stated by way of introduction to the treatment of some subject. To most chapters have been appended lists of topics, which, it is hoped, will be of some assistance in a more thorough treatment of the subject than the limitation of a single chapter would warrant.

The book is primarily intended to be a convenient text for Catholic normal schools and students of education in colleges and graduate schools, but it is hoped that its treatment of the philosophy of education will also appeal to professors and students in non-Catholic institutions still conducted in the spirit of the Christian philosophy of life.

The author wishes to acknowledge his grateful indebtedness to the late Reverend Jaime Castiello, S.J., for much inspiring criticism and the revision of the whole text; to the late Reverend Walter G. Summers, S.J., for many useful suggestions. He also wishes to express his sincere gratitude to the Reverend Gerald G. Walsh, S.J., Professor of History at Fordham University (Graduate School), for his careful reading of the entire manuscript and for many illuminating comments; to his daughter, Miss Marie T. Marique, M.A., for many stimulating suggestions and much help in the final preparation of the volume.

Feast of the Immaculate Conception, 1938.

P. J. M.

Editor's Introduction

TEACHER education is comparatively new, since the assumption was long held that teachers "were born and not made." But, as the demand for public education extended, with a resulting increased attendance of children in the schools, it soon became obvious that teacher education was necessary. The satirizing of schools and teachers by Dickens and others in the nineteenth century hastened the acceptance of the point of view that teachers should be educated for their jobs. Horace Mann led the crusade in America, and, as a result, the first normal school for the training of teachers in America was established. From this beginning, the education of teachers has become a recognized function; today every state has its teachers colleges, every university has its department or school of education, and practically every arts college has courses in education.

Moreover, fundamental in every teacher-education program, the philosophy of education is required as a basic subject and was one of the first subjects introduced as a part of a teacher-training program. Therefore, philosophy or philosophy of education has had a long and changing history as part of teacher preparation. In the century of teacher education in the United States, the most significant fact about the philosophy of education is its changing character and emphasis, for it has followed the evolution of the discipline out of which it grows and from which it gets its emphasis—that is, philosophy.

Space, however, does not permit the discussion of the history of philosophy in this century, but it is necessary to note that the emphasis has been at various times Idealism, Realism, Naturalism, Pragmatism, and Experimentalism, with the experimentalists gaining the dominant and all but exclusive emphasis in the twentieth century. The scientific movement of the mid-nineteenth century provided the inspiration and the basis for the experimentalists, and Dewey, the chief of this school, has practically dominated the thinking of public-school educators of modern times, although idealists have been heard by such outstanding representatives as Horne, but these have been "voices crying in the wilderness." Experimentalism has held sway.

At the present time, however, a growing reaction against the extreme emphasis of the experimentalists is to be noted, and an increasing number of voices is being raised—often by distinguished Catholic philosophers. The author of this book is one of these. Dr. Marique has represented at its best the Catholic point of view of Christian education, and naturally an idealistic emphasis. Obviously, there is truth and reason in all these points of view. The significance of this book, however, is that it represents a point of view, presented at its best, too long neglected in the philosophy that has almost dominated educational thinking in the twentieth century.

E. GEORGE PAYNE

Contents

CONTENTS

CONTENTS

CHAPTER I

Introduction: The Nature, Scope, and Function of the Philosophy of Education

The Various Meanings of the Term "Education"

Like the term *school,* the term *education* has been used and is used today with various meanings. In the broadest sense of the term, education is a life-long process, now conscious, now semiconscious or unconscious. The process begins with the beginning of life, even before the birth of the child, for the influence of the mother's life is constantly brought to bear on the unborn child, increasing or decreasing, be it ever so slightly, the capacity for education with which it will start in life. In infancy and childhood the process is mainly confined to the home: the rearing of the infant by its mother, the learning of the mother tongue, and the influence of the home environment upon the child. Gradually, however, the process extends beyond the family circle, gaining in breadth and fullness all the while with the widening of the individual's environment, his coming under the influence of the multitudinous forms of civilization. Every situation in life is in some way an educative agency. Adults, like children, are constantly influenced by

1

their environment; more or less consciously they adopt the opinions, manners, and sympathies of those among whom they move; they become refined among the refined, and rude among the rude. Life, the whole of it, is a great school.

In the narrower, common sense of the term, education is thought of, not as life, but as a preparation for life furthered by several educative agencies, one of which is the school. Differences in the conception of life will naturally lead to different conceptions of education. If, for example, life is conceived as an end unto itself, education can have no better aim than to fit one for the conquest and enjoyment of what this life can yield. If, on the other hand, this life is conceived as a preparation for a higher supernatural life, whatever temporal aims can be assigned to education must ever be subordinated to the ultimate end of human life.

Further differences in the meaning of education will arise, as history abundantly shows us, from class distinctions, differences in national genius and ideals, foreign influences, different conceptions of man's nature, and of the individual's relation to the state. As late as the 19th century, class distinction was everywhere a determining factor in the kind of education the individual should receive. The meaning of education for the members of a given class of people was, in some respects, entirely different from its meaning for the members of another class. The distinction still holds today, though in a less degree, even in some of our modern democracies. In practice, if not in theory, the education of the children of the poor is far more limited in scope and promises than that of the children of the well to do and wealthy.

The national or racial genius and ideals, national tendencies at different times, and foreign influences are also responsible for differences in education. In ancient Sparta, as in ancient Athens, the practice of a trade or profession was looked down upon as smacking of slavery. Vocational preparation, therefore, could not be considered a part of the free man's education. In both city states, too, military training was an important phase of education. There, however, the similarity stopped. In Sparta, education had no higher aim than to produce a perfect soldier in the service of a communistic military state. The aim of Athenian education, on the other hand, was to refine intellectual life, to prepare the freeborn youth for an active participation in the rich, manifold, political, social, cultural life of his city state.

The history of Roman culture and education shows us one of the most striking illustrations of foreign influence on national culture and education. Previous to the third century B.C. there was hardly any culture worth mentioning in Rome, and schoolwork, whenever it existed, did not proceed beyond the elementary stage. But under the influence of Hellenism, which began to be felt in the third century, a gradual transformation took place, and, by the beginning of the Christian Era, Rome could boast of a culture comparable, in some respects, to that of Greece. Roman education, too, was then thoroughly Hellenized. In method, content, and aim, it differed no less from its earlier counterpart than did Athenian from Spartan education. In one respect, however, the national genius continued to assert itself. While accepting the Greek distinction between liberal and vocational education and, like the Greeks, considering a liberal education as an ornament of life, the Romans insisted, more than the Greeks, on the mastery of language and great stores of knowledge as the net profit of liberal studies. The ideally educated Roman is described for us in Cicero's *De Oratore* and Quintilian's *De Institutione Oratoria*—as the orator, the man that possesses the philosopher's knowledge, both of things and human nature, together with a mastery of language; and thus he can turn his knowledge to practical ends by influencing his fellowmen.

The more radical differences in the meaning of education, however, are not due to differences in national genius and ideals or foreign influence, but to different conceptions of the nature of man and his relation to society and state. If, as Rousseau and his followers contend, human nature is essentially good, then education is a work of freedom; the teacher's task in the main will be limited to removing, so far as it can be done, whatever may hamper the work of the great teacher, that is, nature. If, on the other hand, we see in man a mixture of much evil and some good, education will have to be what it has been for ages: a work both of authority and nature, repressing undesirable dispositions and encouraging, correcting, and improving the good ones.

Again, materialism will impart to education a vastly different meaning from that which it will receive from Christian spiritualism. Man, says the materialist, is but one of the products of the blind forces of nature to which, some day, he will return. Human life is entirely subject to the laws of physics, chemistry, mechanics and biology. Social problems are essentially problems of economics: questions of wages, hours of work, housing conditions, pauperism and the like. Education, then, should be concerned with the body, should stress the study of the sciences of nature, and should be a preparation for economic life. Over against this materialistic conception of life and education stands

Christianity, teaching us that if man's body does perish, his spirit will continue to live; that he is accountable to an Almighty Lord and Maker, not only for his deeds, but for his every thought and feeling. It is needless to insist on the consequences of these doctrines for education and the irreconciliable differences between the materialistic and Christian conceptions of education.

Finally, as a source of differences in the meaning of education, there is the question of the state-individual relations. Does the State exist for the individual, or is it the individual that exists for the State? Does the child belong to its parents or does it belong to the State? Does education pertain to the State in the same way it pertains to the family and the Church? What are the respective rights and obligations of the Church, the family and the State in matters of education? Obviously, differences in the answers to those and kindred questions will carry differences in the meaning of education.

In a still more restricted sense than the above, education may be, and commonly is today, viewed from the standpoint of the school, the one institution whose specific task is to assist in the educative process. By the school is meant here, of course, the whole school system, from the kindergarten to the university and professional schools. If the school system is well organized, the meaning of education in any given stage is determined not only by the philosophy governing the system as a whole, but also by the particular conditions and requirements of that stage. It would not be correct then to say, for example, that the meaning of education in the American elementary school is identical with that of the high school or college; still less, with that of the professional school.

This brief examination of the meaning of education leads us to the obvious conclusion that the character of education changes with time and country, that different philosophies of life will inevitably lead to different conceptions of education. Shall we then say, Sophist-like, that there is in education nothing permanent, essential, and fundamental, except perhaps its ever changing character. Such is the contention of those sponsoring the modern movement which goes by the names Progressive Education, School of the Future, New Education, and the like. According to them there is no universal principle or ideal of education. Man and civilization are a product of evolution. Like nature, to which they belong, they are in a perpetual flux, a perpetual becoming. How could we, under such conditions, think of universal principles and ideals? The best we can do is to gather facts, observe, and experiment, in order to reach some theory or law that works under the conditions of present-day civilization. With the passing of those conditions, other working laws will have to be found and tried. Our answer to this contention is and should be a most emphatic "No." Variations in education are bound to occur as a consequence of variations in time and locality. But those variations are mere accidents. Faith, tradition, and reason tell us that beneath the diversity of appearances there are in education as in man, essential, permanent, and fundamental elements, the real, vital issues in educational theory and practice and those with which the philosophy of Christian education is primarily concerned.

The Various Meanings of the Term "Science"

Subjectively speaking, in other words, from the standpoint of the knowing subject, the term *science* (*scio,* I know) means certitude in the possession of truth, a state of mind opposed to ignorance. Halfway between those two poles stand doubt—in which the mind hesitates between affirmation and denial—and opinion—a belief mixed with doubt. Science, however, is more commonly defined, from the objective viewpoint, as a system of truths on any given subject; a system, that is, a body of knowledge whose elements have been arranged according to one and the same principle and in such a way that there is a clear, logical progression or regression from one item to another; geometry, for instance, is such a body of knowledge concerning spacial magnitudes.

In its most general sense, science, like philosophy, is the explanation of things, a search after the reasons of things, of which there are two kinds: causes and laws. Causes answer the question "why"; laws answer the question "how." Thus, the cause of a natural phenomenon is the force that produces it; the law of that phenomenon is the constant manner in which it happens—the constant relation between two successive stages of the phenomenon. More explicitly, however, we should speak, not of two but of four reasons which help us understand and explain things; cause, law, end, and principle. A cause is a reason of things with reference to some effect flowing therefrom; a law refers to a succession of facts, an end to the means that we use in order to reach it, and a principle to the consequences it may involve.

The last type of the reasons of things is one of the characteristics of the abstract sciences. What is to be explained in those sciences is not a succession of facts, such as we have in physics and chemistry, but some concept, some definition or theorem, from which are derived, or rather developed, a number of consequences. An abstract science, for example, algebra, might then be defined as a body of necessary relations between some truths we call principles and others that are their necessary consequences. We sometimes refer to those relations as laws (for example, the laws of geometry, of mechanics), but there is this difference between such laws and those of physics: that the first express a relation of coexistence, whereas the second express one of succession. The corollaries developed from a given theorem are contained in, coexistent with, that theorem. Not so with the facts of nature, which follow one another in chronological sequence. The relation of coexistence may, of course, also be found in the natural sciences. What we call a type of living organism may be thought of as a principle involving a certain number of consequences or, as we commonly say, characteristics inherent in that organism.

The foregoing remarks on the nature of science have made it evident, it is hoped, that not all knowledge is scientific. A man may know, for example, that a certain kind of water will be a contributing factor in the cure of a certain disease; another man knows why the water is an aid in the cure. In the first case, knowledge is said to be empirical, in the second, scientific. Empirical knowledge is limited to a mere registration of facts; scientific knowledge proceeds from fact to law, from effect to cause, from consequence to principle; it explains. Scientific knowledge, however, is not all of the same type. If it is confined to the direct, immediate causes and the laws governing phenomena, knowledge is said to be purely scientific or positivistic. When it reaches beyond immediate causes, it is said to be metaphysical. Thus, a scientific, positivistic explanation of heat will state the direct cause of the phenomenon and show

how it takes place. Should we go beyond these direct causes and laws of heat and inquire into the nature or origin of matter, we leave the province of the science of physics and enter that of its philosophy or metaphysics. Likewise, there is a science and a metaphysics of psychology. The first studies the facts of psychical life and their relations; the second is concerned with the spiritual essence of the soul and its consequences. Those two aspects of scientific inquiry are not exclusive but complementary of each other. After determining the immediate causes of phenomena, there still remains open the question of their ultimate causes, the "why" of the "why."

Each and every science has an object or subject matter of its own and a method or form adapted to the treatment of that object. Thus, the object of biology is organic life and its various manifestations; its method is observation and experimentation. Of the other important characteristics of science two should be mentioned here. Science is universal, in the sense that it is concerned with the general, permanent elements in things and individuals. It will study the fall of some particular body in order to determine the laws of falling bodies. It will examine the organism of a given animal in order to determine the general character of the genus or species to which it belongs. Psychology is interested in the laws or general character of psychical phenomena, physiology in the general character of functions in living organisms. Another essential characteristic of any science is connectedness. No amount of isolated facts or propositions constitutes a science. There must be system, coördination according to some directing principles; facts or propositions must form a well organized whole, a unit.

The ideal of scientific knowledge would be a synthesis of

all the particular sciences, a perfect, general knowledge of the universe as a whole and every one of its parts. Such knowledge, however, belongs to God alone. Man cannot reach it, though he strives after it through the particular sciences which coexist in universal science as distinct, though not isolated parts, in a whole. There is, then, no hard and fast boundary line between sciences. History shows that progress not only tends to make each science more distinct from every other, but, at the same time, to bring out more clearly their relations and mutual dependence. In physics, for instance, there are subjects that belong to the province of mathematics as well, or that of mechanics or chemistry or even physiology, as in the treatment of optics. Psychology is at some points closely related to physiology; history to geography, chronology, and many other sciences. Studies should, therefore, never be specialized in the strict sense of the term. Mastery in any one subject depends to a great extent on an adequate knowledge of related subjects.

The Various Classifications of the Sciences

Various classifications of the sciences have been suggested by philosophers and scientists. Here are a few, by way of illustration. Aristotle's classification is objective and three-fold: the theoretical sciences, which have truth, as such, for their object (mathematics, physics, and "first philosophy"); the practical sciences, which guide us in our actions (ethics, politics and economics); the poetical sciences, the object of which is the beautiful. Francis Bacon's classification, like Aristotle's, is threefold, but subjective, corresponding, says Bacon, to "the three faculties of the soul" (memory, imagination, and reason); history, which includes the history of literature, civil history and natural history; poetry; and philosophy, which he divides into natural theology, natural philosophy, and human philosophy. Auguste Comte divides the sciences into two groups: abstract, general sciences concerned with the discovery of laws (mathematics, astronomy, physics, chemistry, and biology); and the concrete, particular sciences that apply laws to beings or facts (for instance, natural history and pathology corresponding to biology). According to Herbert Spencer there are abstract sciences (logic, mathematics) concerned with relations; abstract-concrete sciences (mechanics, physics, and so on) concerned with phenomena; and concrete sciences (biology, sociology, and psychology) concerned with the study of beings. Spencer, like Comte, like all positivists, considers metaphysics as being outside the pale of science.

There is no classification of the sciences that is not open to some criticism, but some classifications are more satisfactory than others, which is also true of the countless curriculum arrangements that have been suggested and tried in the last few decades.

The following is the more common classification nowadays: mathematical sciences divided into pure or theoretical mathematics (arithmetic, algebra, geometry, calculus) and applied mathematics (astronomy, mechanics, mathematical physics); the natural sciences divided into physical, concerned with the general properties of matter (physics, chemistry) and the natural sciences commonly so called (geology, minerology, biology), dealing with inorganic or organic bodies; the social sciences, sometimes referred to as moral sciences or ethico-political sciences, subdividing into more or less arbitrary, overlapping groups as in the the preceding groups. They include such sciences as psychology, ethics, jurisprudence, theodicy, economics, history, philology, pedagogy, and so on. The sciences in the first two groups of this classification can be brought into a single group, the mathematical-natural sciences, because they all deal with some phase of the same subject, subhuman nature, whereas the social sciences are concerned with man and God. Whatever the mathematical-natural sciences and the social sciences have in common has been made clear, it is hoped, in the foregoing remarks on the meaning of science; there now remains to bring out their differences.

Differences Between the Mathematical-Natural Sciences and the Social Sciences

As stated above, the mathematical-natural sciences are concerned with matter, either inorganic or organic, whereas the social sciences, aside from theodicy and metaphysics, are concerned with man as a thinking, free agent. From this fundamental difference in the nature of their object, there arise between these two groups of sciences differences in the laws with which they deal and the methods they use. The laws of nature are formulas telling us of that which is, of that which is taking place; they are fatal, indicative, and never imperative. With the characteristics common to all those laws, however, go certain differences between the laws of mathematics and those of the natural sciences, properly so called. The laws of mathematics (and logic) express a necessity, both rational and empirical, that we realize at once in any such statement as: two quantities, respectively, equal to a third quantity are equal; that must be so, and, as a matter of fact, it is so. Such laws belong to the world of abstractions. They transcend facts and cannot be demonstrated through them, though facts, the data of experience, will help illustrate and fix a mathematical truth in the mind. The reason why mathematics is the exact science "par excellence" is not far to seek; its subject matter being altogether *a priori* determined, all the properties therein contained can be reached with certainty.

The laws of the natural sciences (physics, chemistry, and the like) merely express a necessity of fact, as, for instance, a free material body will of necessity fall. They express that which is, that which happens in the material world that we know, not that which must absolutely be, or happen; they are contingent; they can be conceived as being nonexistent or different in a different world. The history of natural sciences shows that the validity of their conclusions depends upon accuracy in observation and experimentation. Any error in the observation of the fact under consideration will automatically react upon the general law, and the detection of new data in the case will necessarily lead to new rules or principles or laws superseding others which for ages, perhaps, were considered scientific truths. Illustrations by the score of this fact could be cited from the history of astronomy, physics, chemistry, physiology, and medicine. Among the better known let us mention the substitution of the heliocentric for the Aristotelian planetary system; the discard of the principle that "nature abhors a vacuum"; blood circulation, superseding the old view of blood oscillation.

In order to reach that precision upon which rests the validity of scientific truth, the natural sciences have been led to appeal more and more to mathematics. Astronomy and mechanics led the way at an early date; then came geography and physics, much of which today can be considered a branch of applied mathematics; chemistry has its formulas and equations; meteorology uses barometers, thermometers, and other mathematical instruments; in physiology can be mentioned, among others, the application of mathematics to the study of the eye and the ear. The movement for mathematical precision in scientific investigation has extended even to the domain of the social sciences. Today economics, politics, and sociology have their statistics and graphs; experimental psychology has borrowed the methods of physics; pedagogy has its statistics and measurements with their graphs and equations. No serious objection could be made to the use of mathematics in the social sciences so long as it is restricted to the measurement of the physical or physiological phenomena that accompany life and mental states; but the use becomes wholly ridiculous when its purpose is to measure life or thought or will, all of which transcends the world of material quantity.

In striking contrast to the laws of nature stand the moral laws that govern man insofar as he is an intelligent free agent. The moral laws include: (a) the natural law, so called because it is an essential element in man's nature; it is the rule of conduct which is prescribed to us by the Creator in the constitution of the nature with which he has endowed us, or, in the words of St. Thomas, the rational creature's participation in the eternal law; (b) positive laws, which determine and explain the natural law. The laws of nature (subhuman nature) are the laws of necessity; they are fatal, inescapable; they are the laws governing the animal world; man, too, is subject to these laws, but only in such processes as blood circulation, breathing, and digestion, which take place automatically. The moral laws, on the other hand, express what ought to be; they are obligatory; they govern free agents; they command, but do not compel; we are bound to obey them under penalty of falling from the perfection of our estate as free, rational beings.

The mathematical-natural sciences and the social sciences not only differ in the nature of their object and laws, but also in the methods mostly resorted to in their advancement and teaching. Accuracy in definition and deductive reasoning is the keynote of mathematical method, whereas the natural sciences mostly depend on observation, experimentation, and induction. The social sciences being at once concerned with that which is and with that which ought to be, use, in turn, the rational and the experimental method. Through observation and induction they determine the laws governing the phenomena which they study. Then, deductively, they draw practical consequences from those laws. Thus, observation and induction lead us to the discovery and formulation of the laws governing economic life; then, in accordance with those laws and in the light of the moral law, we can deduce the measures to be taken to forestall economic disaster.

Aside from the foregoing general characteristics common to all sciences in a given group, there are details of method peculiar to each science. As a matter of fact, each one of them has its own particular method or methods, a detailed treatment of which obviously belongs to treatises on special methods. It has already been remarked that there is, at present, a widespread tendency to apply to the social sciences the methods used in the sciences of nature. The social and natural sciences have this in common: they deal with facts and phenomena, and they aim at the discovery and formulation of the laws and causes of the facts under consideration; they differ by all the differences that exist be tween the phenomena of physics and physiology on the one hand, and those of psychology and ethics on the other.

The Science of Education

Education was from the first and must ever remain essentially an art, the doing of something to attain a given end. To be educated, the individual must engage in certain activities in which he is assisted by others. But like agriculture, medicine, and engineering, in fact all the efficient arts of society, education ultimately falls back upon a science that receives assistance from a number of allied sciences, and places the art of teaching upon a rational basis. The science of education describes, analyzes, and criticizes the factors that enter into the actual process of education, factors of organization, administration, discipline, and instruction; of late, it has been very much given to experimentation, and the purpose of it all, as in the case of the physician or engineer or architect or lawyer, is to afford a basis for a critical comparison and for improvement, to raise the art of teaching above blind routine work, and to put the teacher into intelligent possession of the tools at his command.

The science of education is essentially a social science. The essential part of its program is concerned with the intellectual, moral, religious, aesthetic life of the rising generation, which is distinctly the subject matter of the social sciences. Questions of educational content and objectives, of methods and guidance, can not be intelligently treated, except in the light of culture, economic and social conditions of the time and nation, and that, too, by using the methods peculiar to the social sciences.

By some of its aspects, however, the science of education belongs in the mathematical, natural-science group. Problems of the purely material aspect of education (school building, lighting, ventilation, and seating arrangement), problems of physical education (physical defects, physical exercise, instruction in hygiene), problems of the physiological aspect of learning (length and succession of the teaching or study periods, fatigue, recreation) all relate the science of education to the natural sciences. The methods of treatment in dealing with those problems will be of the natural-science type, insofar as the facts under consideration are physical or physiological. The relations thus established with the natural sciences cannot fail to benefit the science of education. Far more important, however, are the relations with the social sciences, because, as it has already been stated, the science of education is essentially a social science, in fact, an offspring of sociology. The history of education, with its record of past educational views and theories, educational systems, curriculums, and methods, of their successes and failures, will help us understand existing conditions and it warns us not to be ever ready to expect new and startling discoveries in education. Closely related to the history and science of education are the histories of philosophy and the sciences, of religion, art, and language. Great benefit to the science of education may also come from researches in anthropology, in economics and sociology, but the sciences upon which the science of education should mostly depend for aid are psychology and ethics, both individual and social.

The Various Meanings of the Term "Philosophy"

Philosophy of life. Like the terms *education* and *science* the term *philosophy* has been used and is today used with several different meanings, a few of which we shall presently examine.

Of late, much currency has been given to the phrase *philosophy of life* when referring to a man's world outlook. In that sense everyone of us is a philosopher, because everyone of us, at least every normally developed individual, has some standpoint from which to view life, some beliefs, by which he weighs its values. In that sense then and to that extent, everybody may be said to have a philosophy; it may or may not be sound, may or may not have been well reasoned out; but, for all that, it is, in the words of G. K. Chesterton, "the most practical and important thing about a man," [1] because it is, in the last analysis, the determining factor in the shaping of his conduct.

No individual, however, is the sole originator or builder of his own philosophy, whether that philosophy be some carefully worked-out system of doctrines or the kind of unreasoned body of beliefs just referred to above. The history of philosophy shows us that even the greatest of philosophers, the founders of systems of philosophy, were influenced by the facts and trend of their education, the beliefs, traditions, customs, moral code, literature, art, science, and current philosophical thought of their own or other times. Plato's philosophy abounds in evidences of the educational ideals and practices of the Greek city states; so it is with Aristotle. St. Augustine's philosophy reminds us of the Academy; and St. Thomas's, of the Lyceum. Bacon's *Instauratio Magna* bears all the earmarks of the Protestant Revolution and early scientific movement; Locke is intellectually a product of Cartesianism; Rousseau, the mouthpiece of eighteenth-century naturalism.

For the great majority of men, a philosophy of life is

---

[1] Chesterton, G. K., *Heretics,* p. 15.   London, John Lane, The Bodley Lane Limited, 1905.

and has ever been that of their immediate surroundings, unquestioningly accepted and carried out all through life. It was fundamentally the same for all Western nations from the third to the sixteenth century. Life had then for all men, one and the same meaning and ultimate purpose, of which their whole environment reminded them from the cradle to the grave. In the last three hundred years, however, the disruptive influence of the sixteenth-century Revolution has given rise to philosophies which challenge the validity of principles that were supposed to have become part of the wisdom of the race. Confined for a time to the inner circle of philosophers, those newfangled theories gradually found their way into the university halls, then into the normal schools, and today they permeate the instruction of millions of children.

Philosophy as a "mental attitude." To say of a man that he has a philosophical turn of mind, that he is philosophically minded, essentially means (at least should mean) that he observes and thinks, that he tries to discover the reasons of things, to get a clear, adequate notion of everything through a thoughtful consideration of facts. The philosophically minded man is, above all else, a lover of truth, an independent thinker, free from prejudice or bias or passion. He carefully analyzes and verifies the data he receives from the senses or reason and then proceeds to a synthesis of his materials, marshalling all his data in their proper order, arranging them into a well-organized whole. Not to be confused with philosophical-mindedness is its counterfeit, philosophism, or sophistry, the very mark of superficiality and narrow-mindedness. Philosophism is an affectation, an abuse of philosophy; it is a good enough adept in the terminology of philosophy, but it lacks its spirit.

Closely related to the philosophical is the scientific turn of mind. Both are expressions of what may be termed *critical curiosity;* the difference between them is this, that the first is general, interested in all things, whereas the second is particular, interested in a special object. The essential questions raised by man's curiosity were stated long ago by Aristotle as the material, formal, efficient, and final causes of being. A chair, for instance, is made of wood (matter), has a certain shape (form), is made by a carpenter using tools (efficient cause), and is intended for seating purposes (final cause). Science, for example, physics, is mostly interested in the first two causes. It formulates the laws or forms of things and tells us of what they are made. As a rule, it does not tell us by whom or by what a thing is made, nor for what purpose it is made. Philosophy, on the other hand, is mostly interested in questions related to the efficient and final causes. As remarked before, in connection with the scientific and metaphysical knowledge of things, there is no antagonism between the philosophical and scientific spirit. They complete, supplement each other for the greater benefit of both. The scientist who is lacking in philosophical training, who, for example, does not believe in causality or minimizes its importance, can hardly expect to discover causes, which is another way of saying that he can hardly expect to contribute any worth-while discovery to the advancement of science. He may succeed in making some invention, finding a new application to life of a scientific discovery; most likely he will fritter away precious time and energy in a bewildering maze of facts. On the other hand, the philosopher who loses sight of the facts of science will soon find himself lost in the realm of unrealities. The ideal man in this case, it seems, is the philosopher-scientist, or, shall we call him, the scientist-philosopher.

In a somewhat different sense from the preceding, though very akin to it, the term *philosophical-mindedness* would convey the same meaning as the more popular expression "taking a thing philosophically." To be a "philosopher" in that sense is to take life with equanimity, to accept quietly whatever it may bring us, to bear misfortune with serenity, and to accept one's good luck without undue elation. This, of course, does not mean that anyone is philosophically minded who is undisturbed by the vicissitudes of life. Only that man is a "philosopher" in this popular usage of the term, whose reason has led him to a just valuation of human life and all its changes.

Philosophy as a science. We are now to consider philosophy in the traditional and more common sense of the term, that is, philosophy considered as one of the higher branches of learning, a subject studied in colleges and universities. The term *philosophy,* which literally means love of wisdom, a search after the true, the beautiful and the good, was in ancient times coterminous with the terms *science, wisdom,* and *knowledge,* and so the first Greeks who devoted themselves to a study of philosophy or science for its own sake assumed the rather pretentious name of "wise men." With some Greek philosophers, the term *wisdom* or *philosophy* not only implied knowledge, but also virtue; they believed that the knowledge of what is true and beautiful and good would inevitably lead to right living. It is in that sense that we should read the Socratic-Platonic maxim that "knowledge is virtue."

A glance at the curriculum of a medieval or even eighteenth-century college or university will show that philosophy long retained the encylopedic character it had among the ancient Greeks. In point of fact, it was only in comparatively recent times, as a consequence of the expansion of science and its imperative demand for specialization, that the teaching of physics, astronomy, botany, zoology, and other subjects became independent of the course in philosophy.

Each and every special science is concerned with a group of facts or notions which it seeks to explain or develop into some sort of system, or theory, resting upon those facts or notions, but, in so doing, it does not go beyond immediate causes or reasons. Thus, chemistry rests satisfied with the explanation that H_2O will yield water. Philosophy, on the other hand, rises above particular groups of facts or notions, immediate causes or reasons of things. It endeavors to explain the universe as a whole, to give the ultimate reasons of things. It might be called the science of sciences in the sense that it claims as its specialty the general notions and principles involved in every science, or again in the sense that it gives us a synthesis of all the sciences.

A synthetic conception of the nature and scope of philosophy could be expressed in this way: Philosophy is one in this, that it seeks to give to us a unified view of all that exists, that is, being or reality. Now, being exists as matter and spirit, more explicitly, as nature, man, and God; hence, there follows a first division of the subject into metaphysics or ontology concerned with the study of being as such; cosmology or the philosophy of nature; natural theology or theodicy, the science of God; and psychology, the science of the soul. Again, being appears to us under a threefold aspect, the threefold aim of our activity: the true, which appeals chiefly to the intellect; the beautiful, appealing to intellect, imagination, and feeling; the good, particularly relating to the will. Corresponding to that threefold aspect of being, we have logic, the science of right thinking; aesthetics, the science of the beautiful; and ethics, the science of right living.

A complete system of philosophy would thus include the following:

I. *Logic,* divided into:
  (a) Formal logic concerned with the study of thought processes (concepts, judgments, deduction, induction, sophisms);
  (b) Material logic, more commonly called, nowadays, epistemology or criteriology, which inquires into the nature and value of the thought content (knowledge), the criteria of truth, evidence, certitude, and so on;
  (c) Applied logic or methodology, the application of logic to the study of any particular science or art.

II. *Metaphysics* or *ontology,* the science of being as such, treating of the general principles underlying all reality and knowledge.

III. *Theodicy* or *natural theology,* the science of God, closely related to the preceding.

IV. *Cosmology* or the *philosophy of nature.*

V. *Psychology,* the science of the soul, in which the study of mental phenomena should lead to an inquiry into the nature of the principle from which they proceed; in the last 100 years, psychological investigation has divided into distinct branches, each claiming recognition as a new psychological science.

VI. *Ethics,* the science of the good, of right living, that is, of ordaining one's conduct according to the principles of the natural law, a science at once normative and practical.

VII. *Aesthetics,* the science of the beautiful, like ethics, is at once normative and practical; it treats of the conceptions of

beauty, of art, of the universal laws of artistic activity.
Politics and economics, which formerly belonged to the practical
branch of philosophy, are now treated as separate, individual sciences, like so many natural sciences that have
branched off from the trunk of natural philosophy.

The Philosophy of a Science or of Art

The sciences receive from philosophy the principles and
method that govern their formation (the validity of knowledge, the principles of identity, causality, analysis, synthesis,
deduction, induction), together with a knowledge of the
relations connecting the various sciences. On the other
hand, the sciences supply philosophy with its empirical
basis through the data that constitute their subject
matter, together with the general notions evolving therefrom; and the sciences also bring to philosophy a means of
checking its own theories through facts which either con-
firm or belie these theories. Again, since the general conclusions reached by the special sciences tend toward a few
fundamental theories, philosophy claims the privilege of
examining, checking up, and connecting those conclusions.
In the words of Herbert Spencer, we could then define philosophy as "completely unified knowledge," and science as
"partially unified knowledge."

From this brief examination of the relation of philosophy
to the special sciences we can draw the meaning of the phrase
"the philosophy of a science." Such a philosophy is nothing
more than the body of principles derived from the study
of that science in the light of philosophy properly so called;
or else we could say that the philosophy of a science is a
particular application to that science of some system of
philosophy or philosophy of life.

Every science has its own philosophy, a theory that

systematizes its principles, its methods, and its results; what we commonly call *philosophy* is nothing more than a general synthesis of all those particular philosophies. There is a philosophy of mathematics that examines the validity of axioms and definitions, the processes of higher analysis and the nature of the concepts of space, time, and number; there is a philosophy of the natural sciences discussing the nature of matter, of the vital principle, of the laws of physical nature; a philosophy of grammar dealing wit.. the general laws of language; a philosophy of art concerned with the laws of the beautiful; a philosophy of history, trying to formulate the general causes and effects of historical events; a philosophy of law, examining the conditions under which human laws have come into existence.

The history of philosophy, like the history of science, discloses the fact that there may be two or more philosophies of a special science, which is not surprising, in view of the close relation, noted before, between the philosophy of any special science and philosophy proper. A naturalistic, idealistic, or skeptical conception of life is bound to lead to a naturalistic, idealistic, or skeptical conception of the philosophy of history, law, or education.

Plato's *Symposium,* a sort of embryonic philosophy of aesthetics, is an application of Platonism to the realm of the beautiful. St. Augustine's *City of God* and Bossuet's *Discourse on Universal History* are illustrations of the Christian conception of the philosophy of history. Montesquieu's *L'Esprit des Lois* is an illustration of the 18th-century conception of the philosophy of law. Rousseau's *Emile* might be described as an expression of a naturalistic philosophy of education. Dewey's *School and Society* is an application to education of the tenets of pragmatism, socialism, and naturalism. Taine's *History of English Literature* is an illustration of a positivistic philosophy of literature. Hegel's *Dialectics of History* shows us a thoughtful consideration of the past in the light of Hegelianism.

The Philosophy of Education

Beyond the scientific account that education can give of itself, there still remain questions, vital questions, that have to be answered. Science can tell us of that which is, never of that which should be; of itself, it is powerless to solve the problem of life's values, to set an ideal before the educator. "It is sometimes claimed," writes Professor Claparède, "that science can provide us with an ideal. That is an error . . . physiology, for instance, tells us of the effect of morphine, but it does not say whether it should be used to relieve or kill patients; all it says is, 'if you wish to relieve take such a dose, if you wish to kill, proceed to such a dose.' And that is all; its prescription once made, it does not concern itself with the use that will be made of it." [2]

The problem of educational ideals, like the problems of educational aims and values, does not then belong to the science of education, but to its philosophy, and one could not insist too much on the fact that those are the most fundamental problems in educational theory and practice. A system of education might be scientifically adequate and very efficient, the principles underlying it might be sound, insofar as their application would lead to the desired end, and yet the whole spirit and trend of the system might be fundamentally wrong, because they are derived from a false philosophy.

---

[2] Claparède, J., *Psychologie de l'Enfant*, p. 106. Genève, Kundig, 1924.

The time was when Western education received inspiration and guidance from an age-tried system of philosophy, the *philosophia perennis* of Plato and Aristotle, adapted by the early Church Fathers and the schoolmen to Christian principles and ideals. In the last three hundred years, however, it has been gradually displaced in the schools by new philosophies that ignore or reject principles which Christianity considers as fundamental.

Francis Bacon opened the way with his philosophy of nature; then came Descartes' rationalism, Locke's empiricism, Kant's criticism, Hegel's idealism, and a host of minor systems more or less closely related to the preceding. It is no exaggeration to say that during those three hundred years speculative thought has been stirred as it had never been before, except, perhaps, in the post-Socratic period of Greek philosophy, or in the age of Abélard, Albertus Magnus, Thomas Aquinas, and Roger Bacon. All the problems that have puzzled philosophers for ages have been reëxamined, new suggestions made for their solutions, new vistas opened on man's nature and his habitat, and a powerful impetus has been given to scientific research. But this otherwise remarkable, intellectual movement has been accompanied by a tendency to overlook the higher superscientific values of life, bringing in its wake all kinds of newfangled educational theories that discard age-tried educational aims, methods of teaching, and systems of studies because they are, we are told, "old fashioned."

The Philosophy of Christian Education

We have defined the philosophy of a special science: a particular application to that science of some philosophy of life or system of philosophy. A simple and clear definition of the philosophy of Christian education would then be: the application to education in all its phases of the Christian philosophy of life, that is, of Christian beliefs and ideals. The Christian philosophy of life, it hardly needs saying, is formulated in the simplest and clearest of languages in the catechism, that wonderful little book which is at once a *Summa* of theology and metaphysics, of psychology, and of ethics. And it is explained in the light of reason, in its fullness and all implications, by scholastic philosophy.

Like the philosophy of life from which it springs and the system of education for which it provides inspiration and guidance, the philosophy of Christian education is first of all essentially religious, because it is religion, meaning here, of course, Christianity, that reveals to philosophy the true goal of life and, therefore, of all education, together with its full significance for the individual and society. And through this revelation of the supreme end of human life religion at once solves the problem of life values and educational aims, because their one true norm is their relation to the supreme end of life. Religion spiritualizes and energizes the whole educative process, because it calls into play and uplifts all the forces of the human mind and satisfies the higher aspirations of the human heart. Religious motives, of all motives, most effectively free the will from the bondage of self-interest and passion. Man's moral nature can supply a basis for right and wrong, but history, no less than everyday experience, tells us that the appeal of "lay" ethics to the will is weak, unless it be supported by religious motives and sanctions. Religion, in short, has been and remains the mightiest of the many forces that shape human conduct and civilization.

The doctrines of Christianity, its rites and history, will then be the core around which will be gathered the whole content of education. ᐟ The Christian norm of values will be the touchstone for the evaluation of educational aims and ideals, of educational objectives and the hierarchy of subjects in the curriculum. Christian ethics will be the standard in moral education, and the Christian conception of human nature will be the standard of educational psychology with its applications to classroom work. But Christianity, as its very name tells us, is something else, something more vital than a body of doctrines, a ritual, and a history. It is a Person, the ideal Person, Christ, the Way, the Truth, and the Life, the ideal Teacher and perfect Exemplar of human life and, therefore, the goal of Christian education.

The philosophy of Christian education is catholic, that is, universal in the widest, most comprehensive meaning of the term. It is not an educational philosophy devised for one age or nation or class or form of government. Its appeal is to all men, irrespective of the circumstances of time and country, of racial or political or social distinctions. It is today, in all essentials, what it was nineteen hundred years ago; it is today, in any one country, what it is in any other country. The philosophy of Christian education is also catholic in the sense that it welcomes truth and progress from whatever quarter it may come, and it is catholic in the further sense that it embraces the whole man, both as an individual and a member of the social organism, and, therefore, embraces all phases of education.

The philosophy of Christian education is essentially religious and catholic; it is also essentially traditional, that is, closely related to history, particularly the history of education.

The Contributions of the History to the Philosophy of Education

Insofar as it purports to be a survey of the whole of education in the past, the history of education is at once an account of educational theory and educational practice. As a record of educational theory, it tells us of the views, opinions, and doctrines of educationists, of the books these educationists wrote and the influence they had. With the aid of science, philosophy, and religion, it helps us form a correct estimate of educational theories and their authors.

The history of educational theory is closely related to the history of religion, philosophy, and science, because advanced educational opinion cannot fail to be influenced by the trend of religious and philosophical speculation and the progress of science. Plato's idealism is at once evident in the educational theory he sets forth in the *Republic* and the *Laws*; Cicero's *De Oratore* reflects his philosophical eclecticism and the practical bent of the genius of ancient Rome; Hugh of St. Victor's *Didascalicon* breathes the spirit of medieval mysticism, and the pedagogical essays of sixteenth-century Protestant educationists that of the Reformation; educational theory in the last one hundred and fifty years shows unmistakable signs of the progress of the natural sciences and the trend of philosophical speculation from Locke to Bergson.

As an account of educational practice, the history of education tells us of educational systems, of national aims and ideals, of great teachers, of subjects taught, of books and methods used, and of the relation of educational practice to the general history of the nation or time.

While engaged in the study of educational practice the

historian cannot fail to become aware of the intimate connection between his subject and political events, social and economic conditions, national traits, customs, traditions, culture, laws, and institutions. The loss of national independence by the Greeks was partly responsible for a change in their educational aim and practices, and Roman expansion through Italy led to a Hellenization of Roman education. The Greek love of beauty was not confined to works of art; it found an outlet and expression in every phase of Greek life and education. The practical bent of the genius of ancient Rome is no less evident in the Roman conception of education than it is in Roman law and government. The Renaissance worship of the classical age was responsible for the emphasis upon the classical element in the secondary-school curriculum in the fifteenth and following centuries, and the progress of the natural sciences in the last one hundred and fifty years has led to another reshaping of school curriculums, this time in favor of the sciences. Finally, the history of educational practice should not lose sight of the possible influence of educational theory upon schoolwork. The educational "realism" of the seventeenth century was translated into the practices of many secondary schools, and it would not be difficult to trace some of the present-day educational aims and methods to the theories of eighteenth- and nineteenth-century educationists.

The history of educational practice is thus closely related to political history and to the history of language, literature, art, science, philosophy, educational theory, and religion; in general, to the history of culture, which supplies the content and, to some extent, the spirit and purpose of education.

As a separate branch of the science of pedagogy, the history of education is of comparatively recent origin, but the traditional, that is, the historical character of educational aims and ideals, of subject matter, methods, and institutions has ever been implicitly recognized when it was not actually emphasized. To preserve and transmit from one generation to the next the views of life and ways of doing things of the forebears was the chief purpose of education among the ancient Oriental nations, and it has remained, even to this day, one of the outstanding features of education in the East. The ancient Greeks, though ready to welcome change in their educational systems, never lost sight of the relation between past and present or failed to appreciate the contributions of past generations to the culture and education of the present. Aristotle's theory of education, though critical of certain views and practices in his own time, is nothing else in substance than a systematic exposition of what he considered best and worth preserving in the traditions of Greek education. Plato's educational theory, it must be admitted, is highly speculative, but even he does not lose all contacts with the past. In his *Republic,* he adopts many of the national educational practices. The *Laws,* too, share in the speculative character of the *Republic,* but, time and again, the dialogue reminds us of the conditions obtaining in Plato's time and the social, that is, the historical function of education in transmitting intellectual treasures from one generation to the next. *Mos majorum* was the motto of early Roman education, as it was of Roman life in general, and so it remained, even after Rome had assimilated the Hellenistic culture, now considered a part of the national patrimony. With the advent of Christianity, a new, higher purpose was assigned to life and education, new elements were introduced into civilization and culture, but there was not, on that account, any attempt to cut the thread of tradition. Christianity preserved all that was worth preserving in pagan culture, and it has ever maintained the position that the first condition for genuine progress is a realization of the past achievements of the race.

A departure from this age-long tradition in Western culture and education begins with the Renaissance and Protestant Revolution, but it should be noted that the purpose of the humanists and the reformers, in breaking away from the immediate past, was to return, so they claimed, to the fountain head of classical culture and religion in pagan Greece and Rome and early Christianity. Likewise, the seventeenth-century innovators, Ratke, Mulcaster, Comenius, among others, though insisting upon changes in educational methods and subject matter in accordance with the Baconian philosophy, were no less insistent upon retaining Christian ideals, together with classical studies. Far more radical was the attitude of the eighteenth-century philosophers. Rousseau's advice "always to do the opposite of the traditional procedure, if one wished to do what is right in education," is but an extreme view of the general trend of the times.

With the rise of interest in historical studies in the nineteenth century, there returned a saner view of the relation of present to past and a better realization of the value of tradition for the theory and practice of education. If extended far enough into the past and carried on through the broader field of culture, of social and political conditions, the survey of the history of education will reveal to us the origins and evolution of our educational aims and ideals, educational institutions, subject matter, and methods. It will show us that, great as we may consider the educational achievements of the present, they are small indeed when compared with those of the past. To the Phoenicians, we are indebted for our alphabet; to the Hindoos, Babylonians, and Egyptians, for our elementary mathematics, our calendar, and many of our fables. The Greek and Latin classics are still an important factor in our curriculum; they have been a source of inspiration and have served as models for many of our literary masterpieces. The teaching of mathematics is still based on the elements of Euclid and the formal study of language in grammar, rhetoric, and prosody still follows the ancient models. Of late much progress has been made in the natural sciences, but it would not be difficult to show that this progress was made possible by the discoveries of the ancient Greeks, partly preserved during the middle ages, partly revealed to the West by Renaissance scholars. We have abandoned the medieval terminology in the arrangement of school subjects, but the larger medieval classification into trivium or humanities and quadrivium or nature subjects is still with us in our schools. Many of our universities and secondary schools can trace their origin back to the middle ages. Our educational aims and ideals show the unmistakable influence of ancient Greece, Rome, and Christianity; and our educational terminology is replete with reminders of the same influence.

The study of the history of education then, by cultivating a sense of justice to the past, will help us appreciate at their true value the achievements of the present. It will prove a safeguard against the adoption of hasty changes by showing us the fate of reforms that were carried out without due consideration for age-tried educational practices. Then, too, the study of the history of education cannot fail to broaden the educational outlook of the teacher, so apt to be held within the narrow confines of classroom work, by showing him the relation between schoolwork and political, social, and economic conditions and needs. It will help him realize the complexity of the problems facing him. Human nature ever remains essentially the same and so does education, but the successful solution of its problems depends on a number of factors that vary with time and place.

Summary

Summing up our inquiry into the nature, scope, and function of the philosophy of education, we shall say:

I. A philosophy of education is a general theory of education based upon some system of philosophy or some body of beliefs concerning man and society.

II. It is the most comprehensive and unifying of all pedagogical subjects, embracing education in all its phases.

III. It is interested in every phase of education, but especially in its aims, its ideals, its place and importance in society, the various elements of its content and the principles that determine their selection and organization, the essential qualifications of the teacher, and the relative importance of the various educative agencies.

IV. The philosophy of education is closely related to the science of education and allied sciences.

V. The philosophy of Christian education shares in all those characteristics, but it has three of its own:

A. It is essentially religious, because religion alone, not economics, can successfully meet the vital issues in life and education.

B. It is catholic in the most comprehensive meaning of the term.

C. The philosophy of Christian education is also fundamentally traditional. The philosophy of education should not limit its gaze to the present. Educational aims, institutions, curriculum, and methods can be fully understood and evaluated only in the light of their historical development and the social, economic, and political conditions under which they have developed.

The past may be likened to an immense laboratory in which the race has been constantly at work, investigating, trying, comparing, and testing ways and means to solve this life's problems, and what has been found educationally sound for ages past will very likely prove just as sound today. A historical study of education is, therefore, no less "scientific" than the new "experimental pedagogy," while it is vastly superior to it in its scope.

Scope and Divisions of the Survey

Education, in the widest sense of the term, is coextensive with life, because there is no situation in life which, for good or evil, does not in some way educate the individual. A philosophy of education thus understood, however, would defeat its own purpose, inasmuch as it would lead to the analysis of an unlimited number of elements. We shall limit our inquiry to those factors that contribute to the education of the rising generation during the formative period, especially the factors entering into the conscious educative process. Even then the program is an extensive one, calling for a number of divisions and subdivisions suggested partly by the nature of the educative process, its purpose and agencies, suggested also, and mostly, by the nature of the individual to be educated.

The plan of treatment is the following:

To the study of the subject itself, there is prefixed, with their educational consequences, a brief, critical survey of a few philosophies, particularly of the three more important modern trends, naturalism, socialism, and nationalism. The purpose of this prefatory chapter is twofold: (1) to illustrate the close relation between any given philosophy and its corresponding system of education; and (2) to show the antagonism to Christian education of non-Christian philosophies.

The exposition of the philosophy of Christian education is then taken up, first from the viewpoint of society, then from that of the individual, the latter viewpoint leading to the following subdivisions: physical, intellectual, aesthetic, moral, and religious education. A chapter on aims and ideals introduces the treatment of education from the individual's viewpoint. The exposition closes with a general survey of educative agencies and the preparation of teachers.

All through the book, the teachings of scholastic philosophy are taken for granted; but now and then, in order to avoid possible misunderstanding, they are briefly stated by way of introduction to the treatment of some topics.

TOPICS FOR FURTHER STUDY

1. Analyze the concept *belief*.
2. Contrast *belief* and *opinion*.
3. Show the importance of belief in the educative process, in everyday life, in any profession.
4. Analyze the influence on any one ancient or modern philosopher, of previous systems of philosophy and contemporaneous trends in culture.
5. Show the indebtedness of patristic or medieval philosophy to Greek or Roman philosophy.
6. State with a brief comment on each the fundamental tenets of the Christian philosophy of life.
7. State the fundamental tenet of Protestantism and show its logical consequences for religion, philosophy, morality, and education. How do you account for the fact that the disruptive influence of that tenet was not at once evident?
8. Compare the course of study in philosophy in any college

or university in the 18th century and today, accounting for differences, if any.

9. Describe briefly the general trend of (a) ancient Greek philosophy, (b) patristic philosophy, (c) medieval philosophy.

10. State and briefly comment on the basic thesis of the history of philosophy.

11. Compare and criticize any two historical classifications of the sciences.

12. "Science versus Sciences." Discuss.

13. Compare the exact, natural, and social sciences showing their similarity and differences.

14. Illustrate from the viewpoint of classroom work, the relation of the science of education to the exact, natural, and social sciences.

15. Account for the religious origin of both philosophy and science.

16. "There is no antagonism between science and religion." Explain.

17. "The historical viewpoint has ever been present in educational theory and practice." Explain.

18. Give a brief account of our indebtedness to the past for our educational aims.

19. Give a brief account of our indebtedness to the past for our educational methods.

20. Illustrate from actual classroom work, the bearing of the philosophy of education upon the teaching-learning process.

SUGGESTIONS FOR READING

Bergson, H., *Introduction to Metaphysics* (New York, 1932).

Bode, B., *Modern Educational Theories* (New York, 1927).

Bréhier, E., *Histoire de la Philosophie* (Paris, 1933).

Coe, G., *The Motives of Men* (New York, 1926).

Cresson, A., *Les Systèmes Philosophiques* (Paris, 1929).

Dewey, J., *Construction and Criticism* (New York, 1930).

Eddington, A. S., *The Nature of the Physical World* (New York, 1928).

Graves, P., *History of Education* (New York, 1924).

Horne, H., *The Democratic Philosophy of Education* (New York, 1932).

Jeans, J., *The Universe Around Us* (New York, 1931).

Marique, P., *History of Christian Education* (New York, 1932).

Martin, E., *The Meaning of a Liberal Education* (New York, 1926).

Poincaré, H., *Science and Hypothesis* (London, 1914).

Shallo, M., *Scholastic Philosophy* (Philadelphia, 1916).

Shields, T., *The Philosophy of Education* (Washington, 1917).

Turner, W., *History of Philosophy* (Boston, 1903).

Ueberweg, F., *Grundriss der Geschichte der Philosophie* (Berlin, 1928).

Whitehead, A., *Science and the Modern World* (New York, 1925).

Willmann-Kirsch, *The Science of Education* (Beatty, 1921).

CHAPTER II

Philosophies and Education

Even a cursory examination of the evolution of philosophical thought will reveal a bewildering variety of doctrines, methods, viewpoints, and opinions that often contradict one another. Socrates sums up all philosophy in the maxim "know thyself"; he would have it grounded on psychology and concern itself in the main with a rational solution of the question of right living. Descartes uses the same starting point but his purpose is more speculative than practical, and he relies on mathematical deduction instead of experience and induction as Socrates did. Kant's conception of philosophy is also more or less Socratic, but unlike Socrates he does not confine his investigation to the field of ethics and his method is essentially deductive. Plato and Aristotle assign to the search for the first cause the place of honor in their philosophical system, whereas the positivist school (Comte, Huxley, Spencer) ignores the question entirely. Some philosophers, as, for example, Plato, Aristotle, St. Thomas and Descartes, are convinced of the ability of the human mind to reach an objective knowledge of things; others, skeptics of all shades, doubt or deny it outright. Rationalism favors *a priori,* deductive reasoning; empiricism insists on observation and induction. Some systems of philosophy are founded on the dualism of spirit and matter;

other systems admit only of one principle, matter, according to some; spirit, according to others. The list of conflicting differences might easily be continued.

But with all their differences philosophical systems have at least this in common, they center around all or some of the following fundamental questions.

The whole universe, man included, is in a perpetual state of change. It shows us only phenomena, appearances which are subject to change or disappearance. Is there anything permanent, a "substance" that endures, an "ultimate reality" beyond this world of appearances, which is all we perceive through our senses?

If there is an "ultimate reality" what kind of thing is it?

Is there only one or more than one kind of "substance" or "reality"?

Is this single or manifold "substance" eternal, or was it created by a Supreme Being and endowed by Him with the laws of its development according to a divinely ordained plan?

What is the purpose of human life?

Are there rules, founded in the very nature of things and human nature which determine our conduct?

Is man a free agent?

Is the human mind capable of answering those questions? In Kant's words, "What can I know?" [1]

The history of civilization shows that the doctrines woven around those questions are vital forces that have determined to a great extent the culture and the political and industrial life of nations, and the influence of those doctrines has been

---

[1] For a sane, critical discussion of those and kindred questions, the reader is referred to scholastic treatises on metaphysics, cosmology, ethics, psychology, and epistemology.

and is no less paramount on educational theory and practice. The following illustrations, among many others, will make clear, it is hoped, this close relation between philosophy and education.

One of the most striking, if not the best, illustration of the close relation between education and a given system of philosophy is shown in ancient Chinese education.

In the sixth century, B.C., K'ung-fu-tze, better known in the West as Confucius, developed around Chinese traditions as a core, a system of semireligious, moral, and social philosophy, which, added to and commented upon by his disciples, has dominated Chinese life and Chinese education down to the beginning of this century. Like Socrates, Confucius was intensely interested in the reformation of morals; like him, he taught that knowledge is virtue, that no man is willfully bad, and that vice springs from ignorance. But whereas Socrates appealed to reason in his search for principles of good conduct, Confucius appealed to the authority of the past. Virtue, according to him, is the knowledge and observance of whatever has been sanctioned by the practice of past generations and has received the approval of Confucius. There is no place for metaphysical speculation in Confucianism. With a minimum of dogmatic religious teaching, it is made up of wise sayings of the Chinese sages, moral precepts, rules of conduct, down to the minute detail for every sphere of human activity. Preservation of the past is the avowed purpose of the system as it is of education. "What Heaven has conferred," says Confucius, in the opening sentence of the Kung-Yung, "is called nature; an accordance with nature is called the path of duty. The regulation of this path is called instruction." What is meant here by nature, is the form of government and social relations sanctioned by ancestral usage, explained and approved by Confucius. The purpose of education is twofold: to prepare a body of leaders steeped in ancient learning respecting government and society; to train the masses in all the details of doing things in the way of the forebears. To this entire dependence of education upon an ethico-religious system of philosophy, aiming at the maintenance of an unchanging order, China owes it, in the main, that for centuries she enjoyed political and social stability, though, it must be said, the price she paid for its "unprogressiveness" is, in Western eyes, a heavy one.

Plato's *Republic* offers another illustration of this close relation between education and philosophy. Social justice is the subject of the dialogue, but it expands into an exposition of much of Plato's philosophy and a plan of education for the ideal state. "Knowledge is Virtue" is no less axiomatic with Plato than with Socrates; both believed that the knowledge that is conducive to virtue should be the basis of a healthy, peaceful, happy, social, and political life. Plato further agrees with his master that this knowledge consists of general notions as opposed to individual opinions, that the germs of this knowledge are implanted in every man and can be developed through reflection and reasoning. At this point, master and disciple part company. Socrates was satisfied with the formulation of the purpose of life and education and, through the dialectic method, content to try to develop in any willing disciple the power of thinking for himself and therefore, so he believed, of formulating the principles of right living. Plato, on the other hand, being deeply interested in the metaphysical aspect of the question, was led to inquire into the nature of knowledge. To the question, "what is knowledge?" his answer is in substance:

that mental state which conforms with reality. And the only true reality, in the Platonic sense of the term, is the "idea," the eternal prototype, the life-giving form of the phenomenal object which is but its pale, ephemeral reproduction. The more nearly the phenomenal object corresponds to the "idea" from which it emanated, the more nearly does it perform the function for which it was created, the more nearly does it approximate its own good. Each and every being has its own good to attain, to enter into harmony with its own corresponding "idea." Knowledge, true knowledge conducive to virtue, is a clear recognition of this harmony between phenomenon and the corresponding "idea." Such knowledge, however, is attainable only by those who have a sixth sense, a sense for "ideas." Those who have this sense will form the ruling class, because they alone can see the truth and, therefore, direct their own conduct and the conduct of the other classes. And the aim of the scheme of education elaborated in the *Republic* is the selection of this class of philosopher-kings, the guardians of the state.

Ancient Chinese education illustrates the close relation between philosophy and education in actual educational practice; the plan of education elaborated in Plato's *Republic* is an illustration of the same relation in educational theory. Other examples of this relation might be cited by the score. As a matter of fact, the whole history of both educational theory and practice is, in a certain sense, an account of the influence on education of beliefs respecting man, life, society, whether those beliefs are merely religious or philosophical, or both. There is not a system of education or a scheme for educational reform that is not the mirror of a general philosophy and scale of life values. The following illustrations of this truism today are treated at some length, because they have become the gospel of thousands of theorists and teachers outside of Catholic institutions.

Naturalism

The beginnings of modern naturalism can be traced to the revival by a few Renaissance scholars of the naturalistic philosophies of ancient Greece and the new metaphysics born in the 16th century of the enthusiasm for the study of nature. The influence on Western thought of this neo-naturalistic movement, hardly worth mentioning at first, became noticeable in the speculations of the leading 17th-century philosophers, especially Francis Bacon and John Locke, whom we may consider as the originators of the naturalistic trend in modern thought, life, and education. To Bacon's influence we can trace, in a large measure, the beginnings of the shifting of interest from humanistic to scientific school subjects, and the emphasis upon the acquisition of knowledge for utilitarian purposes. Locke's *Essays* opened the way for the more outspoken expression of naturalism in the 18th-century "enlightenment," when it assumed a twofold character.

During the first half of the 18th century, it was essentially skeptical and rationalistic; its fundamental principle at this stage is reliance upon human understanding, unbounded faith in reason, which is proclaimed self-sufficient and the final arbiter on all things. In the name of reason, the leaders of the movement wage relentless warfare against tradition, revealed religion, its dogmas and rites which they deride as so many forms of ignorance and superstition; they rebel against all authority in Church, State, society and morals which they look upon as tyranny of thought, government, social relations, conduct. . . .

The other phase of the enlightenment can be characterized as a sort of reaction against the preceding tendency; over and against the cold calculations of reason it sets the claims of sentiment as a fuller and truer expression of our nature; the skepticism, infidelity, atheism of the "intellectuals" it would replace by some sort of "natural religion" which would more or less exclude the supernatural elements of Christianity but accept the bulk of its morality; for the government of the few, it would substitute that of the masses for whom, at least in theory, it professes unbounded sympathy.[2]

In the course of the 19th and 20th centuries, naturalism has asserted itself more and more openly in Western civilization. It is, today, the keynote of the philosophy of life and education for millions. Its doctrines are expounded or taken for granted in hundreds of universities and colleges, in normal schools, and in treatises on educational theory and practice, and they are applied in one form or another in thousands of classrooms and textbooks.

What then is naturalism? In its modern form, it is not so much a system of philosophy as it is a tendency to consider nature as the fountainhead of all that exists and, therefore, to explain or at least to try to explain everything in terms of nature. On this fundamental tenet of the doctrine all "naturalists" substantially agree, differing only in their interpretations of the term *nature*. Materialistic naturalism denies or ignores the existence of a Creator, professes to believe in the eternity of matter, considers the whole universe as some sort of gigantic machine subject to none but mechanical laws. Pantheistic naturalism admits a dualism of mind and matter as a twofold manifestation of one underlying, immanent cause of the whole universe. According to a third type of naturalism which we may, for lack of a better term, refer to as *transcendentalism,* there is a First Cause, a

---

[2] Marique, P. J., *History of Christian Education,* Vol. III, pp. 44ff. New York, Fordham University Press, 1932.

Creator, but the universe once created never has been and never will be interfered with by its Maker. The order of nature, man included, once established, remains unchangeable. Man, in particular, possesses within himself all that he needs to achieve his destiny.

As it has just been remarked, whatever be their differences on other points, all "naturalists" substantially agree on the dogma of the primacy and all-sufficiency of nature, whence follow a number of important consequences for man, culture and education. Man's supremacy over nature under God's sovereignty is done away with. Man, so says naturalism, is in nature and a product of nature, as evolution amply shows us. There is no difference in kind, only one of degree, between man and the brute. He is but a higher animal. What tradition calls his spiritual life is but one aspect of his organic life, subject, like every other phase of organic life, to the laws, of physics, mechanics, and chemistry. Thought is a function of the brain; free will is an illusion. Man's activities, whether we call them physical or spiritual, belong to the realm of nature and are subject to its laws which are sufficient to account for everything that happens in this world, the only one we can know anything about. Man is naturally good, endowed by nature with all that is required to achieve his destiny. Human reason is the only source of knowledge, the only criterion of truth. It is idle talk, so argues the naturalist, to speak of prophecies, miracles, and mysteries. Those words are but the expression of our ignorance or gullibility. If we knew all the facts, we would discover that so-called mysteries or miracles or prophecies are natural events or figments of a deluded mind.

Society is looked upon by naturalism as a "vast organism" which, like the individual, is subject to fatal laws of development. Ethics is not the science of what ought to be, dealing with eternal laws existing antecedently to human actions; it is the science of what actually is useful and agreeable to the individual and the community in which he happens to live; ethical standards vary with the variations in time and surroundings. In trying to explain the past, the task of history is to record events and then to trace the laws of their sequences, just as physics and chemistry trace laws of sequences in their respective fields. Literature and the fine arts should give us a picture of nature as it actually is, without any idealizing and without any regard for the laws of morality. Philosophy is at best an adjunct to science—not a very useful one at that, since its province is that of the unknowable. Religion, in the popular sense of the term, is nothing more than an expression and an exploitation of ignorance and fear. There is no place for it in naturalistic culture. If man must have a religion, let it be a religion dictated by reason, the religion of nature.

Naturalism and Education

The details of the application of the naturalistic creed to education, now in a somewhat moderate form, now in a more radical one, have been treated in thousands of books, essays, and articles published in the last 150 years from Rousseau's *Émile* to John Dewey's *School and Society,* and the Progressive Education literature.

The fundamental educational tenets of naturalism are expressed in the opening sentence of the *Émile*: "Everything is well as it comes from the hand of the Author of things; everything degenerates into the hands of man." Human nature, then, is essentially good and should be allowed to develop freely. The task of parents and teachers is, in the main, one of noninterference: to remove, so far as it can be done, whatever may hinder the work of the great teacher, nature. And since nature never uses authority but resistance, it follows that authority should be banished from education. Parents and teachers have no right to deprive the child of the "pleasure of living now," under the pretence that through developing discipline, self-control, they prepare for a happier life in the future.

The frankest and most widely known exposition of the naturalistic philosophy of education is probably that of Herbert Spencer (1820–1903), an English philosopher and publicist, whose influence has been paramount in many educational circles of the English-speaking countries. Spencer's views on nature, man, and life are set forth in his *System of Synthetic Philosophy* or *Principles of Biology, Psychology, Ethics and General Principles.* His educational creed, a corollary of his philosophy, is formulated in *Education, Intellectual, Moral, Physical,* a book consisting of four essays, each of which appeared at first as a magazine article.

Spencer's philosophy can be summed up in the word *agnosticism;* we know nothing, nor can we prove anything of a hereafter; so far as we can ascertain, human life is all of this world, it begins and ends in nature. Let us then see what man is, and examine the conditions under which man has to live this earthly, "natural" life which, so far as one can see, is all that he can hope for. Man is primarily a living organism, an animal endowed with senses, and, therefore, the first and most essential prerequisite for the individual's success in life, for the nation's prosperity and welfare, is that man be a good animal, healthy, sturdy, endowed with a strong nervous system and well-developed, keen senses. Human life is made up of certain activities which, according to Spencer, can be classed as follows, in the order of their importance: activities related to preservation of life and health; vocational activities, related to earning a living; domestic activities, related to family life and the rearing of children; social and political activities related to citizenship; leisure activities, related to the gratification of the tastes and feelings. The purpose of educaton, which can be formulated as a preparation for all those activities, for complete living, demands both knowledge and training. What knowledge then answers best the purpose of education? What knowledge is of most worth? For centuries, the child had been taught that man is created to the image and likeness of God, that man's first duty is to know Him, to love Him, and to serve Him, in order to be happy in this life and the next; that the only knowledge which really counts is that which concerns our Lord and Creator, our origin and destiny, and the road thereto. Rubbish, says Spencer. Man is a product of nature, belongs to nature, lives and will entirely vanish in nature. The knowledge that he needs in preparing himself for the life he is to live is supplied by the sciences that deal with nature.

He needs a knowledge of biology, physiology, and hygiene because such knowledge is essential for the preservation of life and health; of mathematics, physics, chemistry, biology, in order to be able to eke out a living under existing conditions of industrial life; family life and the rearing of children demand for their proper functioning a knowledge of biology, hygiene, psychology, and ethics; political and social activities, a knowledge of the sciences of history, economics, and politics. Last and least, man needs a knowledge of music, aesthetics, and literature which belong to the leisure part of life and, therefore, should occupy a corresponding position in the curriculum. It is hardly necessary to remark that Spencer's conception of psychology, ethics, economics, politics, history, even art and literature, is in keeping with the naturalistic trend of his philosophy. His psychology and ethics are nothing else than some kind of "transcendental physiology." Thought life is brain life; conscience, duty, free will, moral responsibility, supernatural sanctions he ignores; his ethics is concerned with the intellectual development, physical well-being, material comfort and prosperity of the individual and the race. Historical events, economic, social and political conditions, art and literature are so many manifestations of the hidden forces constantly at work in nature. A knowledge of the natural sciences is therefore a prerequisite for the understanding of past and present conditions of the race, the problems that face it, even for the enjoyment of art and literature.[3]

During the past fifty years, the tenets of educational naturalism have been taught and applied in one form or other by a school of innovators who preach their gospel under various banners: "The New School," "The New Education," "The School of the Future," "The Activity School," and "Progressive Education." Here it is not meant that all those innovators, insofar as they have one, share in the same, identical philosophical creed. John Dewey, for example, the best-known of them all, is sometimes referred to as a pragmatist or instrumentalist, at other times as an agnostic or a socialist or a materialist. But whatever may be the differences in this respect, the educational innovators, consciously or unconsciously, lend their support to the educational doctrines of naturalism, which is all too evident in the following propositions which more or less sum up their educational creed.

Coercive discipline and dogmatic instruction should be banished from the school.

The true method of learning is by doing and experimenting.

The child is to be left free to choose and execute his tasks.

The child's desires and feelings are sacred, and so on.

Not everything, it must be admitted, is to be condemned

---

[3] *Ibid.*, pp. 102–103.

in the program of the "progressives." Many of their positions are sound, but their soundness is not derived from naturalism, and they have nothing to lose but much to gain by being freed from the connection.

Criticism

A detailed, systematic criticism of naturalism properly belongs to the various provinces of philosophy and natural science. To the expert in physics and chemistry must be referred the contradictions into which naturalism is involved as a consequence of the progress of the sciences in the last fifty years: the discovery of the X ray, the changeableness of the atom, once thought of as unchangeable, the conversion of matter into radiant energy and vice versa, the interdependence of space and time. Our own criticism, within the narrow compass of this exposé, must be limited to a brief consideration of the fundamental naturalistic doctrines concerning man, human life, and education.

Body and mind, says naturalism, are substantially the same, both are a product of matter and motion. If such be the case, we should expect thought, the product of the mind (in naturalistic parlance, the product of cerebral energy), to display the same properties and characteristics as brain, the thought producer. But then, how shall we account for the following differences? The brain has weight and dimensions. No man, in his senses, would speak of a thought as being so many inches or feet long and weighing so many ounces or pounds. The brain is all in the present. Thought dwells not only in the present but in the past and the future. The brain is a set of facts and a register of facts. Thought passes from fact to its meaning. A red light along a railway track is a fact registered through the retina and optic nerve in some cortical area where thought reads it not merely as a red light, but as danger. To send a bullet into somebody's head is a fact, but thought calls it murder. Truth, says naturalism, varies with temperament, time, and place, which amounts to say, for instance, that whereas, in the temperate zone two plus two make four, at the poles, two plus two might make three or five. Again and again we are told by its devotees that naturalism is the very essence of science just as science is of naturalism; the two are identical. And yet it would not be difficult to draw up a list, even a long one, of eminent physicists, chemists, and biologists who had no interest in naturalism, even professed a philosophy of life diametrically opposed to it. The truth of the matter is that science is one thing and philosophizing about science, as "naturalists" do, is quite another. Science belongs to no particular time or country or philosophical or religious creed. Its only concern is the search after truth, the study and explanation of reality, and, in that search and study, it refuses to be bound up to any preconceived theory or to commit itself to the use of any uniform procedure. Any hypothesis it makes to explain reality is discarded as soon as it is not verified by fact; the method it uses is determined by the nature of the subject it considers: mathematics has its own specific method and so have physics, chemistry, biology, physiology, ethics, and history.

One of the fundamental tenets of naturalism is that there is no difference in kind between inorganic and organic nature, both being governed by the same set of fatalistic laws. But in the last fifty years the progress of the biological sciences has brought to the front the doctrine of vitalism, which disproves this naturalistic contention. It tells us that living beings belong to a province of their own, apart from inorganic nature, showing finality and preordained arrangement.

As stated above, naturalistic ethics flows from the doctrine that man, like the rest of the universe, is subject to none but the laws of matter. His behavior is the resultant of heredity and surroundings, of forces over which he has no control. Free will is an illusion. Carried out to its logical conclusions, this proposition leads to the destruction of the whole of civilization; community life becomes impossible, since all its activities and relations are based, either explicitly or implicitly, on the assumption of free will. Why should a murderer or a thief be penalized, if there is no responsibility? And there can be no responsibility, unless there is freedom.

Not very consistent either is the attitude of naturalism toward philosophy which it considers one of the born enemies of science, though not a very dangerous one, since, according to naturalists, it is concerned with barren speculation. Now, a glance at the history of science or the history of philosophy will show that, far from being the enemy of science, philosophy was responsible for the rise of science. Both were for centuries so closely related to one another that their nature and purpose seemed to have been identical. Thales, Pythagoras, Plato, Aristotle, Roger Bacon, Descartes, Leibnitz, to mention only a few, were both scientists and philosophers. Science, knowledge, philosophy, and wisdom were for a long time practically identical terms. As late as the 18th century, a college or a university course in philosophy included, with other studies, courses in physics, botany, zoology, politics, and economics. It was only during the last one hundred years that a distinction between science and philosophy gradually took place. The amusing thing about this naturalistic attitude toward philosophy is that naturalism itself, with all its scoffing at philosophy, whether its devotees realize it or not, is nothing more than a certain type of philosophy, and not a very consoling one at best.

As to the repeated assertions of "naturalists" that there is opposition between religion and science, that religion is but a relic of a superstitious past, that it is the refuge and opium of the ignorant and unintelligent, let it be said that there have been and there are today many eminent and deeply religious scientists, that religion is no less deeply rooted in human nature than the love of scientific truths, that it has survived once-mighty empires and philosophies which would ignore it or sneer it out of existence.

Socialism

In its modern form socialism is both a philosophy of life and a certain type of industrial organization, whereby it is hoped that existing social ills would be removed or at least greatly mitigated. As a philosophy of life, socialism is closely related to naturalism, viewing human life and all its activities from a purely economic, that is, material standpoint. As a system of industrial organization, it would substitute state monopoly of the sources and means of production for private ownership. In that sense, socialism is a distinctly modern movement, though features of this conception of community life can be found in the writings of some political theorists, as in Plato's *Republic,* St. Thomas More's *Utopia,* Campanella's *City of the Sun,* or in actual social practice, as in the Spartan State, in some of the early Christian communities, a few medieval sects, and, in general, most religious congregations. The extreme form of

socialism, commonly referred to as communism, insists upon
state ownership of all property, whereas moderate socialism
advocates only the collective ownership and management
of material agencies of production; consumption goods,
such as food and clothing, can be owned privately. Col-
lectivism, another form of socialism, is primarily interested
in the economic features of the system, only casually in its
ideology.

The old dictum that "man is by nature a social animal"
sums up socialistic philosophy, if we read it in this way:
that man becomes a man in the full sense of the term
through society, that he owes to society all that differentiates him from the brute. Language, literature, arts,
science, philosophy, and religion are all a product of social
life; they are our inheritance as members of the social
group. Society then, not the individual, is the reality we
should keep in mind in dealing with mankind. Now, if
society is the only reality, it follows that sociology, the new,
modern science dealing with society as a whole, has precedence over all sciences. There were, of course, social sciences long before the appearance of sociology. At the beginning of the 19th century, there were at least half a
dozen: economics, politics, jurisprudence, ethics, psychology,
and history. Each one of those sciences studies social relations from some definite standpoint; it has a limited but
well differentiated field of inquiry. Sociology on the other
hand, views society as a whole; its purpose is to serve as a
sort of introduction to the special social sciences and, at the
same time, to offer a general survey of all social activities.
The sociologist is thus led to insist on the relations to one
another of the various social sciences, that is, to view social
facts from a number of standpoints. Thus, for example, in

studying the relation of employer to employees, sociology would examine it from the viewpoint of economics, politics, ethics, and psychology. Thus again, in the study of the family, sociology will not only consider the relation of husband and wife, of parent and child, but also the relation of the family to the state, its status today in any country with its status in other countries today or in the past. In a most general way, the method of sociology is both inductive and comparative, supplemented by the use of statistics; gathering, classifying, comparing facts in order to reach some conclusion. The application of the method varies, of course, with the particular field of investigation or particular standpoint one takes. Outside of Catholic circles, the general trend of sociology is, today, substantially what it is in the writings of its founders, Auguste Comte and Herbert Spencer. Assumptions are made which are alien to Christian philosophy, or else factors of social activities are ignored which Christianity considers vital. Sociology of this type is concerned with the description and interpretation, from a naturalistic viewpoint, of social relations; never does it concern itself with what ought to be. Christian sociology, on the other hand, while no less interested in "what is," never loses sight of the standard to which social relations should conform. Illustrations, at once clear and authoritative, of the Christian treatment of sociological questions are the Encyclicals *Rerum Novarum* and *Quadragesimo Anno*.

Sociology (naturalistic sociology) is the science of sciences. So declares socialism, and from that premise it draws the conclusion that sociology alone can give us an intelligent outlook on life. Answers to such questions as "What am I?" "What relations bind me to my fellowmen?" "What destiny awaits me?" are not to be sought, says the socialist, from the traditional metaphysics or ethics or psychology, but from the new science of society. Language, art, literature, science, and religion must be thought of from the social viewpoint, because they are all a product of the social mind and, therefore, cannot be understood or explained except from the viewpoint of society, that is, through sociology. Traditional psychology, for example, inasmuch as it is concerned with the individual man, cannot account for the growth and development of, say, language, because language is essentially a social product, just as individual psychology is but a reflection of social psychology, whether it be a question of examining and explaining thought or emotion or volition. Free will is one of the fundamental tenets of traditional, that is, Christian psychology and ethics. Free will, says naturalistic sociology, is but a figment of our imagination. No individual is free. Our thoughts, feelings, and conduct are determined by the laws of heredity and the influence of our environment.

Positive religion, founded on revelation, leading man into supernatural life, never enters, of course, into the socialistic conception of life. Whenever the socialist treats of religion, he does it from a purely naturalistic standpoint. Man is religious, not because he is a man, but because he belongs to some community whose religion becomes the religion of each one of its members. Whether we consider religious doctrines or religious sentiments or religious rituals, we have to deal with the religion of some group of men. And the purpose of all religions is likewise essentially social: to idealize the community, to develop in its members, sentiments of sympathy and solidarity, which is particularly true of the Christian religion. Is not "Love thy neighbor as thyself" its fundamental tenet? Religion, therefore, must adapt itself to the needs and aspirations of the natural man; its kingdom is of this world: the kingdom of the ideal natural society whose advent every man should do his utmost to bring about.

Socialistic ethics are the natural corollary of the doctrine of social supremacy. Society determines what is right and what is wrong. It has first claims on the gratitude, devotion, self-sacrifice of the individual, because he owes all that he is and all that he possesses to society. Now, self-renunciation is the very soul of social life as it is of moral acts. It is, then, the business of social ethics to make clear to the individual his dependence upon society, in order to awaken in him those sentiments of solidarity, sympathy, and love of community which will ensure social stability.

Remarks similar to those just made on the socialistic conception of psychology, ethics, and religion could be made on the other elements of culture; all of them, we are told, as well as all the activities of life must have but one aim: the improvement of existing social conditions, the building up of an ideal community, whose motto is "work, in common, and for a common aim."

Socialism and Education

Socialism, with its full naturalistic significance, has found its way into the theory and practice of education under a variety of labels: "the working man's school," "the school of activity," "the school of the future," and so on. Its best-known representative is probably the American, John Dewey. His educational creed may be considered in all essentials as typical of the radical socialist school. According to Dewey, the conditions under which we live today call for a new kind of education, drawing its inspiration and purposes from the spirit of the three revolutions—intellectual, industrial, and democratic—that ushered in the modern era. It should be thoroughly democratic, it should emphasize manual work and prepare for intelligent participation in industrial activities. This new, scientific, industrial, democratic education is the very opposite of traditional education, which is a class education, is passive, static, out of harmony with child psychology, the keynote of which is activity, doing, and achieving something. The school of the future must be active, the pupil must produce something in cooperation with his fellow pupils. Schoolwork is traditionally considered a preparation for life; according to Dewey, education is life, it must bring into the school the conditions and activities that obtain in today's civilization. Manual work should be an integral part of its work, not so much as a preparation for the practice of some craft or trade, as a means of introducing the child to the life he will have to live as an adult, of developing social habits.

All studies and school activities should be viewed from the pragmatic and social standpoint; they should lead the child and youth to a realization of the demands of social life upon all the members of the community. This new, progressive school, the school of the future, will be a school for moral training, because its spirit and work will develop the qualities that we look for in a useful, worthy member of the community. Needless to say, there is no room for religion in the curriculum of the socialist school.

The integral socialist program was put into practice on a huge scale, in Soviet Russia in 1918, with an orgy of "new" methods of teaching, "new" methods of discipline, "new" courses of study, "new" objectives, and "new" school organizations. In 1932, the experiment was officially pronounced a dismal failure. In spirit, Soviet education is still socialistic and naturalistic; for the rest, it has returned to the old, traditional ways of doing the things educational.

Criticism

Socialism claims that it can bring to an end the age-long conflict between the interests of the individual and those of the many. In order to do this, it requires the state to establish a substantial equality of material goods and keep this distribution compulsory. Of a hereafter, of spiritual values, it professes to know nothing. Its interest is in the material aspect of life, and it tells men that the one goal of life is the accumulation and enjoyment of material commodities. The realization of this socialist dream, the materialistic Eldorado, would require at least two conditions: that there be an unlimited amount of material goods; that everybody will be satisfied with what he receives. Unfortunately, since the amount of earthly things is rather limited and human nature is what it is, the best that can be hoped for is satisfaction of a kind for those individuals who personify the supreme owner, the state, at the expense of the great mass of toilers.

Religion, declares socialism, is a product of society. At least insofar as Christianity is concerned, it is the reverse proposition that is true. Christianity came from the East as a new religion unknown to the pagan West, and, in the course of a few centuries, it transformed its civilization. In the fifth century the Roman Empire with its splendid political organization and brilliant culture had become a thing of the past; society was heading toward barbarism. Social reconstruction in the sixth and following centuries, culminating in the splendid civilization of the thirteenth century, was, in the main, the work of Christianity.

Morality, we are told, is a product of society, but here again, facts belie theory. The comparative study of morality and ethics reveals divergence as to the theories of ethics and diversity of moral judgments, which might be taken to favor the socialist position. Far more impressive, however, is the fact that, in all ages and all countries over which we have records, we find a fundamental agreement among men on the essential features of ordinary morality. There are differences in the actual rules of conduct, but the principles of right and wrong are everywhere the same, because they are written deep in human nature.

Radical socialism fails to give a satisfactory explanation of historical events, because it refuses to take into consideration the essential element in the fashioning of national life and international relations. Climate, nature of soil, vicinity to or distance from the sea are, each and all, important factors in shaping the life of nations, but their social value depends on the intelligence and will of man. The immense opportunities for wealth in the American continent remained practically unused until the coming of Europeans to its shores. The sudden expansion of the Greek world in the third century, B.C., will remain a riddle for us if we leave out of consideration the genius and will of Alexander the Great; nor can we account for the changes that took place in the Roman world in the first century, B.C., without considering Julius Cæsar, or the medieval west without Charlemange, or the France of Louis XIV without Richelieu. And so it is in the realm of literature and the fine arts. The *Divine Comedy* is unexplainable without a Dante, or the *Last Supper* without a Da Vinci, or *Macbeth* without a Shakespeare.

Nationalism

The third type of a philosophy of life and, therefore, of education, which comes up for a brief consideration in this chapter, is nationalism. It can be defined in a very general way as a sense of loyalty and devotion to a group of men sharing in a common tribal origin, common dialect, common traditions and beliefs, social and political organization, common interests, or at least in some of those bonds of union. Like socialism, with which it has much in common, nationalism is an expression of that deep-rooted tendency which prompts man to seek the companionship of other men and is responsible for the existence of economic, political, religious bodies and of guilds, clubs, fraternities, in a word, associations of all kinds. In a very general sense, nationalism appears in some form or other in all times and climates. The tribes of primitive and barbarian society were so many small nations, and so were the city states of ancient Greece and the chartered towns of medieval Europe. We are here concerned, however, with modern or rather contemporary nationalism, which is mainly a product of political and economic rivalries in the last one hundred and fifty years.

Closely related to nationalism, though not necessarily identical with it, is "statism" or "politism," the doctrine of the "totalitarian state," that is, the absolute supremacy of the state in every phase of the national life. Italian Fascism, German Nazism, Russian Bolshevism are the best-known, though not the only illustrations of this union or, rather, confusion of state and nation in which, as a third element, socialism may enter with or without its naturalistic background. Soviet totalitarianism might be termed *socialistic nationalism,* inasmuch as the Soviets have adopted integral socialism as their sociopolitical creed and suppressed from national life and national culture anything that would not fit into Marxian philosophy. In Germany and Italy, on the other hand, totalitarianism is more aptly described as national socialism (its official German name), because it retains only those features of socialism that do not seem to conflict with national aims and ideals.

Nationalism does not assume everywhere the aggressively militant character it exhibits in Italy, Germany, or Russia, but it seems to be committed everywhere to the expression of the same tendency, to further national aims and interests at all cost and by all the means at the nation's disposal.

All sorts of theories have been advanced in answer to the question: What constitutes a nation? According to some, the element that is paramount in the making up of a nation is the racial element; others will stress geographical position; others still, language, religion, or a common past. None of these theories taken singly will account for all types of nationality. The race theory alone could not easily account for the existence of such nations as the French or the Swiss or the Italians or the English. The territorial or geographical theory alone could not account for the Polish nation before the World War, or the German nation in 1918 if we are ready to admit that it included, in addition to the population of the Reich, millions of Germans in Alsace, Austria, and Czechoslovakia. A common religion is one of the strongest bonds of national union, but there are very few nations that enjoy it today. A common culture is also a most important constituent element of nationality, but that, too, is not sufficient. The Italians of the 15th century could claim a common culture, but, as yet, they hardly thought of themselves as one nation. The most important element, it would seem, is the national consciousness, the idea, feeling, and conviction, in the individual members of a nation that they belong to some sort of great family. This national consciousness is contributed to chiefly by two factors: a rich bequest of culture, traditions, past achievements —which is felt to be a common possession of the whole community—and the will to preserve this common heritage, to improve it, and to share a common destiny.

This divergence of views on the question of nationality is due in no small measure to the fact that the distinction between nation and state is overlooked. The term *nation,* as its etymology would suggest, refers to a common origin, and, therefore, a community of language, religion, and customs. The term *state,* on the other hand, refers to a group of men living on a territory that is their property, under a common government; the latter term itself referring to the group of individuals representing the state. Community of origin, language, religion, and tradition will contribute to the strength and stability of the state but is not necessary to its existence. The Austro-Hungarian Empire was made up of at least a dozen different nationalities. The chief difference between state and nation is this, that the first is a community, the members of which are held together by political relations; whereas the relations of the second are chiefly cultural and moral. A nation will constitute a state so long as it preserves its independence, but it will remain a nation even after the loss of that independence.

Nationalism and Education

The French Jacobins were the first to realize the value and need of a new type of education for national propaganda. They realized that "the republic, one and indivisible," the new France of their dreams, would never become a reality without a new school system "the nation in public schools," a system of state-supported, state-controlled schools, which all French children should be obliged to attend, where the national language and the doctrines of the French Revolution should take precedence over all other subjects. The elaboration of this theory and its translation into practice has been carried on in France by its successive governments, from Napoleon to the present Republic. With variations in ideology, purposes, and the extent of state control, the theory of the nation in school for national ends has, today, been put into practice everywhere. In some lands there is a complete state monopoly of the schools, even of other agencies that might be considered educative. Private initiative is banished. A hierarchy of powers has been established which controls and enforces uniformity in purpose, subjects taught, and methods of teaching. In other lands, the principle of freedom is still maintained with safeguards against possible abuse. Private schools exist side by side with the public schools. But the tendency everywhere seems to be toward more and more state support and control. In most countries religious instruction is barred from the public schools. In its place there is given "neutral" instruction in morals and civics, with an emphasis on the duties of the citizen to the nation. The purpose of the instruction is to make boys and girls feel the superior excellence of the national and political institutions and to make them willing to bear their share of the national burden, because they prize the nation's institutions and traditions.

The instruction in the native tongue is designed to fill the rising generation with pride in the national idiom; to make them conversant with its masterpieces and, through the selection of suitable materials commented upon and learned by heart, to arouse patriotic enthusiasm. History is taught, not to get at the truth, but to inculcate the national point of view, to glorify national heroes and national virtues, to recall ancient hatreds, and to praise courage and self-sacrifice in the national cause. The teaching of national and local geography is intended, in part at least, to acquaint the pupil with the scene of great national events, with national economic and military problems, and to convince him of the justice of the national policies.

Criticism

Patriotism, love of country, is just as natural as love of one's family. The criticism of nationalism, therefore, cannot be aimed at nationalism as such, but at its abuse, especially the invasion in the name of nationalism of the rights of the family and the Church in the matter of education. This question is admirably treated in the following excerpt from the *Encyclical on the Christian Education of Youth.*

In the first place, it pertains to the State, in view of the common good, to promote in various ways the education and instruction of youth. It should begin by encouraging and assisting of its own accord, the initiative and activity of the Church and the family, whose successes in this field have been clearly demonstrated by history and experience. It should moreover supplement their work whenever this falls short of what is necessary, even by means of its own schools and institutions. For the state, more than any other society, is provided with the means put at its disposal for the needs of all, and it is only right that it use these means to the advantage of those who have contributed them.[4]

---

[4] Discourse to the students of Mondragone College, May 14, 1929.

"Over and above this, the state can exact, and take measures to secure that all its citizens have the necessary knowledge of their civic and political duties and a certain degree of physical, intellectual and moral culture, which, considering the conditions of our times, is really necessary for the common good.

"However, it is clear that in all these ways of promoting education and instruction, both public and private, the state should respect the inherent rights of the Church and of the family concerning Christian education, and, moreover, have regard for distributive justice. Accordingly, unjust and unlawful is any monopoly, educational or scholastic, which, physically or morally, forces families to make use of government schools, contrary to the dictates of their Christian conscience, or contrary even to their legitimate preferences.

"This does not prevent the state from making due provision for the right administration of public affairs and for the protection of its peace, within or without the realm. These are things which directly concern the public good and call for special aptitudes and special preparation. The state may therefore reserve to itself, the establishment and direction of schools intended to prepare for certain civic duties and, especially, for military service, provided it be careful not to injure the rights of the Church or of the family in what pertains to them. It is well to repeat this warning here; for, in these days, there is spreading a spirit of nationalism which is false and exaggerated, as well as dangerous to true peace and prosperity. Under its influence, various excesses are committed in giving a military turn to the so-called physical training of boys (sometimes even of girls, contrary to the very instincts of human nature); or, again, in usurping unreasonably on Sunday, the time which should be devoted to religious duties and to family life at home. It is not our intention, however, to condemn what is good in the spirit of discipline and legitimate bravery promoted by these methods; we condemn only what is excessive, as for example violence, which must not be confounded with courage nor with the noble sentiment of military valor in defense of country and public order; or, again, exaltation of athleticism which even in classic pagan times marked the decline and downfall of genuine physical training.

"In general, also, it belongs to civil society and the state to provide what may be called civic education, not only for its youth, but for all ages and classes. This consists in the practice of presenting publicly to groups of individuals, information having an intellectual, imaginative, and emotional appeal calculated to draw their wills to what is upright and honest, and to urge its practice by a sort of moral compulsion, positively by disseminating such knowledge, and negatively by suppressing what is opposed to it.[5] This civic education, so wide and varied in itself as to include almost every activity of the state intended for the public good, ought also to be regulated by the norms of rectitude and, therefore, cannot conflict with the doctrines of the Church, which is the Divinely appointed teacher of these norms.

"All that we have said so far regarding the activity of the state in educational matters rests on the solid and immovable foundation of the Catholic doctrine of the Christian Constitution of States set forth in such masterly fashion by Our Predecessor Leo XIII, notably in the Encyclicals *Immortale Dei* and *Sapientiae Christianae*. He writes as follows:

---

[5] Taparelli, P. L., *Saggio teor. di Diretto Naturale*, n. 922; a work never sufficiently praised, and recommended to university students (*cf. Our Discourse of December 18, 1927*).

God has divided the government of the human race between two authorities, ecclesiastical and civil, establishing one over things Divine, the other over things human. Both are supreme, each in its own domain; each has its own fixed boundaries which limit its activities. These boundaries are determined by the peculiar nature and the proximate end of each, and describe as it were a sphere within which, with exclusive right, each may develop its influence. As however, the same subjects are under the two authorities, it may happen that the same matter, though from a different point of view, may come under the competence and jurisdiction of each of them. It follows that Divine Providence, whence both authorities have their origin, must have traced with due order the proper line of action for each. The powers that are, are ordained of God.[6]

"Now the education of youth is precisely one of those matters that belong both to the Church and to the state, 'though in different ways,' as explained above.

Therefore [continues Leo XIII], between the two powers there must reign a well-ordered harmony. Not without reason may this mutual agreement be compared to the union of body and soul in man. Its nature and extent can only be determined by considering, as we have said, the nature of each of the two powers, and in particular the excellence and nobility of the respective ends. To one is committed directly and specifically, the charge of what is helpful in worldly matters; while the other is to concern itself with the things that pertain to heaven and eternity. Everything therefore, in human affairs that is in any way sacred, or has reference to the salvation of souls and the worship of God, whether by its nature or by its end, is subject to the jurisdiction and discipline of the Church. Whatever else is comprised in the civil and political order, rightly comes under the authority of the State; for Christ commanded us to give to Cæsar the things that are Cæsar's, and to God, the things that are God's.[7]

---

[6] Ep. Encyc. *Immortale Dei*, November 1, 1885.
[7] *Ibid.*

"Whoever refuses to admit these principles, and, hence, to apply them to education, must necessarily deny that Christ has founded His Church for the eternal salvation of mankind, and maintain instead that civil society and the state are not subject to God and to His law, natural and Divine. Such a doctrine is manifestly impious, contrary to right reason and, especially in this matter of education, extremely harmful to the proper training of youth, and disastrous as well for civil society as for the well-being of all mankind. On the other hand, from the application of these principles there inevitably result immense advantages for the right formation of citizens. This is abundantly proved by the history of every age. Tertullian in his *Apologeticus* could throw down a challenge to the enemies of the Church in the early days of Christianity, just as St. Augustine did in his; and we today can repeat with him:

Let those who declare the teaching of Christ to be opposed to the welfare of the State, furnish us with an army of soldiers such as Christ says soldiers ought to be; let them give us subjects, husbands, wives, parents, children, masters, servants, kings, judges, taxpayers and taxgatherers who live up to the teachings of Christ; and then, let them dare assert that Christian doctrine is harmful to the State. Rather let them not hesitate one moment to acclaim that doctrine, rightly observed, the greatest safeguard of the State." [8]

Topics for Further Study

1. "Naturalism is not science." Discuss.
2. State and comment on the fundamental positions of the theory of evolution.
3. Show the application of the notion of evolution to any of the following: history, language, literature, art, science, and philosophy.

---

[8] Ep. 138.

4. Contrast, with illustrations, the idealistic and naturalistic conceptions of either literature or the fine arts.

5. Compare, with illustrations, realism and naturalism in (a) literature, (b) education.

6. Discuss the application to the teaching of other subjects of the methods used in the teaching of the natural sciences.

7. Discuss the relation to naturalism of either positivism or pragmatism.

8. "What constitutes a nation?" Discuss.

9. Differentiate state from nation, giving illustrations.

10. Differentiate objective from subjective elements in nationality.

11. Discuss the relative importance of any two of the following as constituent elements of nationality: race, language, literature, geography, history, tradition, religion, and national consciousness.

12. "Sound versus extreme nationalism." Discuss.

13. "Sound versus extreme internationalism." Discuss.

14. Discuss the influence of nationalism on educational aims.

15. "State control of education." Discuss.

16. Discuss the influence of nationalism on the school curriculum.

17. Show the relation of naturalism to socialism.

18. Discuss the influence of socialism on (a) school administration (b) school curriculum.

19. "The social versus the socialistic positions on education." Discuss, citing representatives with their views.

20. "The school of activity." Discuss.

Suggestions for Reading

Adams, G., and Montague, W. (eds.), *Contemporary American Philosophy* (New York, 1930).

Boutroux, E., *Questions de Morale et de Pédagogie* (Paris, 1895).

Cathrein, A., *Der Sozialismus* (Freiburg, 1910).

Chesterton, G. K., *Orthodoxy* (London, 1915).

Coe, G., *A Social Theory of Religious Education* (New York, 1922).

Counts, G., *The American Road to Culture* (New York, 1932).

Demiashkevich, M., *An Introduction to the Philosophy of Education* (New York, 1935).

Deploige, S., *Le Conflit de la Morale et de la Sociologie* (Louvain, 1915).

Eucken, R., *The Meaning and Value of Life* (tr.) (London, 1910).

Eymieu, A., *Le Naturalisme devant la Science* (Paris, 1911).

Fouillée, A., *Education from a National Standpoint* (New York, 1892).

Gurian, W., *Bolshevism* (New York, 1934).

Hayes, C., *The Historical Evolution of Nationalism* (New York, 1931).

Hocking, W., *Types of Philosophy* (New York, 1929).

James, W., *Pragmatism* (New York, 1907).

Jordan-De-Hovre, *Philosophy and Education* (New York, 1931).

Kane, W., *An Essay Toward a History of Education* (Chicago, 1935).

Kuehner, Q., *A Philosophy of Education* (New York, 1936).

Marique, P., *History of Christian Education,* Vol. 3 (New York, 1932).

O'Connell, G., *Naturalism in American Education* (Washington, 1936).

Pinkevitch, A., *The New Education in the Soviet Republic* (New York, 1929).

Pius XI, *The Encyclical on Christian Education of Youth* (tr.) (New York, 1930).

Reisner, E., *Nationalism and Education Since 1789* (New York, 1922).

Schneider, H., and Clough, S., *Making Fascists* (Chicago, 1929).

Willmann-Kirsch, *The Science of Education* (Beatty, 1921).

CHAPTER III

Education and Society

The Social Trend in Educational Theory

Educational theorists have ever emphasized the social character of education. In Plato's *Republic* and *Laws,* as the very titles of the dialogues would suggest, education is essentially treated from the social viewpoint. Plato's chief concern in both dialogues is the welfare of the state, and the schemes of education which he offers are his solution of the problem of social justice, peace and happiness. When "philosophers are kings or the kings and princes of this world have the spirit and power of philosophy, and political greatness and wisdom meet in one," [1] then indeed, so Plato believes, shall justice reign in the state. The purpose of education, according to him, is essentially a social one: to prepare a class of rulers that will perpetuate the ideal state outlined in the dialogues.

Though passages dealing with education can be found in Aristotle's *Ethics* and *Poetics,* the subject is, in the main, treated in his *Politics,* a fact indicative, as in Plato's case, of the social importance attached to the subject by Greek philosophers. The nature and function of education, according to Aristotle, are determined both by the nature of the in-

---

[1] *Republic,* V, p. 473. Jowett translation, Clarendon Press, 1871–1895.

dividual and his function as a citizen, that is, by the constitution of his own state, which is an outgrowth of the character of the nation and the particular conditions under which it has developed. All political and social agencies should coöperate in the work of education, whose end is the maintenance, safeguarding, welfare, and perpetuation of the state.

Latin literature offers no parallel to the philosophical treatment of education by the two leading Greek thinkers. The practically minded Roman had little sympathy for or inclination to speculative discussions. Whenever Latin writers treat education they do it for the purpose of stating or criticising, or improving existing conditions, but they, too, do it from the social viewpoint, as the very title of the treatises would suggest: the *De Oratoribus* of Tacitus, the *De Oratore* of Cicero, and the *De Institutione Oratoria* of Quintilian. To the Roman, oratory meant efficient public interest and activity. The ideal orator was he who could combine in his person the functions performed today by the pulpit, the press, the bar, the forum, the university chair, as well as those involved in legislative and judicial activities. Since efficiency in those varied activities depended on oratory, *fari posse* in public life was the purpose assigned to Roman education by Latin writers on the subject.

Christianity emphasized from the first and has ever since insisted upon the social character of human life and, therefore, the social function of education; but whereas the social horizon of Jew and Gentile of old was limited to their own nation, that of Christianity extends to the whole human race. "And, behold, a certain lawyer stood up tempting Him, and saying: 'Master, what shall I do to possess eternal life?' But He said to him: 'What is written in the

Law? How readest thou?' He, answering, said: 'Thou shalt love the Lord, thy God, with thy whole heart, and with thy whole soul, and with all thy strength, and with all thy mind; and thy neighbor as thyself.' And He said to him: 'Thou hast answered right. This do and thou shalt live.' But he, willing to justify himself, said to Jesus: 'And who is my neighbor?'"[2] In the admirable parable of the good Samaritan, and again in His command to His disciples and their followers: "Go ye into the whole world, and teach all nations."[3] Christ has made clear, once and for all time, the true conception of society and the social character of education. His Church, founded on faith in His divine wisdom, hope in His promises, and charity toward all for the love of our common Father, is the one true, ideal society that knows no other limits to its membership and existence than those of the human race and eternity. Christian education was then from the very beginning, as it is today, and will ever be, essentially a moral process, which is another way of saying that it was, is, and will ever remain essentially social. Of this ideal character of Christian society and the social nature of education, the world was again reminded recently by one, who of all men, can speak with authority on matters of this kind. Pope Pius XI, in his *Encyclical on Christian Education of Youth,* stated:

Education is essentially a social and not a mere individual activity. Now, there are three necessary societies, distinct from one another and yet harmoniously combined by God, into which man is born: two, namely, the family and civil society, belong to the natural order; the third, the Church, to the supernatural order. In the first place comes the family instituted directly by God for

---

[2] *Luke,* x, 25–37.
[3] *Matt.,* xxviii, 18–20.

its peculiar purpose, the generation and formation of offspring; for this reason it has priority of nature and therefore of rights over civil society. Nevertheless, the family is an imperfect society, since it has not in itself all the means for its own complete development; whereas civil society is a perfect society, having in itself all the means for its peculiar end, which is the temporal well-being of the community; and so, in this respect, that is, in view of the common good, it has pre-eminence over the family, which finds its own suitable temporal perfection precisely in civil society. The third society, into which man is born when through Baptism he receives the divine life of grace, is the Church; a society of the supernatural order and of universal extent; a perfect society because it has in itself all the means required for its own end, which is the eternal salvation of mankind; hence it is supreme in its own domain. Consequently, education, which is concerned with man as a whole, individually and socially, in the order of nature and in the order of grace, necessarily belongs to all these three societies, in due proportion, corresponding, according to the disposition of Divine Providence, to the co-ordination of their respective ends.

A departure from the traditional trend in the Christian theory of education can be noticed among educational writers of the fifteenth and sixteenth centuries. Though socioethical motives were not foreign to Humanism and Protestantism, both were opposed to the Middle Ages and its conception of life and education; both stressed the subjective, individual consciousness: the Humanists, in their conception of a new culture harking back to pagan Greece and Rome; and the Protestants, in their interpretation of the teachings and practices of early Christianity. In this as in some other tendencies, Humanism and Protestantism were the lineal ancestors in modern times of the eighteenth-century Enlightenment.

The first reaction against this educational individualism appeared with the so-called didacticians or sense realists of the seventeenth century: Bodinus, Ratke, Mulcaster, and Comenius among others. Their purpose was to build up a science of education on a broader foundation than the theory and practice of their own time. Comenius's *Great Didactic* may be taken as the best exposition of the views of those pioneers of a modern science of education. Every human being, we are told, is entitled to some degree of education; everyone has the right and the duty to acquire the knowledge that is needed "to prepare himself for all the actions and desires of life, within what bounds he shall advance, and how his present situation shall be secured." [4] In that sense the purpose of education can be called social. Comenius outlined a state school system bearing a striking resemblance to our own, but he overestimated the importance of the school at the expense of other educational agencies and the educational value of factual knowledge. His Protestant prejudices also blinded him to the importance of the past in accounting for existing social conditions.

The *Great Didactic,* like Mulcaster's *Positions* and other works in the same vein, had very little influence on the educational theory or practice of the age. For the next hundred years and more, theorists and teachers continued to view education chiefly as a personal, individual process; witness Locke's demand that the end of education be "a sound mind in a sound body," that the teacher respect the individual character of each one of his pupils; witness, too, the fierce individualism of Rousseau who brings up his imaginary pupil in complete isolation, away from the influence of the community past and present. The reaction against this one-sided view of the educational process began

---

[4] Keatinge, M. W., *The Great Didactic* (tr.), p. 65. London, Adam and Charles Black, 1896.

in Rousseau's own time. Though starting from the doctrines of the *Emile,* the eighteenth-century Philanthropinists were led, through their own experience as teachers, to recognize the one-sidedness of a conception of education which ignores man's social nature and the social forces contributing to his making or unmaking.

Social regeneration was the end which Pestalozzi pursued .among the little beggars at Stanz and Neuhof, and the ultimate purpose of his experiments at Burgdorf and Yverdun, we are told, was the material, intellectual, and moral improvement of the masses through the proper training of teachers, and, therefore, a more intelligent, more efficient schoolwork than was the rule in his own time. Froebel made the principle of social participation with that of self activity the keynote of kindergarten work. On the other hand the educational doctrines of Herbart are but an echo of eighteenth-century individualism; notwithstanding his insistence upon the ethical side of education, the trend of his theories is individualistic; what he sponsors under the name of character is nothing more, in the last analysis, than an egoistic type of culture. English pedagogy, too, was still following, late in the nineteenth century, the lead of Locke's individualism; witness the pedagogical doctrines of Alexander Bain and Herbert Spencer, the more commonly cited English theorists of the nineteenth century. Bain's treatment of education is confined to the process of instruction in the classroom, and Spencer merely reproduces Rousseau's doctrines in a somewhat more scientific garb. Viewed as a whole, however, the trend of educational theory in the last hundred years shows a decided departure from the narrow pedagogy of the Enlightenment. The change was brought about, partly at least, by the romantic movement and the

revival of historical studies which, after a lapse of over a
hundred years, again turned men's minds to the rich educational bequest of past generations and showed them once
more that through education, society, past and present, lives
in every one of us. Of greater importance still, for the return to a saner view of education, was the Renaissance of
the Christian and national spirit which followed the lessons
of the French Revolution and Napoleonic wars of conquest.
Men had at last realized that the vaunted ideology of the
Enlightenment and the French Revolution headed them
towards the destruction of all existing institutions and nationalities, and they frantically grasped and held fast to anything that would help them escape the hated tyranny of the
French invaders. Limited at first to the furtherance of
nationalistic, political ends, this neosocial trend of educational theory has in the last fifty years received a new impetus through the progress of the social sciences and the
spread and challenge of Marxian theories.

The Social Trend in Educational Practice

If we now turn from the survey of educational theory to
the history of educational practice, we see everywhere, in
all ages and stages of civilization, education treated as an
essentially social process, oftentimes, notwithstanding the
individualistic views of contemporary theorists. The education of the young savage culminates in the "initiation" ceremonies that usher him into the full membership of his tribe.
The purpose of old Chinese education was the twofold one
of familiarizing prospective leaders with the ancient national learning, wherein are minutely described all the relationships of life, and developing among the masses a deep-
rooted habit of doing all things in the hallowed spirit and

manner of the forebears. So it was, *mutatis mutandis,* of all Oriental nations: education had for its purpose the maintenance of tradition, the transmission from one generation to the next of the national religion, views of life, language, literature and arts as so many bonds between succeeding generations. Among the ancient Greeks education was practically identical with their political life or, as we would say today, the whole political, cultural, religious, and social life of the community. In Rome the common practice for centuries was to prepare the young for life, through actual participation in all its activities, by the side of the father, who was at once teacher and a living model.[5]

It was left for Christianity, however, to give the social function of education its highest and fullest development, to bring it into complete harmony with the rights and the needs of the individual. With the ancient peoples the social concept never extended beyond the nation, or race, to which the individual happened to belong. Even the Greeks, the most enlightened of the pagans, considered all other peoples as barbarians, peoples outside the pale of Hellenistic, that is, real society. The Jewish distinction between Chosen People and Gentile and the *Civis Romanus* of the Latins conveys the same political or national connotation of the social concept. Christian society, on the other hand, is not bound to race, or caste, or government; it rises above and extends beyond the confines of particular nationalities. It is a universal heavenly nation into which all are welcomed, who are willing to follow Christ. And the primary purpose of Christian education is to lead men through Christ to their common Father and Lord.

---

[5] See Graves, F. A., *History of Education,* Vol. I. New York: The Macmillan Company, 1922.

This social character of Christian education is seen at its best in medieval society. Whether he was preparing for the professions or the life of the artisan or knight, the child was made to realize that he was being prepared to be, some day a loyal and worthy member of a brotherhood whose rights, interests, and good name he must ever be ready to uphold. At the same time his whole environment constantly reminded him of the fact that he belonged to the great Christian family, in duty bound to deal in all justice and charity with all his fellowmen, whatever be their race or occupation or station in life.

With the advent of the Renaissance, there developed in the practice as in the theory of education a tendency to stress self-development, self-expression, ambition, and individual interests, irrespective of the rights or claims of society upon its members. This spirit of selfish individualism, all too evident in most of the leading personalities of the fifteenth and sixteenth centuries, was gradually caught by education in and out of school, particularly in the education of the sons of the higher aristocracy. Its extreme form appears in the formal skepticism, artificiality, selfish indifference to the welfare of the masses so characteristic of eighteenth-century aristocratic society, and so well reflected in Chesterfield's letters to his son. A reaction set in at the beginning of the nineteenth century, but it has failed thus far to fulfill its promises. If the selfishly individualistic education of Enlightenment days is not so much in evidence today as it used to be, there has been reared in its place, a no less selfishly nationalistic, no less dangerous type of education.[6]

---

[6] See Marique, P. J., *History of Christian Education,* especially Vol. III. New York: Fordham University Press, 1932.

Why Emphasize the Social Aspect of Education?

This brief historical survey has shown us the importance attached everywhere to the social character of education, both in theory and practice, but it has revealed little, if anything, of the inner nature and actual functioning of the process and, therefore, of the reason or reasons why it should be viewed as an essentially social function. A line of approach to our subject is suggested by an old simile, which has been used time and again by philosophers, historians, and orators, to illustrate social concepts, social processes, and social relations. Though much abused of late by sociologists of the radical school, this simile will serve our purpose, if we keep in mind that the notion it conveys is nothing more than a certain analogy between biological and social facts.

Society, like the living organism, is composed of a number of unions or systems, made up of various parts, each one of which has its own definite function, all of them being closely related to one another, and contributing to the harmonious functioning and well-being of the whole. But the terms *social body, social organism,* and similar expressions which social terminology has borrowed from biology have a deeper and, from our standpoint, more fruitful meaning. There is going on in the living body a constant process of waste and reconstruction, through the discharge of worn-out elements and the assimilation of new ones; yet, in spite of and all through the changes affecting its component elements, the animal body preserves its identity. Social life shows us an analogous process of tearing down and building up, in the departure of old individuals and the arrival of new ones who must be assimilated in order to insure the existence and proper functioning of the social organism. And here again the identity of the whole is preserved in spite of the ceaseless change taking place in the component elements. Unity in complexity, reconstruction through assimilation, identity preserved throughout and in spite of change, those are characteristics common to the animal and the social body, but there the similarity ceases, at least in its essential features. Organic reconstruction is a purely mechanical process, whereas social reconstruction, though contributed to by material elements, is essentially a psychical process. Of the many forces furthering this process we are here interested in education and the closely related subjects: heredity, environment, and free will.

Heredity, Environment, and Free Will

Great as the importance of heredity must be acknowledged to be, it is yet supremely necessary to distinguish between that which can be inherited as a reality and that which is transmitted as a disposition. Furthermore, materialistic thinkers have hopelessly obscured the whole question by making all habits the result of biological necessity, leaving nothing to the free, independent determination of man. Let us make it perfectly clear, then, that character is not and cannot be inherited. For, character is the voluntary shape a man gives to his inborn tendencies. Temperament, on the contrary, is transmitted to one by one's forbears, with the bodily structure one may have inherited. According to Kretchmer,[7] there are three bodily structures with three corresponding temperaments: the fat structure, which tends

---

[7] Kretchmer's *Theory of Temperament* is the only one with a solid scientific basis. See his *Körperbau und Charakter.*

to strong emotional oscillations of depression and exaltation; the thin structure, which is peculiar for its relatively
mild affectivity and for its rather strong introspective tendency; the muscular structure, which seems to be a mixture
of the former two and turns out to be the most harmonic.
It can be recognized by the hard muscles which are characteristic of this type, even when relatively little bodily exercise is made. Bodily structure then, and the corresponding
temperament, is inherited. The acquired habits of one's
parents are not. At least there is not a single experiment
which proves that an acquired habit can be transmitted by
birth. For centuries, the Chinese women have been shorten-
ing their feet, and yet the feet of their children will always
grow normally, if not put into the short shoes. The scars,
which for centuries have been inflicted on the backs of certain savage races, have never become hereditary. As for
illnesses, it seems that some do penetrate as far as the genes
and are hereditary. Such are the different kinds of insanity.
Others are transmitted only as dispositions, as, for example,
cancer and tuberculosis. Whether these predispositions
come to be actualized or not will depend on the kind of life
an individual lives.

The arguments brought up in favor of the transmission
of acquired habits do not stand a severe criticism. That in
certain families a certain predisposition for music exists is
not necessarily the result of heredity, but of the atmosphere
in which these families live, which naturally influences the
children. A boy who from his earliest childhood has heard
excellent music, who always plays with instruments, who
starts learning two or more instruments when he is six or
seven years old will naturally have an enormous advantage
over children who start their musical career at the age of

12 or 14.   However, it will not be the result of heredity, but simply of the milieu in which he has lived.

In reality, then, a man is the result of three important factors: first of all, of the hereditary mass which he receives from his parents and which constitutes his temperament (moody, agressive, quiet, alert, and so on); secondly, of the surroundings in which he lives.   It has been found, in Chicago, for example, that no factor correlates so highly with crime as that of milieu.   What a man is depends very much on the family life he lives. ´ Finally, there is the individual's own free will.   Each man can make of his natural, inborn urges what he chooses.   His habits naturally will always be highly colored by his temperament and inborn dispositions.   But whether these or those habits do or do not come to be, whether he integrates his life in terms of animal instincts or high moral ideals—all that will depend in a great measure on himself.

As for the thesis propounded with so much fervor by eugenists with an axe to grind—that intelligent parents will necessarily have intelligent children—it is simply false.   We refer our readers to such fundamental books as Professor Jennings's *Biological Basis of Human Nature* (New York, 1930).   It will be seen that selective breeding does make it somewhat more probable that the intelligent parents will have intelligent children, but it is by no means certain. Each individual in a series has the capacity of reproducing any other individual of that series.   Bright people can have dull children, and vice versa.   However, by mating those that are similar, the probability of reproducing the type is heightened, but that is all.

Heredity, then, is an important factor in the life of any man.   As Napoleon used to say, men start to live one hundred years before they are born. The riotous living of an ancestor, dead fifty years ago, may be the cause of epilepsy in this or that child, or may predispose him to this or that type of illness. We are all born with certain natural urges, whose intensity depends on a temperament which is, within certain limits, hereditary. But there is nothing fatalistic about this. If we owe it to heredity to come into this world with a greater or lesser tendency toward good or evil, we cannot, nor should we ever hold it responsible for vice and virtue; vice and virtue are not inherent in the tendencies, either within us or outside of us, that would drag us into the mire or lift us above it; they are a product of our own making, of our willingness to be carried downstream or determination to go up against it. There is probably no clearer, or more sweeping recognition of the influence of heredity than that contained in the doctrine of original sin; yet, Christianity is no less emphatic upon the freedom of the will, that we are responsible for our own acts, that heredity merely supplies the primitive data of nature out of which it is our duty, with the aid of our fellowmen and the grace of God, but mostly through our own efforts, to fashion our personality, in other words, to be educated.

The Broader View of Education

Education is ordinarily thought of as a formal, well-regulated process, centering around the school, and lasting from ten to twenty years according to the length of the individual's period of school life; but we can conceive it as a lifelong process, at times formal and conscious, but mostly informal, unconscious, or semiconscious, which is furthered by the whole environment of the individual. This broader and, withal, truer conception has for us the advantage of making at once apparent the close relation between the educative process on the one hand and the process of social assimilation and social reconstruction on the other, though the two processes should not be identified. Education has other aims besides the social one, and, on the other hand, it is but one of the many forces at work in the preservation and perpetuation of the social organism; religion, language, culture, national ideals and interests, a common past, and a common form of government are so many forces that may and should make for social union, but it will be noted that their influence upon the rising generation is felt through some kind of educative process.

Education has its real starting point and first incentive in an instinct that is closely related to that of reproduction and is shared in common by man and the lower animals: the tendency, namely, which prompts parents to care for and watch over the young. Its manifestations are connected with the period of helplessness of the offspring, which, in the animal world is of short duration, but lasts for years in the human race and has been rightly considered a great boon both to the child and parents. For the child it means a slow, but broad and deep development of all its inherent capacities, while it demands from the parents long years of tender and loving care which cannot fail to have a refining, ennobling influence upon their character.

This close association between parent and child, which marks the beginnings of the educative process and social assimilation, has at first no set, definite purpose, such as education will assume later on in the home, the school, the church, and the vocation. Rather, it is a sort of extension of the unconscious process of physical growth and development into the spiritual field, and it is only by degrees that it becomes conscious, though remaining essentially informal. It is in that way that the child first learns the mother tongue, the very name of which is suggestive of the informal method through which it is at first transmitted from one generation to another; it is in that way, too, that the various influences of home life, which will prepare the ground for formal teaching and discipline, are being brought to bear upon the child. But this process of informal assimilation is not limited to the home; it proceeds beyond its confines, gaining in breadth all the while, as the environment of the child becomes wider and wider through his coming into contact with the many forms of civilized life, the many products of the labor of the past generations, which at every step elicit from the child wonder and questions.

Aids to the Philosophy of Education

When surveying education from the social viewpoint, we should not fail to take advantage of the progress made in the social sciences during the last one hundred years. Biological anthropology which deals with the anatomy and physiology of the human body, as found in different races or in different social groups of the same race, may help us understand and explain differences in capacity for culture and education; ethnology, with the aid of philology and history, will give us an account of the growth and development of the intellectual possessions of nations, their language, literature, traditions, customs, and beliefs, which are the essential elements of their educational content; social and comparative psychology, which study the psychic phenomena of community life, will throw some light on the national spirit of different countries, which may help us understand differences in national types of education. Further gains for the philosophy of education may be expected from the closely related sciences of economics, social ethics, and politics which must be appealed to whenever we try to determine the influence upon education of the wealth of nations, the relations of capital and labor, national ethical standards, the form of government, and the conception of state's rights and duties. Nor should we neglect the data supplied by statistical researches in various fields: statistics of morality; statistics of crime, school attendance, school mortality, illiteracy, book reading, and so on. Statistical data, however, may lead us to false conclusions if we do not carefully check up the data gathered in one field by those gathered in other fields; if furthermore, we do not read all our information in the light of the right ethical standards.

The philosophy of education may also receive valuable aid from the science of sociology, provided it be free from the naturalistic, Marxian incubus which weighs it down in such systems as those of Auguste Comte and Spencer. The analogy between society and the living organism, which was referred to before in a figurative sense, is treated by those sociologists as a reality; for them, the individual bears to society the relation that actually exists between the living cell and the organism; man's individuality is engulfed in his social surroundings ultimately reduced to economic, that is, physical forces; language, literature, art, science, philosophy, morality, r ligion and education are merely by-products of social, that is, economic life. The theory may have the merit of simplicity but it ignores the one essential factor in social life, the individual consciousness.

Masses of men, though one in language, customs, and interests, do not constitute a nation, they must be conscious of being bound together by the ties of a common nationhood. A number of men imbued with the same ideas on religion do not constitute a religious body; to be a religious body, they must be conscious of being united by a common faith. The animal organism needs but a union of forces to be a reality; but social forces must produce an act of consciousness before the social organism can be said to possess reality; without this act—which is an act of the free will—no social organism exists.

Therefore consciousness is of vastly greater importance for the social organism than the organic individual, the cell, is for the living body. The cell is but a part of the animal organism, whereas the consciousness of the individual is not only a part of the social organism but the source of its continued existence. Compared with the organism, the cell is a unit of a lower order; the organism is its end; but in the relations between the individual and the community, the latter is not superior to the individual; both are complements of each other, and neither of them is merely a means for the other.[8]

Topics for Further Study

1. "Plato's conception of education is at once socialistic and aristocratic."   Comment.

2. Contrast the Platonic and the Aristotelian conception of the educative function of the family.

3. Contrast the educative influence of the family in, (a) the Athenian and Spartan city states, (b) in Pagan and Jewish society, and (c) in Pagan and Christian society.

4. Contrast the Greek and Roman state policy in education.

5. From the social viewpoint show the unnatural character of Rousseau's conception of education, according to nature.

6. Differentiate the social from the political view of education.

7. "The function of the state as an educational agency is to supplement the educative function of the family."   Discuss.

8. On what grounds can you justify compulsory school attendance?

---

[8] Willmann-Kirsch, *The Science of Education*, Vol. I, p. 39.   Archabbey Press, Beatty, Pa., 1921.

9. What is the meaning of *environment?*

10. Differentiate "perceptive" from "conceptual" environment.

11. To what extent can we speak of the past as part of our environment?

12. "Heredity versus environment as factors in the shaping of personality." Discuss.

13. Differentiate *growth* from *development.*

14. Discuss education as "growth" and "development."

15. Discuss the importance of social inheritance.

16. "Physical versus social heredity." Discuss.

17. Discuss the relation of general to vocational education.

18. "Democratic education should provide opportunity for the elite." Discuss.

19. "Liberal education as a prerequisite in preparing for the professions." Discuss.

20. "Tradition versus progress in education." Discuss.

Suggestions for Reading

Aristotle, *Politics.*

Bagley, W., *The Educative Process* (New York, 1905).

Bryce, J., *Modern Democracies* (New York, 1921).

Conklin, E., *Heredity and Environment* (Princeton, 1929).

Counts, G., *Dare the School Build a New Social Order?* (New York, 1932).

Dewey, J., *The School and Society* (Chicago, 1915).

Finney, R., *A Sociological Philosophy of Education* (New York, 1928).

Foerster, F., *Christentum und Paedagogik* (München, 1920).

Graves, F., *History of Education* (New York, 1924).

Kidd, B., *Social Evolution* (New York, 1894).

Kilpatrick, W., *Education and the Social Crisis* (New York, 1932).

Learned, W., *Realism in American Education* (Cambridge, 1932).

Lindsay, A., *The Essentials of Democracy* (London, 1929).

Lippmann, W., *A New Social Order* (New York, 1933).

Myers and Williams, *Education in a Democracy* (New York, 1937).

Payne, G., *Readings in Educational Sociology* (New York, 1937).

Pius XI, *Encyclical on the Christian Education of Youth* (tr.) (New York, 1930).

Plato, *Republic.*

Willmann-Kirsch, *The Science of Education* (Beatty, 1921).

CHAPTER IV

Psychological Survey

Man's Dual Nature

"Man is a creature composed of body and soul, made to the image and likeness of God." This simple truth, taught throughout the ages to the Christian child, will be our starting point and our guide in the more detailed study of education that is to follow. Evidently, there can be no intention here of going into an elaborate consideration of the questions raised in the opening sentence of this chapter. Our task will be the more modest and simpler one of presenting, in a rather condensed form, the teachings of Scholastic philosophy as a sort of introduction to the study of the educative process.

Considering, first, man's nature, we shall say, in the language of the School, that it is made up of two substances: one spiritual, the soul; the other material, the body. Man's personality is the resultant of the intimate union of the two substances, neither of which is by itself complete. Life is imparted to the body by the soul which in turn receives its present visible individuality from the body, and this intimate union of the two substances is expressed by the word "I," that is, a certain person actually distinct from other persons, endowed with a permanent unity amidst the complexity and transitoriness of psychical states. This unity and permanency of the ego are asserted by consciousness and constantly referred to in the language of everyday life. When I say, "I hear," I do not refer the sensation to the body alone or to the soul alone, but to their union in the ego. When I say, "I thought," "I promised," "I regret," "I will go," I affirm the identity of the ego of the past with the ego of to-day or the future.

"The soul is the principle of life," is probably the simplest and most satisfactory of many definitions that have been given of the soul. Life is more easily described than defined, though many definitions of it have been suggested. The following, *vita in motu*, "life consists in movement," has become a sort of axiom, and, because of its paramount importance for the understanding of life and education, it is worth while to dwell at some length on this notion of movement.

Activity, the Keynote of Life

Activity or movement, the capacity for action of some kind, to be the cause of some effect, belongs to the very nature of things; it is a natural consequence of existence. Its opposite, inertia, is not the absence of activity, but the inability of material bodies for self-activity. To say that a body is inert does not mean that the body is deprived of all activity, but that it cannot of itself start movement, change its position. Every being then is active, but not in the same way, or in the same degree. The lowest type of activity found in inorganic nature may be characterized as mechanical and external, though it is also internal in some measure, as a result of physicochemical processes. Organic matter, while subject to the laws of inorganic matter, is possessed of a higher type of activity that may be termed *spontaneous,* manifesting itself in various ways. In the plant, spontaneity is shown in the processes of nutrition, internal growth and development, and reproduction, the essential functions of vegetative life. In addition to those forms of activity the animal is endowed with the capacity for sensation, implying appetency, and locomotion. Over and above the preceding types of activity there is, in man, intellectual and voluntary activity.

The Threefold Character of Human Life

The essential characteristic of life, then, is a type of activity which may be called spontaneous or immanent action —the faculty of any organic being, in some measure, to direct its own activity towards a definite end. Spontaneity, neither implies nor excludes freedom or reflection, and, as just pointed out, it is exhibited in varying degrees in plants, animals, and man. Vegetative life, that is, organic life in its lowest form, needs material organs and is characterized by nutrition, self-development, and reproduction; sensitive or animal life involves the preceding and is characterized by sensation, appetency, and locomotion; human life is at once vegetative, sensitive, intellectual, and moral; its characteristics are intelligence, free will, and sentiment. In man, all three lives, together with all the phenomena that are peculiar to each, have their source, their principle and natural relation to one another in the human soul. Each one of the three lives is an integral part and a peculiar expression of human nature, and none of the three can be left out of consideration by either psychology or education, whenever they intend to give a complete account of themselves. Beyond and above these three lives, but closely related to them is the supernatural life, the life of faith and grace which corresponds to and prepares for man's ultimate end.

Though body and soul are intimately related they may be studied separately. The living body with its functions is properly the object of physiology. The soul, its faculties and activities, form the subject of psychology which is either empirical or rational. Empirical psychology is the science of psychical facts and their laws, whereas rational or metaphysical psychology is concerned with the nature of the soul and its destiny. The two "psychologies" should not be confused; each has its distinct province; but they should not be entirely separated either, because both are concerned with the same object viewed under two different aspects: the human soul and its activities.

The intimate union of body and soul points to a more or less similar relation between physiology and psychology. Many facts of consciousness, such as sensations, images, and recollections, are closely related to the actual condition of the organism, whether as effects or causes. In general, there is no psychical state that is entirely free from some physical or physiological concomitant, and it is therefore impossible to gain an adequate knowledge of psychical facts, without some knowledge of the corresponding physiological and physical facts.

This close relation between psychology and physiology has given rise to new sciences like physiological psychology and psychophysics, the purpose of which it is to study and measure psychical phenomena directly related to some physical or physiological antecedent. Research in those new fields of scientific investigation cannot fail to be useful, and it should be welcomed by students of psychology and education, so long as its purpose is to determine the share that physical and physiological elements have in psychical phenomena, the distinction between body and soul being always kept in view. Whenever, as is so common in the "psychologies" of the last fifty years, the existence of the soul is ignored or denied, the best that can be said of those investigations is that they are pseudoscientific.

The Materials of Experience

All the facts that come within our experience fall into one of the following classes:

(A) Physical, that is, the facts of material nature considered independently of life, such as form, color, weight, attraction, height, electricity;

(B) Physiological, the facts of organic life, like nutrition, circulation of sap or blood, reproduction, muscular movements; and

(C) Psychological, the facts of psychical life, such as sensation, sentiments, thought, volitions.

Physical and physiological facts belong to the realm of matter, either organic or inorganic; extension and form are their characteristics; their cause is perceived only in its effect, and their end in organic bodies is the preservation of the individual and the species. Psychological facts, on the other hand, are independent of extension; they happen in time rather than in space, and their end, insofar as man is concerned, is the development of psychical life, the true, the good, the beautiful; and their cause is at once perceived as being the ego. I am not conscious, under normal conditions, of my having anything to do with the processes of my digestion and blood circulation, but I am conscious of my being the cause of my thoughts and volitions.

The Scope and Method of Psychology

Like every science, psychology has its own specific method, introspection, the faculty of inner observation, or the turning inward of the mind on itself. This subjective, introspective method is supplemented by other sources of information which, taken altogether, may be referred to as the objective method. The psychologist may appeal to the results of other men's observations of their own mind; to language, history, animal psychology, physiology, experiments, in order to check up the findings of his own introspection; but all those objective means of psychological investigation are secondary; introspection is and should ever remain the core around which should center all the particular methods devised for psychological analysis.

One of the first tasks that confronts the psychologist, as it does the student of every science, is the proper distribution of the facts he intends to study, and he soon discovers that these facts admit of a threefold classification.

(A) There are, first, intellectual phenomena, such as perceptions, ideas, remembrances, judgments, the first characteristic of which is that they are representative; they give us an intellectual representation of some object. A second feature of intellectual phenomena is that they are objective, in the sense that any idea or representation of any being implies the dualism of a thinking subject and known object. Intellectual phenomena finally are fatal and at once active and passive; fatal, in the sense that in the face of absolute evidence the intellect is not at liberty to accept the contrary notion; active to the extent that they are influenced by attention; passive, in the sense that knowledge does not produce its object, but presupposes and represents it.

(B) Secondly, there are emotional phenomena, such as fear, anger, admiration, respect, and awe, which are affective and therefore subjective, passive, and fatal. A feeling of whatever kind is not a representation of an object, but a modification of the subject. Emotional phenomena are passive and fatal to the extent that they cannot be aroused or stopped at will, but flow naturally from certain given antecedents.

(C) The third class of mental states comprises volitional phenomena such as intentions, resolutions, and tendencies which imply an effort—an act of which we are more or less conscious of being the author—and these phenomena are essentially active.

This threefold classification of psychical phenomena corresponds to a threefold capacity or faculty: thinking, feeling, and willing, the three modes of expression of the ego, which constantly copenetrate one another. Psychological analysis deals with thinking or feeling or willing or any particular element in one of these divisions, independently of all other psychical phenomena, but in actual life we are never faced by a case of pure thinking or feeling or willing. Every situation that we may come across is a complex one. A volition, for example, is eminently an act of the will, but it presupposes a knowledge of the situation facing the self, which pertains to the intellect, and motives of action, which partly belong to the province of feeling. Over against the classification just outlined there is, among others, the traditional Scholastic division of psychical faculties into cognitive or apprehensive, and conative or appetitive. Each one of these in turn subdivides into sensuous or lower psychical powers and higher or rational or spiritual capacities. To the lower group of cognitive faculties belong perception, sensuous memory, and imagination; to the higher belong conception, judgment, and reasoning. Likewise on the appetitive side of psychical life we have all kinds of instinctive tendencies over against the rational appetite or will in the true sense of the term. Feeling is not adjudged to a specific class, but is treated as the affective element in cognitive and appetitive phenomena. The division of psychical life into lower or sensuous and higher or rational holds, of course, in our classification, as it does in the Scholastic arrangement. There is this difference, however, that since affective phenomena belong to a class of their own in our classification, we must keep in mind a distinction between, say, such feelings as anger and the love of truth.

Psychical Growth

'The order in which psychical facts should be studied is suggested by nature itself. It is the order of genetic development. First come the faculties and processes of sensitive life such as sensation, perception, memory, imagination, desire, appetites, instinctive tendencies; next come intellect and will, properly so called, and sentiment. This order is not only genetic or chronological, but logical as well. Intelligence presupposes sensation, percepts, and images, which supply the material for intellectual operations; sentiment, though sometimes semiconscious, even entirely subconscious in its origin, usually starts from an idea and therefore presupposes intelligence; the functioning of the will, free will, that is, is inconceivable without a knowledge of what is to be done and a desire to attain it. On the other hand, we should not, as Rousseau does in the *Emile,* lose sight of the unity of psychical life and the solidarity of all the elements that compose it. All the capacities and tendencies that unfold during life are present in the newborn child and they all grow and develop at the same time, though not at the same rate. To confine the educative process first to the body and instinct, next to the intellect, and last to sentiment and will is not then "education according to nature" but an artificial process that all along violates the mandates of nature. To the extent that the age and capacity of the child, boy or girl, will permit, the education of body, instinctive tendencies, sense perception, memory, imagination, sentiment, intellect, and will, should be simultaneous.

Such is, in general outline, in the light of tradition and common sense, the psychical situation facing the educator. In subsequent chapters, by way of introduction to some particular phase of the educative process, we shall have occasion to return to the various divisions of the above outline for a more detailed consideration. For the present, it will serve our general purpose to contrast the traditional conception of psychical life and psychology with the more widespread theories outside of Catholic circles during the last thirty years.

Neopsychologies

Common features. While there are many and, in some instances, radical differences between one neopsychological system and another, they all have in common the following characteristics:

They ignore or else betray a strange ignorance of the status and progress of psychology before this century. They all seem to take it for granted that the systematic, scientific study of psychical phenomena began with the wholesale application to the study of psychical life of the methods used in biology, physics, and chemistry.

Their language, though bristling with supposedly scientific terms, often lacks the clarity and precision that one expects to find in works claiming scientific accuracy.

The general trend of these psychological theories is materialistic. Psychical phenomena are explained—at least the attempt is made to explain these phenomena—in terms of physics or chemistry or physiology, without any reference to an inner principle distinct from the body.

There is a tendency on the part of some of the neopsychologists not to assign to psychology a particular province of its own. They consider psychical phenomena as one phase of physical and physiological reality, and thus they are led to do away with a distinct science of psychology.

Other innovators of the same class would rather consider psychology as a branch of, or, at the most, a mere adjunct to sociology. Psychology has for a long time been thought of as one of the social sciences, but it has ever preserved its autonomy, claiming as its own the study of the human soul and all its manifestations. According to the sociopsychologists, it should be thought of only in social terms, as an aid in the solution of the problems we meet in ethics, economics, politics, education, and history. Each one of those sciences is concerned with some aspect of human group behavior but all of them, like the new psychologies, are made to view it from the Marxian, materialistic conception of society, which brings us back to that characteristic of the neopsychologies which is most far reaching in its consequences for education.

If we assume that man's nature is all reducible to material principles, man's behavior is entirely subject to and determined by the laws governing matter. Freedom of action, in the common, Scholastic sense of the term, does not exist, nor can it exist. In business or social or political relations, or in the process of education, man's behavior is determined by forces, both internal and external, over which he has no control. Frankly admitted and taught by psychologists of the behavioristic school, this determinism is more or less happily disguised under a mixture of half-hearted admissions, restrictions, and limitations by psychologists of other schools, but they cannot escape it as the logical conclusion of their ignoring the existence of a spiritual soul.

Distinctive features. While the above-mentioned characteristics belong in a greater or less degree to all new schools of psychology, they are differentiated from one another by their particular viewpoint in the study of psychology.

Structural psychology is concerned with the analysis of mental states and the discovery of the "laws" according to which the elements of mental states combine. The knowledge phase of consciousness is ultimately reduced to sensory elements which combine according to the "laws" of association, to produce percepts and ideas. Feeling is reduced to the two elements of pleasantness and unpleasantness. The study of the will is confined to the consideration of the kinesthetic sensations involved in activity. On the whole, structural psychologists seem to be interested in feeling, particularly sensation and its contributions to the cognitive side of psychical life.

Functional psychology is closely related to the adjustment aim, so popular among educational theorists and teachers some thirty years ago. Like structural psychology it is primarily concerned with feelings, sensations, images, and with their contribution to the knowledge side of psychical life.

But it stresses them as mental functions, dynamic forces in the process of adapting the individual to his environment, whereas the structural psychologist is rather interested in their static form. Mental functions, say the functionalists, parallel bodily functions in man's behavior, through the central nervous processes. The interest of the functionalists in the problem of adjusting the individual to his environment leads them to emphasize the importance of instinct which they consider as the original and most fundamental equipment of man in the process of adjustment.

Behaviorism is primarily interested in motor activity, in the belief that physical behavior is the only thing about man that can be studied directly and can lead to reliable information concerning the neurological conditions involved in any particular act. Man is treated as a piece of machinery concerning which physics, mechanics, chemistry, physiology, and anatomy can tell us all that is worth knowing. In explaining visual sensations and subsequent visual images, for example, the only facts that we must take into consideration are the wave lengths of light, the structure of the end organ and the neurological mechanism that reacts to the impression received. The traditional explanation of instinctive behavior must be discarded, we are told, in view of the importance of reactions learned under controlled conditions. Behaviorism has shown a marked interest in the study of animal and child behavior, through which it has developed an objective technique that it considers of great value in the study of adult behavior.

Purposive psychology is a type of psychology that recognizes in human nature the presence of tendencies toward some end, some goal, or some purpose. It is opposed to the mechanistic explanation of mental and bodily activity, and

it considers instinct as a purely mental force just as important for the explanation of human behavior as gravitation,
cohesion, and other physical forces. As human beings we
possess not only inborn tendencies to act in a certain way,
but capacities to act in that way and reach a goal which is
foreseen.

Psychoanalysis, another one of the new psychologies, grew
out of the treatment of nervous and mental disorders. It
originated at the close of the last century, with the publica-
tion of the works of the Viennese physician, Sigmund
Freud. All mental abnormalities, according to Freud, have
their origin in some interference with the sex instinct, which
can be traced even as far back as early childhood. Freud
not only considers the sex instinct responsible for mental
aberrations, but he also considers it as the deciding factor in
the shaping of personality and character, in the interest
which we manifest in any particular aspect of the life about
us. According to Adler, one of Freud's disciples, conflicts
between individual and social interests are not due to the
sex instinct, but to the desire for power. For Jung, another
Freudian, the preservation of one's individuality is the great
driving force in life. Far more deserving of serious consideration than their one-sided explanation of psychical life
is the attention paid by psychoanalysts to the subconscious
self, growing out of their practical experience in the treatment of nervous and mental disorders.

The last type of new psychology to be mentioned here,
Gestalt psychology, is of German origin like the preceding
and in a certain way its very opposite. Instead of assigning
a single, definite cause to any given reaction, say, a given
stimulus for a given visual sensation, it prefers to insist upon
the entire psychical situation at any given moment. In the

above illustration, for example, it would say that the visual sensation depends not only on the stimulus operating at the time, on the particular condition of the end organ and neurological mechanism, and on the amount of attention the sensation received, but on other sensations arising in the subject at the time, and the whole complexus of images, ideas, and dispositions of the subject. A more general expression of the Gestalt viewpoint would be the following: Anything happening in the psychical life of the individual influences and is influenced by all the other elements in the past and present psychical life of the individual. This position would lead one to believe that Gestalt psychology is founded on the assumption of the existence of a spiritual soul, but the works in which the theory is expounded, though more or less conveying that impression, never state the case very clearly.

The types of psychology which have just been sketchily described are all offshoots of naturalism, and they all share, more or less, in its fundamental weaknesses and shortcomings as an explanation of human psychical life and a guide in education. As one may readily see from the textbooks used in the teaching and study of these new psychologies, their interest lies in the lower aspects of psychical life: sensations, percepts, images, desires, and instinctive tendencies. Those are mental states into which there enters an important physical and physiological factor, and they lend themselves more or less readily to the application of the methods used in physical or physiological sciences. When the neopsychologists attempt to explain the higher psychical phenomena they miss the issue. The neopsychologies certainly have contributed much to a better knowledge of the lower mental processes, but this gain has been made at the cost of an immense harm done to many, by the spread of all kinds of false notions on mental life and education.

Topics for Further Study

1. "The principle of self-activity in education did not originate with Froebel." Discuss.

2. Explain the meaning of the term *faculty* in psychology.

3. "Man is a moral being because of the threefold character of his nature." Prove or disprove that statement.

4. Show the indebtedness of the science of psychology, if any, to any three of the following: Socrates, Plato, Aristotle, the Stoics, St. Augustine, St. Thomas Aquinas, Vives, Locke, Condillac, Hamilton, Bain, Sully, Wundt, and Binet.

5. Trace educational psychology as a science to its origin.

6. Explain the relation to educational psychology, if any, of any two of the following: physics, statistics, comparative and social psychology, psychiatry, and animal psychology.

7. Show the contributions of child study to methodology.

8. Show the contributions of the psychology of adolescence to methodology.

9. "Psychology is one of the social sciences." Explain.

10. "Man's nature is not reducible to material principles." Prove.

11. "The soul always functions as a unit." Explain and illustrate.

12. "There is nothing in the intellect that was not before in the senses." Explain.

13. Contrast the Scholastic and sensualist interpretation of the preceding statement.

14. From actual life or classroom work, show the contribution of feeling to the cognitive side of psychical life.

15. Give a brief description of the central nervous system.

16. Discuss the "localization of functions" in the nervous system.

17. Differentiate mental from physiological functions in psychical life.

18. Show the relation of behaviorism to evolutionism.

19. "There is a fundamental difference between child and animal behavior." Explain and illustrate.

20. Explain the meaning of the term *mental hygiene* and submit a critical evaluation of its services to education.

SUGGESTIONS FOR READING

Bode, B., *Conflicting Psychologies of Learning* (Boston, 1929).

Castiello, J., *A Humane Psychology of Education* (New York, 1936).

Fearon, A., *The Two Sciences of Psychology* (New York, 1937).

Froebes, L., *Lehrbuch der Experimentellen Psychologie* (Freiburg, 1928).

Hollingworth, H., *Educational Psychology* (New York, 1933).

Jennings, S., *The Biological Basis of Man's Nature* (New York, 1930).

Maher, M., *Psychology* (London, 1915).

Marechal, J., *Science and Psychology* (New York, 1927).

McDougall, W., *Outlines of Abnormal Psychology* (New York, 1926).

Morgan, J., *The Psychology of the Unadjusted School Child* (New York, 1927).

Ragsdale, C., *Modern Psychologies and Education* (New York, 1932).

Spranger, E., *Types of Men* (Halle, 1928).

Symonds, P., *Diagnosing Personality and Conduct* (New York, 1931).

Terman, L., *The Intelligence of School Children* (Boston, 1919).

Thorndike, E., *Educational Psychology* (New York, 1927).

CHAPTER V

Educational Aims and Ideals

Instinctive Educational Motives

Viewed from the standpoint of the individual, all educational aims can be traced back to various motives that can be referred to as direct or indirect educational interests. We may be interested in education, its content, and its activities, for their own sake, because the acquisition of knowledge or skill will satisfy the instinctive craving for intellectual activity. But we may also be interested in education because we consider it as an aid, a means to secure something beyond it. We may value education for its refining or steadying influence upon personality; we may value it because it is a means of acquiring wealth or power or honor; again we may be interested in education because it may serve as an introduction into a certain class of people, or because it furthers one's supreme end in life.

The direct, instinctive interest in education is best observed in children. It appears in their eagerness to listen to stories, in the questions they are likely to ask at any moment on all kinds of subjects. At first the ever recurring question is "What is this?" or "What is that?" and the child's curiosity can be satisfied with a name. Gradually other questions follow, showing that the child's speculative interest is awakened: "How do you do that?", "What is that for?", "Why?" This instinctive desire to know is probably the best of the teacher's aids in intellectual education, but it cannot be summoned or controlled at will. The child's intellectual capacity and the natural development of its intellectual interest must be the teacher's guide in his appeal to the child's curiosity.

Another evidence of this instinctive, direct interest in education is the eagerness of all healthy children to do something, to use their hands at all kinds of little tasks, which has been turned to such good account in the manual exercises of the school. Further evidences of the direct, instinctive interest in education appear in the native tendency to imitate, to express our thoughts and feelings, to collect things, to share what we have learned with others. Children delight in repeating sounds, words, gestures; in imitating parents, teachers, playmates; in collecting all kinds of things; in relating what they have seen or heard.

The existence and importance of these instinctive dispositions have been recognized all through the ages, but it is only in comparatively recent times that they have been subjected to a systematic study by psychologists and educational theorists.

If properly taken care of those native dispositions will prove the teacher's surest guides and aids in intellectual education. With the more highly gifted children, under favorable conditions, the native urge to inquire, to know, to express one's sensations, images, and ideas through words or some craftsmanship may develop into the disinterested search of the scientist and scholar for scientic truth, or the striving of the poet and artist for beauty of form in speech or plastic or musical expression. Those interests, however, are rather exceptional and have been neglected by the school, except when a discriminating, conscientious teacher would detect and encourage some budding talent among his scholars. In the present guidance movement there is at least a promise that the gifted child and youth will be better taken care of by the school than they have been in the past.

Educational Aims

The history of education has recorded a rather long list of aims which, at one time or another, have been assigned to education by theorists or social agencies or the national will. A detailed, critical treatment of all those aims would require a volume of its own. We must confine ourselves here to a brief exposition of some of those aims, with such comment as the nature and importance of the subject call for.

The Cultural Aim

The term *culture* has been used and is still used in educational literature with a variety of connotations. Among the Romans the term *culture* (*cultura, colere*) meant originally and literally a tilling, cultivating the soil, in order to improve its productiveness. By analogy, when transferred to the field of education, the term came to mean the cultivation, amelioration, refinement of all our capacities, physical, intellectual, aesthetic, moral, and religious. Thus, through play, gymnastics, games, and sports, the purpose of culture is to develop the latent capacities for strength, agility, gracefulness in bearing and in movements; through appropriate studies and exercises, to stimulate and develop the aesthetic sentiment, the desire for knowledge, and the capacity to think for one's self. The Greek *paideia* and the Latin *humanitas* would more or less convey the same notion as the word *culture.* All three terms, like the phrase "liberal education" refer to the same process of developing, improving, and refining native talents, and appeal to the same interest, which for want of a better term, we shall call the *cultural interest.* This interest is concerned with the materials of instruction, but never for their own sake or their practical value. It is aesthetic, artistic in character, but it should not be confused with the interest of the artist in painting or sculpture or music; it is concerned with language, literature, history, science, and philosophy, but not in the same way as the poet or scholar or scientist is interested in poetry or scientific research or philosophical speculation. It lacks the element of disinterestedness which is one of the characteristics of the devotion of the artist, poet, scientist, or scholar to his particular pursuit.

Education for culture brings the individual into contact with many subjects, but its purpose is never a thorough mastery of subject matter or the acquisition of practical skill; its one concern is the development and enrichment of personality. It will use poetry and art in order to develop the aesthetic sentiment, the ability to appreciate and enjoy the beautiful in all its expressions. It is interested in language, but only insofar as the study of language will be an aid in acquiring the ability to express oneself with ease and elegance. It is interested in science because the man of culture should be acquainted with his physical environment, more especially because scientific studies further a vigorous mental life. Education for culture is interested in customs, habits of life, and social intercourse, because one of the essential characteristics of culture is the ability to move with ease and assurance in social circles.

Physically, culture means dignity in bearing, ease and

gracefulness in movement.   Intellectually, it means, in the first place a wide range of knowledge over which the individual has perfect control; it means, in the next place, a keen, alert intellect that can easily turn from one subject to another, together with a highly developed aesthetic faculty. From the viewpoint of the emotions, culture demands a perfect control of the coarser feelings, the ability to avoid "scenes" in social intercourse; it also demands a genuine, ready sympathy for the feelings of others, which, combined with the quick apprehension of a situation in social gatherings, will enable a person to act with tact.   But the domain of culture extends still further.   In the full sense of the term, it means a refined conscience, a will to do one's duty quietly, unostentatiously, at whatever might be the cost to one's self; it means, above all, a deep realization of one's dependence upon the Providence of God and a will to please Him and do His will to the best of one's ability.

Culture, then, such as we consider it here, is something other than the external polish that goes by the name *accomplishments,* for it reaches deep into the individual's nature. It is not a by-product of education as one may receive in so-called finishing schools.   It begins in early life and cannot be said to be exclusively the product of any one educational agency, because it is advanced or retarded by every influence brought to bear upon the individual in the home, the school, the Church, or society at large.   Like a tender plant, it will grow and blossom and bear fruit only under favorable conditions.

Culture, from the individual's viewpoint, is not synonymous with civilization.   To be civilized means that one lives in conformity with the requirements of community life, but the conformity might be very superficial.   To be cultured

means that the best there is in civilization has sunk deep
into one's nature, has become, so to say, part of one's personality. A crisis is likely to bring into sharp contrast the
merely civilized and the cultured man; witness the horrors
of the Reign of Terror in France.

Culture is interested in the formation of the whole personality and therefore is opposed to early specialization. The
man who began too early his preparation for efficiency in
some trade or profession will start in life with a dwarfed
personality, will be a narrow specialist, out of touch and
sympathy with the broader view of life. Culture, however,
far from being opposed to efficiency, is the best preparation
and foundation for efficiency and leadership in all walks of
life. Education for culture, if it be of the right kind, aims
above all else at the formation of what the French very
aptly call *un bon esprit, un esprit juste,* which more or less
corresponds to the English "a sound mind," that is, a mind
that sees things as they should be seen. Culture, therefore
true culture, is synonymous with intellectual vigor—the habit
of hard, even painful thinking. It is the very opposite of
superficiality. The cultured mind has learned to look for
reality beneath appearances, to look for the scientific truth
that a formula is supposed to convey, to look for ideas and
their relations beneath the words which express them. And
culture is one of the best antidotes against the danger of
narrow-mindedness, to which all specialists are exposed. A
broad, solid culture will ever help us realize that the domain
of knowledge or skill does not begin and end at the frontiers
of our specialty, that beyond the little world of our profession or occupation there extends the great, big world of
other realities, past and present.

Culture is not synonymous with knowledge. A man

might be, as Rabelais says, "an abyss and bottomless pit of knowledge" and yet be an unsufferable boor. Culture demands that the knowledge which has been acquired be thoroughly assimilated, that all its elements be well related to one another and at one's command. Culture is interested in the whole range of school subjects, because every subject is concerned with some phase of our material or spiritual environment and therefore helps us come to a better knowledge of it, while contributing to the process of cultivating and refining thought, feelings, and will. Culture, however, is particularly interested in the humanities, that is, religion, language and literature, art, history, and philosophy, because their very object is man and the revelation of his nature, his relations to his Maker and fellow beings, and his destiny. The capstone of culture from the viewpoint of knowledge is philosophy, a sound system of philosophy which surveys and gathers together in a well-organized synthesis all the scattered elements of knowledge that have been acquired so far, and teaches us, at the same time, the right attitude toward reality and therefore toward life.

Culture demands knowledge, not for the sake of mere information, but for the intellectual activity which the assimilation of knowledge entails. From the viewpoint of knowledge, then, culture depends not so much on the materials as it does on the method of instruction and, therefore, upon the personality of the teacher. Culture means development, refinement, and discipline of all latent capacities, but since they have not all the same importance, there must be proportion in the amount of time and attention each one receives and the importance attached to the various disciplines. Culture aims at an ideal. From a purely mundane point of view, the ideal will vary according to time and country; for the Christian, however, this ideal has been set up for all time in the maxim "Be ye perfect as your Heavenly Father is perfect." This leads up to the last and perhaps most important remark on culture. Culture should be for its own sake. Not in the sense that it should not be ultimately integrated in the social and religious life of the nation, but in the sense that it should not be commercialized, made a mere means of, reduced to a stepping stone for power or wealth or fame or vainglory. Culture, which is intellectual beauty, is and must be for itself. And, being for itself, it will yet be, paradoxical as it may sound, eminently social. For it will make everything it touches beautiful, and, if it stands on the side of virtue and truth, it will make them unconquerable. Think of the power of Newman's culture in the service of God!

The Unfoldment Aim

This educational aim is generally associated with the names of Pestalozzi and Froebel, but many other educational theorists could be cited who hold the same view. Says Pestalozzi:

Sound education stands before me symbolized by a tree planted near fertilizing waters. A little seed which contains the design of the tree, its form and its properties, is placed in the soil. The whole tree is an uninterrupted chain of organic parts, the plan of which existed in its seed and root. Man is similar to the tree. In the newborn child are hidden those faculties which are to unfold during life. The individual and separate organs of his being form themselves gradually into unison, and build up humanity in the image of God. The education of man is a purely moral result. It is not the educator who puts new powers and faculties into man, and imparts to him breath and life. He only takes care that no untoward influence shall disturb nature's march of development.

The moral, intellectual, and practical powers of man must be nourished within himself and not from artificial substitutes.[1]

Similar views, though somewhat complicated by his philosophy, are expressed in Froebel's *The Education of Man*. The child is likened to a plant that grows, develops, and reaches its form and perfection if properly taken care of. Education is defined as a free, natural, harmonious process of development, unfoldment of man's powers or faculties. The ultimate purpose of the unfoldment process and the disciplinary phase of education are seldom emphasized, if mentioned at all.·

The "Formal Discipline" Aim

The doctrine, which is the subject of a voluminous literature, can be treated here only in briefest outline. It can be stated in some such way as this: "The essential value of the educative process does not consist in what is learned but in the mental power or ability that learning develops. The power or ability thus generated, say, through the study of language or mathematics, can be transferred to the learning of other subjects; in fact, according to the extremists, to any other situation.

Some transfer is implied in all systems of education and is today generally admitted, even by former foes of the doctrine. The question is: What amount of transfer takes place? From the discussions and experiments on this problem there seems to be consensus on the following.

The channels through which intellectual improvement is carried from one field of mental activity to another are similarity in content, similarity in procedure, or both. Serious study of mathematics will prove helpful in the study of

---

[1] Bardeen, C. W., *How Gertrude Teaches,* p. 20.   Syracuse, 1898.

physics, because there is much similarity in the content of both subjects. Likewise, a person who knows Latin and French will have many of the difficulties in learning Italian or Spanish removed, because of similarities in the vocabularies in those languages. In a similar manner, the mastery of the procedure in the study of one subject will help a person in the study of another subject in which a similar method is used.

General habits or ideals are transferable from one situation to another in such functions as neatness, obedience, and self-reliance. If properly developed in the home and school, those general habits or ideals will function in everyday life, especially if the person has a native capacity for those ideals.

The extent to which transfer will take place depends largely upon the intelligence of the learner and the method of the teacher. Genius discovers relations between subjects which remain hidden for the ordinary man. The teacher who is master of his specialty and its relations to other specialties, and does not confine his work to a narrow, mechanical treatment of the subject will reveal to his class all kinds of applications, in other fields, of what they are actually learning.

Another important factor to be taken into consideration is that of "attitudes." Likes or dislikes developed in connection with one study or situation are likely to reappear in similar studies or situations. Aversion to one person, for instance, may subconsciously manifest itself against another who looks like the first.

The Knowledge Aim

Knowledge is an important factor in life and men have ever been inclined to consider the acquisition of knowledge, because of its practical value, as the one true aim of education. China is often cited as an illustration of this narrow view of education in ancient times. China, however, was no exception in this matter. In all the ancient East, studies were mostly pursued for utilitarian purposes. Among the ancient Greeks knowledge as such never had the importance it had in the East. Whatever knowledge entered in the national education was mostly valued for its liberalizing effect. It was only in the philosophers' schools, such as Plato's, that the acquisition of knowledge for its own sake and its possible ethicosocial value became the purpose of studies. Though the Romans accepted the Greek distinction between the liberal and illiberal studies and occupations, they never lost sight of the practical side of studies. The school in ancient Rome was expected to equip the youth with the knowledge and training needed for success in one's chosen line of activity.

In the Middle Ages, knowledge was held to be the true aim of academic education. The Temple of Learning and the Tower of Wisdom, with their ladder of ascent, so dear to the medieval imagination, typify this medieval aim of school education. Through the knowledge of the seven arts, the student gradually ascended to the summit of the tower where he learned theology, the truth which tells of God. With the fifteenth-century Renaissance there came a revival of the Greco-Roman conception of a liberal education. Though much was retained of the medieval arts course—the relative importance of the subjects—the method of teaching and its purpose were somewhat modified. Religion and the classics were made the core of the curriculum, and the purpose of teaching and study was no longer knowledge, but intellectual, aesthetic, and moral refinement. This "humanistic" aim held undisputed sway for three centuries in Catholic and Protestant secondary schools alike. With the rise of naturalism, however, knowledge—useful knowledge—has become more and more the motto of general education. "Knowledge is power." Let the individual be equipped with all the information that might assist him in securing financial gain.

The Adjustment Aim

This educational aim, very much in fashion a few years ago, is essentially biological; it is an offshoot of the theory of evolution and very much akin to Herbert Spencer's "complete living" aim, which has been explained in connection with the naturalistic philosophy of education. All along we are reminded by the adjustment theory of the common origin of man and the animal, of similarities in their environment and the consequent adjustment to it. Differences, of course, cannot be overlooked, but they are explained in terms of evolutionistic, that is, naturalistic, philosophy. Education, then, we are told, must be viewed as the adjustment of the individual to the life in which he must participate. More explicitly, "to educate a person means to adjust him to those elements of his environment that are of concern in modern life and to develop, organize, and train his powers, so that he may make efficient and proper use of them." [2]

Adjustment to life, modern life, as the foregoing definition intimates, is both objective and subjective. Insofar as education is concerned, knowledge of the environment to

---

[2] Ruediger, W., *Principles of Education*, p. 39. New York, Houghton Mifflin Company, 1910.

which the individual must be adapted is the objective, content side of the process of adjustment; on the subjective side, the process implies a cultivated intellect and disciplined will. As one might expect from its evolutionistic origin, the theory takes it for granted that everything in man, as well as in his environment, is in a perpetual flux. Education, therefore, should adjust the individual not only to the conditions facing him today, but also those which may face him tomorrow! That there are in man's nature, in his relations and aspirations, and in his environment, fundamental elements which never change and make education possible is, of course, passed over in silence.

The "Progressive" Aims

Mention was made in Chapter II of a group of educational innovators who sponsor aims and practices which, they tell us, are the "new," "progressive" aims and practices demanded from the school by our changing civilization. The questions raised by those "progressives" are mostly questions of school "technique" which belong to the province of methodology. Here we retain only, for a brief consideration, the claim of novelty and progress coupled with the assertion that our civilization is changing.

Taking up the last point first. No one, we take it, would seriously question the changeableness of civilization. Men, not yet sixty today, can remember the time when there were no automobiles, wireless, subways, airplanes, radios or movies; the time when the rulers of China, Russia, Germany, Spain, and Portugal were kings or emperors, when the words *communism* and *fascism* were seldom, if ever mentioned. Their grandfathers could have told them of their wonder, not unmixed with awe and misgivings, at the appearance of the first railroads and steamers taking the place of the horsecar and sailboat; of huge factory towns rising on the site of villages; of the first rumblings of social revolutions. And so it has been all through history. Civilization changes; all civilizations change; and, of course, the only ones that do not change are the dead civilizations. But there are a few things which should not change in civilization, if it is not to be turned into barbarism. And one of those "unchangeables" for which the new pedagogy shows scant regard is respect for authority, whether it be the authority of parent or teacher or state, all of them ultimately deriving their authority from God.

As to the the claims to novelty and progress of the "new," "progressive" movement, it is the same old challenge of all would-be reformers to existing conditions, whether it be in politics or economics or religion or education. Divesting the new creed of its terminology, we find that it stresses self-activity, appeal to the senses, the interest of the child, the value of manual training, and other things that have been a byword in the pedagogy of the last one hundred or more years. This is not to deny in the "new," "progressive" education an element of originality. Some of the devices it sponsors once more illustrate the old truth that there may always be a new, better way of doing old things. But the originality of the educational new dealer lies elsewhere. It does lie in his unqualified endorsement of Rousseau's unnatural conception of education according to nature: that the child should be allowed to develop freely and that parents and teachers have no right to interfere with this freedom under the pretense of preparing him for a better, higher life.

The Utilitarian Aim

One of the most widely accepted educational aims is the practical or utilitarian aim, usually styled nowadays, the "efficiency aim." Now, to be efficient means to be able to do things well and quickly, to obtain results in one's own occupation, trade, or profession. Thus, we speak of the efficient teacher, as one that is a good disciplinarian, who contributes his or her own good share to the smooth running of the school machinery, more especially one who can show that the members of the class are better taught and better trained at the end of the term than they were at the beginning.

Efficiency in providing for the material needs of life is usually called economic efficiency, and it can be viewed from the standpoint of the individual or that of the community, the latter being sometimes referred to as industrial efficiency. Evidently, there is a very close relation between the two. The economic efficiency of a nation demands that each and every member of its industrial army be an efficient unit, that all these individual efficiencies be well disciplined and organized, and that there be intelligent leadership. It is because she fully met those requirements that Germany was so efficient, industrially, before the World War. On the other hand, the individual's efficiency depends on the efficiency of the group to which he belongs. No individual, however efficient he may be, can give the best that is in him if he is handicapped in his efforts by the lack of efficiency among his co-workers. Formerly, economic efficiency was everywhere taken care of by the home and the apprenticeship systems, through which solid moral training could be combined with technical preparation. As a consequence of the Industrial Revolution, the industrial home and the apprenticeship systems have become things of the past in most Western lands, though still considered important educational agencies in the East, as also in farming and some local industries, like lacemaking, in a few Western districts. Today, for economic efficiency, all industrialized nations rely on the work of a variety of schools: continuation schools, trade schools, and vocational and industrial schools more or less related to the trades. Leaders in the economic life are prepared in a variety of institutions of university grade: institutes of technology; polytechnic institutes; and schools of agriculture, engineering, and finance.

In a broader sense than the preceding, education for efficiency is, nowadays, understood to mean education for social efficiency, which is well explained by Bagley in the following passage of his *Educative Process*:

That person only is socially efficient, who is not a drag upon society; who in other words can "pull his own weight," either directly as a productive agent or indirectly by guiding, inspiring, or educating others to productive effort. This requires of a socially efficient individual that he be able to earn his livelihood either in a productive employment or in an employment where his energy will be ultimately if not directly turned into a productive channel. . . . That man only is socially efficient who in addition to "pulling his own weight" interferes as little as possible with the efforts of others. This requires of a socially efficient individual that he be moral in at least a negative fashion; that he respect the rights of others, sacrificing his own pleasure, when this interferes with the productive efforts of others. . . .

That man is socially most efficient who not only fulfills these two requirements but also lends his energy consciously and persistently to that further differentiation and integration of social forces which everywhere is synonymous with progress. This demands of a socially efficient individual that he be positively moral; that he not only refrain from injuring his fellow workers, but that he contribute to their further advancement.[3]

Education for social efficiency, then, means preparing the child to become a healthy, intelligent, self-supporting, upright, socially minded member of the community. That aim is furthered by physical education when it helps build up a vigorous healthy body, the ready servant of the mind. It is furthered by intellectual and moral education if that education has resulted in the assimilation of useful knowledge, the development of a sound judgment, and the formation of good habits of thought and conduct; and social efficiency is furthered by every task performed in a spirit of self-reliance.

But this general preparation for efficiency will not bear all its fruit if it has not been permeated with the spirit of Christianity, if the child and, later, the man and woman are not in their dealings with their fellow-beings prompted by the higher motives which Christianity alone can supply.

The Civic Aim

Preparation for good citizenship, service to the state, will evidently vary according to the conception that is held of the state. Education for citizenship in Locke's commonwealth, for instance, would hardly meet the requirements for civic education in Hobbes' state. According to Locke, the state exists for the good of its citizens. It must not only protect life and property, but insure liberty to all. According to Hobbes, the state is omnipotent, claiming blind subservience from its citizens. Civic education would then be,

---

[3] From Bagley, W., *The Educative Process*, pp. 62–63. New York, 1914. By permission of The Macmillan Company, publishers.

in one case, in and for a democracy; in the other, in and for a totalitarian state.

The civic aim has ever been more or less prominent in educational theory and practice. Plato's *Republic* is perhaps the best illustration of the extreme form of that aim in educational theory. The state is supreme. Education is a state affair and it has a twofold purpose: (1) to discover the special aptitudes of every free member of the rising generation; (2) to prepare each and everyone of them for that position in which they would be of greatest service to the state. Christianity has ever insisted on the politicosocial aspect of human life and, therefore, of education. At the same time, it also has ever insisted on the limits to the state claims on the education of youth. "Render unto Cæsar the things that are Cæsar's and to God the things that are God's."

In modern times, the emphasis on the civic aim in educational theory is contemporaneous with the rise of nationalism at the close of the 18th century. French theorists of the period advocated the establishment of a state school system in which the civic aim would be paramount, and their example has since been followed in other lands. Essentially political at first, this modern civic aim came to be used with the social efficiency aim, but the combination is not a uniform one. It varies, according to the view which is held of the nation, the state, and the society.

If we pass from the theory to the practice of education, we meet again the importance attached to the civic aim. It was very prominent in the education of the ancient Greek and Italian city states. The last four years in the education of the Athenian youth were essentially devoted to preparation for good citizenship under state supervision. In Sparta, education was from beginning to end a state affair. At the age of seven, the Spartan boy became a state ward and so remained until his education came to an end. The purpose throughout the whole process was the formation of brave, sturdy fighters entirely subservient to the command of the state. In Rome, the civic aim was no less emphasized, though there was no state interference. *Mos majorum,* that is, tradition, was the ruling force of education as it was in all aspects in Roman life. Cheerful obedience to the lawful commands of the state, devotion to one's native land, has ever been the teaching and practice of the Church. At the same time, she has always vigorously opposed the monopoly of education by a purely secular state. In practice as in theory, she insists upon the rights of the parents and the rights of the Church in the education of youth.

The extent to which education is a state affair varies from country to country. In democratic lands, we usually find some degree of freedom in education: free, that is, private schools, side by side with public schools. In countries with an autocratic form of government, the tendency is for the state to monopolize all education. We find this policy in its extreme form today in Nazi Germany and Bolshevik Russia. As it was remarked before, it used to be assumed that education for citizenship means a preparation for the intelligent discharge of purely civic duties. Today, however, education for citizenship includes, first and foremost, preparation for economic productiveness.

The Moral Religious Aim

The moral, religious aim need not detain us long here, because the moral and religious aspects of education are treated at some length in Chapter VI and again more fully in Chapters XIII and XIV. To the moral aim belongs the distinction of being the one educational aim that has been, in one form or another, insisted upon all through the ages by educators and educational theorists alike. The purpose of ancient Chinese education, typical in this respect of Oriental education, was to train the individual, as Confucius says "in the path of duty." In ancient Greece and Rome, devotion to the state or the socioethical aim was the supreme end of education, while Greek and Roman theorists from Socrates to Tacitus are of one mind on the importance of the moral aim. Christian education was from the first and has ever remained essentially a moral religious process. With the exception of denominational institutions, the modern school has drifted away from the deeply religious spirit of former days, but the emphasis, in both theory and practice, upon moral instruction and training of some kind has been retained. This consensus of opinion on the moral aim clearly points to the following conclusion: that it must be the standard for evaluating all other educational aims. Culture, aiming at the refinement of man's nature, is one-sided and leads to a selfish enjoyment of one's personality, if it neglects the moral element. Social efficiency implies a consideration of a social, that is, moral relations. Likewise, the moral aim is implied in "preparation for complete living" or "adjustment to environment," two of the more commonly mentioned educational aims in the last fifty years. In short, the moral element is an integral part of all sound educational aims, while false educational tendencies, like the naturalistic *laissez faire* or the sordidly utilitarian aim are best opposed on moral grounds.

Beyond and above all other educational aims, though closely related to each, stands the supreme end of education and life which has been most clearly formulated in the following words of Christ: "Thou shalt love the Lord, thy God, with thy whole heart, and with thy whole soul, and with thy whole mind. This is the greatest and first commandment. And the second is similar to this: Thou shalt love thy neighbor as thyself. On these two commandments dependeth the whole law and the prophets." [4]

This centering of education around the religious aim as a core is the most distinctive characteristic of Christian education. Other aims and ideals are welcomed, of course, by Christianity, but only insofar as they do not run counter to the realization of the ultimate aim of education to which they must always be subordinated. All subjects in the curriculum of the Christian school must be related to the religious core, and they must all, so far as possible, further the supreme end of education.

Educational Ideals

An ideal, as the etymology of the word at once suggests, is, first of all, a thing intellectual, though something more than a mere abstraction. It begins with the perception of some trait, principle, or activity, which appeals to some individual disposition and to which imagination lends a sort of halo. The second element in the formation of an ideal is the sentimental element. The trait, principle, or activity that has been perceived evokes feelings of admiration and sympathy which, in turn, lead to a desire to imitate or acquire the object of one's admiration and sympathy. The third and most essential element in the formation of an ideal is the personal element. There must be tangible, concrete embodiment of the concept reached in men or women of a

---

[4] Matt., xxii, 37–39.

strong personality who may serve as models in the attainment of the ideal.

Ideals are determined, in the first place, by the individual's native talents and dispositions. A retiring, studious disposition coupled with some talent for research and assimilation of knowledge would naturally predispose one for the selection of the scholarly ideal. To an assertive, combative temperament, the military or missionary ideal would evidently appeal very strongly. The influence of immediate, actual surroundings is another important factor in the shaping of ideals. Boys born and brought up on the seaboard are likely to display a bent for seafaring life and admiration for its heroes. Many an American boy has dreamed of becoming some day, a baseball or football star. A strongly religious home life has often been the determining factor in drawing Catholic boys and girls to the monastic or missionary ideals. We are here particularly concerned, of course, with educational ideals whose character, in addition to the aforementioned factors is determined by the ideals that men cherish in life. Beauty was the keynote of the Athenian higher life and so it was of the Athenian educational ideal. Rome, on the other hand, stressed in her educational ideal, as she did in life, all the qualities that make for efficiency. In the same age we may come across different educational ideals corresponding to different classes of people and different vocations. Medieval military life, like medieval monastic, scholastic, or industrial life, called for a distinct type of education. Corresponding to each there was a distinct type of educational ideal: the ideal knight, monk, schoolman, or artisan. In each one of these ideals were combined the fundamental Christian virtues and the traits peculiar to the particular calling. Before those who wished to strive for the attainment of the higher stage in the ideals, the Church held up for imitation the one Person who is the exemplar of all perfection and her great roster of Christian heroes, where each one could select the model of the traits and virtues peculiar to his calling.

Educational ideals are influenced by intellectual movements and political and economic changes. The difference between the fourteenth-century-school ideals and those of institutions like Vittorino da Feltre's at Mantua is accounted for by the Renaissance. The Enlightenment, the Industrial Revolution, and the rise of nationalism are responsible for most of the changes in educational ideals in the last one hundred years. Educational theorists may also influence ideals in education: witness Plato and philosophical speculation as an ideal in ancient Greek education, and Rousseau and the naturalistic tendencies in the modern school.

The essential elements of the educational ideal ever remain the same. They were brought out in our survey of the educational aims. Differences in the realization of the ideal will arise with the stressing or neglect of some of the component elements. On the more practical question of how to deal with the development of ideals in the young, the reader is referred to the related topic of imitation treated at some length in the chapter on moral education.

Topics for Further Study

1. Show the relation to educational aims and ideals of the "collecting," "aesthetic," and "expressive" tendencies.

2. Analyze critically any three historical types of culture, such as the ancient Greek or Roman, the Renaissance, French, or English.

3. Is education for culture consistent with education for efficiency? Explain.

4. Explain the similarities and differences between the cultural aim and the "unfoldment" aim as advocated by Pestalozzi or Froebel.

5. Discuss the respective values of the humanities and the sciences from the viewpoint of the cultural aim.

6. Compare the respective values of the home and the school as agencies for culture.

7. To what extent are the press, moving picture, theatre, and radio agencies for culture today?

8. Show the importance of the religious element in education for culture.

9. State and discuss from the Christian viewpoint the limitations of the "efficiency" aim as it is commonly interpreted.

10. "Knowledge is virtue." Compare the Socratic and Platonic views on this maxim.

11. "Knowledge is power." Discuss.

12. "What knowledge is of most worth?" Compare critically Spencer's and the Christian answer to that question.

13. Compare education for good citizenship in a democratic and an autocratic state.

14. State and comment on the formal discipline aim.

15. Compare the respective importance of knowledge in general and special education.

16. "The moral religious aim is the standard in evaluating any educational aim." Discuss.

17. "Adjustment to life should be the purpose of education." Explain adjustment to life, and comment.

18. Comment on Spencer's "complete living" aim in education.

19. Compare critically any two historical ideals in education.

20. "The ideally educated man today." Discuss.

Suggestions for Reading

Almack, J., *Education for Citizenship* (Boston, 1924).

Bagley, W., *The Educative Process* (New York, 1914).

Bode, B., *Fundamentals of Education* (New York, 1921).

Brunetière, F., *Sur les Chemins de la Croyance* (Paris, 1905).

Chancellor, E., *Motives, Ideals and Values in Education* (New York, 1907).

Charmot, F., *La Teste Bien Faicte* (Paris, 1932).

Davidson, T., *Aristotle and the Ancient Educational Ideals* (New York, 1892).

Hanus, J., *Educational Aims and Educational Values* (New York, 1899).

Martin, E., *The Meaning of a Liberal Education* (New York, 1926).

Meriam, J., *Child Life and the Curriculum* (Yonkers, 1920).

Newman, J., *The Idea of a University* (New York, 1929).

Peters, C., *Objectives and Procedures in Civic Education* (New York, 1930).

Ruediger, W., *The Principles of Education* (New York, 1910).

Rusk, R., *The Philosophical Basis of Education* (Boston, 1928).

Shields, Th., *Philosophy of Education* (Washington, 1917).

Spalding, J., *Means and Ends of Education* (Chicago, 1895).

————, *Education and the Higher Life* (Chicago, 1922).

————, *Thoughts and Theories of Life and Education* (Chicago, 1901).

Willmann-Kirsch, *The Science of Education* (Beatty, 1921).

CHAPTER VI

The Educative Process

Introduction

Education, let it be remarked again, is essentially a social process. The individual is born in society; he must live and achieve his destiny through society; his education involves the coöperation of other individuals and collective agencies, and it presupposes the assimilation of at least the essential elements in the social inheritance. On the other hand, society, being nothing more in the last analysis than the aggregate of all its individual members, it is evident that the process of social assimilation and reconstruction will succeed only to the extent that the social assimilative forces will elicit the coöperation of individuals and influence their personality. Thus, even though we would insist upon considering education merely from the social viewpoint, ignoring the fact that the individual has educational interests prior to and independently of the rights of society, we must consider the nature of the individual to be assimilated and the effect upon his native capacities of the social forces brought to bear upon him in order to make of him a law-abiding, efficient member of society.

Education, a Physical Process

The root meaning of the English *education* is that of the Latin *educare,* related to *educere,* "to draw out, to lead forth," referring, at first, to the process of generation and the work involved in the physical growth, development, and well being of the child. The meaning of the term was later on extended to the intellectual and moral side of the child's nature, and those new, higher implications of the word have somewhat obscured its original meaning. From the individual's viewpoint, we should evidently think of education as an essentially intellectual, moral process, but this higher and truer sense of the term should never lead us to lose sight of its original meaning, of the fact that the body is an integral part of man's nature, claiming its due share of attention from all those who are entrusted with the upbringing and training of the younger generation. No system of education is complete which does not make adequate provision for the body. We may even go further and say that neglect of the physical side is likely to jeopardize the intellectual and moral side of education. Poor nutrition, uncleanliness, and poor clothing and shelter will impair the child's health and, therefore, his capacity for learning; defective eyesight or hearing, unsatisfactory heating or lighting or seating conditions will likewise react unfavorably upon classroom work.

All available educative agencies, therefore, should co-operate in the work for the physical well-being and development of the child, but the greater share of the responsibility for its success naturally devolves upon the home and the school. During the first five or six years of its life what the child needs most are simple food, fresh air, sunlight, and the free movements of outdoor life, all of which should be abundantly provided for by the home; but the parents' responsibility in this matter does not end with the satisfaction of those simple needs.   It is also their duty to develop in the child, habits of cleanliness, moderation, exercise, correct posture, and graceful carriage, the signs and prerequisites of a healthy organic life and the physical counterpart of many aesthetic and moral ideals.

With the beginning of school life, a large share of the responsibility for the development of correct hygienic habits and ideals falls to the teacher.   Doctor Bagley says:

There is no sterner duty laid upon the teacher than the development of those [hygienic] habits and ideals.   A large public school is a fertile ground for implanting the seeds of disease and vice. The mind of the child at any time after the eighth year is predisposed to impulses that are vulgar and degrading.   Some of these reactions may be "natural" enough; they are not always to be looked upon as abnormalities or perversions, but under the conditions of modern life, they are none the less disastrous, and it is precisely at this point that some form of education or external guidance becomes essential to the salvation of the race.   If the dictum, "follow nature" is ever fallacious, it certainly is here, for here, nature is working at cross purposes, pitting instincts and impulses so evenly against one another that the composition of forces, if left to the natural law, could hardly fail to equal zero in practically every case.   In dealing with children between the ages of eight and twelve, there is little room for freedom or liberty. Ceaseless vigilance is, here, the price of success, and this vigilance must extend to every nook and cranny of the child's nature.   Uncleanliness of all sorts grows with the growth.   Filth breeds filth, both mentally and materially.   The germs must be nipped in the bud if infection is to be prevented. . . .   In dealing with adolescence . . . specific methods must be employed, differing radically from those used in the preadolescent period.   Arbitrary rules and summary punishments must give place to reason, and hygienic habits that have been formed largely by mechanical processes in the earlier years, must now be generalized and justified on the basis of ideals.[1]

To this otherwise accurate statement of the case, Christian pedagogy would add one essential element, the influence of religion, which should be felt in all phases of education and all through life, but at no time so strongly as during the formative period of preadult life.   Reason and experience tell us that appeals to law, to order, and to ideals will be of little avail in the storm of the passions unless supported by religious motives.   When the authority of God is ignored, the demands of any other authority are likely to appear as unjustifiable encroachments upon the rights of the individual.

Education, an Intellectual Process

We commonly think of intellectual education as a teaching-learning process, of moral education as one of training and discipline; but that does not nor should it ever mean, of course, that either pair of terms is restricted to intellectual or moral education respectively.   A good moral character is, in the main, the outcome of doing, of habit formation, but it involves some teaching; in order to do what is right, we must evidently know what is right.   Intellectual education, likewise, is not limited to the mere imparting of information; it implies a disciplining of mental powers.   And it should be noted, further, that teaching and discipline, as

---

[1] From Bagley, W., *The Educative Process*, pp. 346ff. New York, 1914. By permission of The Macmillan Company, publishers.

a means of intellectual and moral development and social assimilation, are not limited to the schools, or to the young. Missions, sermons, and religious revivals are forms of teaching that can and do supplement schoolteaching but are not limited to the young. Political propaganda is another form of teaching, though again not primarily addressed to the young. Scientists, scholars, and philosophers, the great men of any age, become the teachers of that age and the following generations by communicating to their fellow men the results of their investigations and speculations, though here again the teaching is not limited to the school or the young. The artist, the poet, or the critic, in short, a master in any province of culture, is a teacher, and it is quite common to use the term *school* when referring to those who accept the leadership of that master, though the disciples are not necessarily young people. The book is a teacher, and so are the magazine, the pamphlet, and the newspaper, but here again, the meaning of the term *teaching* is extended far beyond its usual connotation. And so it is with discipline. Just as we are taught at all ages and through all kinds of agencies, so we are constantly checked and directed by the social institutions that surround us, the home, the Church, the trade, the profession, the club, or any particular association to which we happen to belong, not to speak of the police and the army.

Intellectual education is essentially concerned with the development and training of the intellect. It implies, first of all, an increase in mental power. The acquisition of knowledge is but its material side. Not until knowledge has really contributed to our mental growth and development can it be said to have educated us and to be our own.

"What has been learned by heart or acquired by dint of exercise and practice may be lost in the course of time." [2] What remains with us is the intellectual development and discipline that have been achieved through the assimilation of ideals and the formation of good intellectual habits. [3]

Intellectual education is a social process in the sense that the efforts of the individual to become an intellectually educated person require the coöperation of other individuals, either directly, as in actual teaching, or indirectly, through libraries, museums, the school system, and the theatre and other social institutions. It is also a social process in this further sense that before becoming to any degree the property of the individual, as a result of his efforts to assimilate it, the subject matter of intellectual education is the property of the community, both past and present. Intellectual education, however, is essentially an individual process and a work of freedom; it is a product of the individual mind's free activity, self-activity as the phrase goes nowadays, or, to use an older but more forceful term, a product of free will, of hard intellectual work performed by the individual himself. The most brilliant native talents would have been received in vain, the devotion of parents and teachers would be so much time and energy wasted, if the wholehearted coöperation of the individual were not enlisted in the service of his own education. In that sense can we wholeheartedly agree with Rousseau's plea for education according to nature, and Froebel's principle of self-activity.

But the mind that must be educated is a growing mind, and the process of education, therefore, must be adapted to

---

[2] Willmann-Kirsch, *The Science of Education*, Vol. I, p. 17. Archabbey Press, Beatty, Pa., 1921.
[3] See Castiello, J., *Geistesformung*. Berlin, 1934.

the stages of the mind's natural development. The bane of the old pedagogy was its assumption in practice, if not in theory, that there is no difference between the psychology of the child and that of the adult, that the approved methods of teaching adults could be applied indiscriminately to elementary classroom procedure. It is true that, barring experience, all the forces of adult psychical activity are present in the child and the youth, but many are still in the embryonic stage of development or else are awaiting the discipline of a few years of steady work and the hard knocks of actual life. It has been the great service of psychology to education in the last one hundred years to place at the disposal of the teacher a better knowledge of psychical processes during the period of preadult life. A new pedagogical science, educational psychology, born of this progress in psychical studies, has contributed much to formulate the principles of teaching best adapted to the successive stages of learning in childhood and adolescence.

Of late, educational psychology has come to depend more and more on the methods used in the psychological laboratory, and its investigations have centered around the psychological analysis of the factors involved in learning certain school subjects and the discovery of tests of efficiency. Research work of this kind cannot fail ultimately to prove helpful to the teacher by showing him ways and means to improve his technique. There is the danger, however, that the importance attached to this aspect of the teacher's work will obscure more important issues. The teacher may be so much taken up with the methods of imparting information that he will lose sight of the real purpose of the art of teaching during the formative period, which is to assist in the development of mental power and the formation of character. The acquisition of knowledge and skill in the school, under the guidance of competent teachers, is nothing else, after all, than one of the best means, so far devised by man, to achieve this purpose.

To the extent that the technique of teaching will assist in achieving that end, to that extent only should this technique be insisted upon. For the rest, we must rely upon the teacher's knowledge of the subject; upon his practical knowledge of the psychology of each and every member of his class; his ability to discover their intellectual strength and weakness, to arouse and keep alive their interest in learning, to provide for their intellectual needs; his intellectual insight; his tact; his zeal, patience, and never-flagging sympathy for the young. "Perfect schools are the results not so much of good methods as of good teachers, teachers who are thoroughly prepared and well-grounded in the matter they have to teach; who possess the intellectual and moral qualification required by their important office; who cherish a pure and holy love for the youth confided to them, because they love Jesus Christ and His Church, of which these are the children of predilection; and who have therefore sincerely at heart the true good of family and country." [4]

Education, a Moral Religious Process

The adoption by contemporary psychologists of the threefold classification of the facts of conscious activity into the phenomena of knowing, feeling, and willing would suggest the insertion here of a few remarks on the education of the emotions. We assume with Scholastic philosophy, however, that the phenomena of feeling are mere aspects of

---

[4] Pius XI, *Encyclical on Christian Education of Youth.*

cognitive or appetitive activities, or else complex products of both and, therefore, at least at this stage in our survey, can be considered as involved in either intellectual or moral education.

Stated in briefest form, the purpose of moral education is the disciplining of the will; it is achieved through the formation of good moral habits, the teaching of the moral law and the force of example in the environment of the young. Like intellectual education, moral education is both a conscious and an unconscious or, at least, a semiconscious process. Consciously and purposely, parents and teachers seek to control the conduct of the rising generation, to bring forth influences that will shape their character aright. Unconsciously, through the ever-present, impelling power of imitation, the whole environment is exerting a moral influence which, according to whether it is for good or evil, will assist or set at naught the conscious efforts of the educator for the moral uplift of childhood and youth.

The immediate purpose of moral education, formulated above as "discipline of the will," is sometimes stated in terms of character. In fact the phrase "character education" has been quite frequently used in late years to denote what is referred to here as moral education. This change in terminology would be immaterial if the meaning of the two terms was substantially the same. Such, however, is not the case, and, to avoid possible confusion in the reader's mind, it will be necessary to explain the twofold meaning attached to the word *character* in this and the following chapters.

In the general sense of the term, *character* can be defined as the expression of the personality of a human being, the result of a combination of native and acquired capacities.

We are all endowed at birth with certain dispositions, certain ways of being influenced by our environment and reacting upon it, certain capacities for thought, feeling, and willing which are the materials out of which our character will ultimately be fashioned. Those dispositions, capacities we possess at birth, are constantly modified by the influence of our environment, but particularly by the way in which they are consciously exercised by the individual, who is, in the last analysis, the chief agent in the building up of his own character. Activity in any given direction develops a disposition and a facility to act again in that direction, and, through repetition, it may result in a habit, a trait in the character of the individual. Thus, if it be given free rein, the imagination may lead on into habitual "day dreaming"; frequent indulgence in fits of anger can result only in an "irascible" character; make it a practice to "stop and think" before a decision, and there will be developed a "thoughtful" disposition. But exercise not only strengthens our native disposition in the right or wrong direction, it is also responsible for the character of our will. Frequent yielding to one's whims and fancies, to emotional impulses, must inevitably result in a weakening of the will, and repeated acts of self-control, or self-denial, will no less surely strengthen will power; and this brings us to the second, narrower meaning of the word *character*.

When we say, without qualification, that a man "has character" we intend to convey the notion that the man possesses a certain unity and constancy of qualities, that he shows, in his conduct, energy, perseverance, and independence. *Character* in that sense is essentially a combination of sound judgment and disciplined will power, but not in equal proportions; the will is predominant. A man may possess knowledge and experience in plenty, he may be gifted with the intellectual acumen of a Socrates and the keenest of susceptibilities to ethical values and yet be a despicable character, because he lacks the courage, the driving power to carry out the dictates of his conscience. The man of character is a man who is not at the mercy of his impressions or moods, a man who is not swayed by prejudice or events or opinions. His will has been trained to adhere to the principles which reason tells him to be those of right living. He places honor above honors, conscience above interest; he is not ready to bow before every rising sun, not afraid to displease when truth and right are at stake; he does not say what everybody says, but that which he knows to be true; he does not do what everybody does, but that which he knows to be right. His motto is: "Do what you ought, come what may." We come across men of character in all times and climates, but the true, the ideal man of character is:

The true Christian, product of Christian education, the supernatural man who thinks, judges and acts constantly and consistently in accordance with right reason, illumined by the supernatural light of the example and teaching of Christ; . . . For, it is not every kind of consistency and firmness of conduct based on subjective principles that makes true character, but only constancy in following the eternal principles of justice as is admitted even by the pagan poet when he praises as one and the same "the man who is just and firm of purpose." And, on the other hand there cannot be full justice, except in giving to God what is due to God, as the true Christian does.[5]

---

[5] Pius XI, *Encyclical on Christian Education of Youth.*

CHAPTER VII

Physical Education

In the Past

The nature and purpose of physical education have varied from age to age or country to country, according to the prevailing conception of educational aims. Among the ancient Greeks, bodily training was an important part of education, but aims and practices were not uniform in the Greek city states. In Sparta, physical training was practical; the Spartan youth had to go through a long, hardening process in the practice of gymnastics and military exercises for the sole purpose of preparing for war. Spartan girls also received physical training that they might become the mothers of sturdy soldiers. In Athens, physical training, otherwise similar to the Spartan, aimed at beauty rather than strength of body, and women had no share in it. In other Greek city states, physical education might be here of the Spartan type, there of the Athenian, but there was everywhere an intense interest in bodily training and athletic contests as is shown by the importance in Greek national life of the Olympic and similar games. In Rome, physical education was eminently practical. The aim was to prepare the Roman youth for war. In early Republican days, the hard life of the farm, which was the common lot of Roman families, was in itself an excellent preparation for the hardships of the soldier's life; it was supplemented by the martial exercises of the camp. The practice of gymnastics for aesthetic ends, so characteristic of Greek life, never became popular among the Romans, though proficiency in riding, swimming, hunting, and dart throwing was no less highly valued than dexterity in the use of weapons.

In the early centuries of Christianity, as also during the Middle Ages, with the stressing of the spiritual aspect of life, there was a corresponding tendency to neglect physical education. The most noteworthy exception to this tendency was the education of the prospective knight who was trained in the so-called seven arts of chivalric life: riding, swimming, shooting with bow and arrow, boxing, hawking, playing chess, and poetry writing. In modern times, aside from early humanistic schools like Vittorino da Feltre's "Pleasant House," a few English schools like Rugby and the military academies of the seventeenth and eighteenth centuries, little attention was paid to physical education before the nineteenth century.

Today

The physical nature of the child, more or less neglected by the school before the nineteenth century, has been forced upon the attention of the modern educator by the conditions of urban life, the management of large city schools and the progress of the biological and medical sciences. Prospective teachers are now expected to know at least the essentials of human anatomy, human physiology and hygiene, and to be more or less familiar with the symptoms of the more common physical defects and diseases. They are expected to guide their pupils in the formation of good hygienic habits. They must be able to detect and then refer to the nurse and physician all cases calling for expert remedial measures. In the arrangement of the school curriculum, full cognizance is now taken of the question of physical growth, the cerebral capacity of children in successive periods of growth, and individual differences and the problem of fatigue; schoolhouses must meet the latest requirements in hygienic building; the gymnasium and the playground have become an integral part of the school equipment, and physical exercise, through manual training, play, gymnastics, and athletics, is an integral part of the school activities.

Physical Education and the School

Before passing on to a brief consideration of the more important items in this rather extensive program, it will not be amiss to state anew the reasons why the school should concern itself with physical education.

Efficiency in life depends in no small measure upon a sound physique; no system of education is complete which does not make adequate provision for physical well-being.

Because of the intimate interdependence of body and soul, neglect of the physical well-being of the child is likely to have serious consequences for his intellectual and moral development, as is shown by experimental studies on the correlation between physical defectiveness and school retardation.

For these two reasons, if for none other, all institutions concerned either directly or indirectly with the preparation for life of the rising generation should coöperate in the physical aspect of this preparation. But do they? We, know, for instance, that the sanitary conditions of many, too many homes, are far from satisfactory. We know also that certain aspects of public life—like the observation of the symptoms of infectious diseases, which normally should be assigned to special agencies—will not be taken care of unless the school attends to them. Here, then, we have another reason why the school should concern itself with physical education. Unless the school does take care of it, the physical condition of many children is likely to be sadly neglected.

The Teacher and Physical Education

We now come to the more practical question of what the school can do for the physical well-being of the child. What should be the school program of physical education? What preparation should the teacher receive in order to be able to coöperate in the carrying out of this program? As a minimum requirement for intelligent coöperation in physical education, the teacher should possess a general knowledge of human anatomy, physiology, and hygiene, particularly of the nature and functions of the nervous system; he should be familiar with the characteristics of physical growth and the problem of fatigue; he should finally be equipped to coöperate with the school physician and nurses in the work of medical inspection and also be familiar with the respective values of the agencies for bodily training. We shall here retain the question of fatigue for a few remarks of a practical character, referring, for the other questions, to special works on human anatomy and physiology, on hygiene and the physical nature of the child.

We are concerned with the problem of fatigue only insofar as it affects mental work and its chief physical agent, the brain. Mental work, as we know, is dependent upon brain activity, but the brain can be overtaxed, with serious consequences for brain and body, especially during the period of rapid physical growth, when the body requires for its own development most of the nutrition it produces. If the brain is made to consume more than its normal share of nutrition, there is danger of arrested physical development, which ultimately may result in arrested brain development. The teacher, then, should be familiar, in a general way, with the data concerning physical growth and the brain capacity of children at successive levels in physical growth; he should also, insofar as that is possible, acquaint himself with the individual brain capacity of every child in his class. He should adapt the nature of the subject taught and the method of presentation to the dominant characteristic of conscious life in the successive stages of mental development. While frequent recesses and short recitations are the obvious ways to avoid overtaxing the brain, a knowledge of the nature and functions of the nervous system will show the teacher that a change in occupation may lead to the same result, if it calls into play other brain centers than those actually at work.

The School Program of Physical Education

The school program of physical education includes the following items: the hygiene of instruction, medical inspection and follow-up, instruction in hygiene, and what has been referred to above as the agencies of physical training, that is, manual training, play, gymnastics, and athletics.

The hygiene of instruction, which, to some extent, is beyond the teacher's control, includes such matters as proper ventilation, temperature, lighting, size of print in books, and seating accommodations. Its purpose is to safeguard the vital energy of the child by placing before him school-work that is under the best possible material conditions.

Medical inspection and follow-up properly belong to the province of physicians and nurses, but the inadequacy of the medical staff in most schools makes it necessary for teachers to contribute to it. Besides, the coöperation of the teacher in this phase of physical education will help him to understand and appreciate the handicaps under which some members of his class are working. The teacher's task in this matter is, evidently, merely one of observation, detection, and report, but it requires, nonetheless, a general knowledge of the symptoms of nervousness, the common diseases and disabilities of children.

In the sense in which the term is here used, instruction in hygiene comprises, with a knowledge of the structure and function of the human organism, the formation of sound health habits and ideals. For obvious reasons this part of the school program in physical education should not be carried out in its entirety all at once. In the primary grades instruction in hygiene should be limited to the formation of good habits in such matters as posture, personal cleanliness, and breathing. The principles involved are those of habit formation treated at some length in another chapter. Adherence to this phase of the instruction, the most important phase in hygiene, should, of course, continue throughout the whole period of school life, but in the intermediate and higher grades there is added to it the development of health ideals in such matters as pure food, water supply, the disposal of refuse, and so on. Appeal to the imagination and the feelings through graphic, concrete illustrations and correlation of the lessons on this subject with the program in community civics seem to be the best methods of teaching the subject.

Health knowledge, that is, systematic instruction in the structure and functions of the human organism, properly belongs to the course of study in the higher elementary- and high-school grades. The purpose of the instruction is the practical one of providing a rational basis for the health habits and ideals that have been acquired. Lengthy, elaborate excursions into the field of physiology would be out of place here. What is needed is the stressing and explanation of the rules of sound hygiene in the light of the more obvious facts of physiology.

By way of summing up the foregoing paragraphs, we shall say that the hygiene of instruction helps us to carry on schoolwork under the best possible conditions; medical inspection and follow-up is concerned with the detection, prevention, and correction of possible organic abnormalities; instruction in hygiene aims at equipping the child with sound health habits and ideals and a fairly good stock of health knowledge. In addition to all this, there are included in the modern school program for physical education the following agencies for physical training: manual training, play, gymnastics, and athletics.

Manual Training

Advocated for economic and social reasons by Rousseau and his immediate followers, manual training is today used by the school for general educative purposes, as a means of self-expression, an agent of brain and mind training through metal, wood, and clay when books fail. It is pointed out by its advocates that manual training implies a close coöperation between mind, brain, and hand; that it affords a splendid opportunity for the training of the senses, for the development of habits of accuracy, precision, honesty, and the artistic characteristic of putting the "finishing touch" to one's work, which is something very akin to thoroughness. For the city child, manual training undoubtedly is the best substitute the school can offer thus far for home occupations in the pre-Industrial Revolution days; furthermore, manual training has a prevocational value for those boys and girls who will enter the trades.

Play

Play, "the spontaneous, physical expression of individuality," is best understood by contrasting it with work. Play is free, always pleasant, and exists for its own sake, whereas work is compulsory, may or may not be agreeable, and is done for the sake of reaching some goal beyond it. Whether play is a safety valve for superfluous vitality, a relaxation from the strain and stress of work, or a preparation for the tasks of life is immaterial insofar as the teacher is concerned. Play is probably all of that and something more besides. What really matters is the fact that play is an innate tendency, though forms of play have to be learned; it is just as natural for human beings to play as it is for them to eat, which would seem to be a sufficient reason for its having been enlisted from the very beginning in the service of education. Yet, it is only in modern times that play has been generally accepted as a normal, school activity. One of the first forms of play thus to receive scholastic recognition was dramatic performance. Greece has long since shown the educative value of dramatic performances, and the lesson was taught anew by the Church through the medieval liturgical, mystery, and miracle plays. Instances are also cited of medieval schools staging Latin plays, but the practice did not become general until the latter part of the sixteenth century, when the Jesuits, in particular, made the staging of plays a regular feature of their school calendar.

Games and sports occupied an important place in some secondary schools of the early Renaissance—as, for instance, in the "Pleasant House" of Vittorino da Feltre—and later in the Jesuit schools, the military academies, and the English "public" schools. Elsewhere a gloomy neglect of this cheerful element in the education of childhood and youth seems to have been the rule before the nineteenth century. The full and general recognition of the value of play in all the stages of the educative process is a thing of the latter part of the nineteenth century, and it was due largely to the work of Froebel and his followers. In the kindergarten, which embodies the Froebelian basic principle of self-development through self-activity, play is the very soul of school life. In the elementary school, high school, and college, it justifies the recess, providing, as it does, the necessary relaxation from work, invigorating physical exercise, and a return to the classroom with renewed zest. To the observant teacher, play affords an excellent opportunity to study the character of his pupils. In the freedom of the playground, various traits in personality will appear, which the discipline of the classroom keeps under the surface.

Gymnastics

Gymnastics, which we may define as "consciously directed physical exercise," is not, like play, an end in itself, but a means to physical development. It has this advantage over play, that it can provide systematic, adequate exercise for the various parts of the body, and thus fortify weak points, correct physical defects, and develop certain vocational aptitudes. Gymnastics, however, could hardly take the place of play as a means of relief from fatigue, because of the mental strain it involves.

Athletics

Athletics, "play to win," have been and still are a target for much criticism. It is said in condemnation of athletics that they provide exercise only for the few, that they discourage scholarship, that the time which they consume is out of all proportion to the benefits students derive from this kind of amusement, and that they demoralize the student body. It cannot be denied that there is an element of truth in those strictures, but they should be aimed at the abuse of athletics, rather than athletics as such. England might be our teacher in this matter. For generations her national games have been an integral part of the school activities in her "Public Schools," in the belief that sport is a school of virtue, that, if properly run, sport trains in instilling ideals and developing certain definite habits.

Topics for Further Study

1. Give a critical account of the ancient Greek system of physical education.

2. Discuss the educative value of the Olympic games.

3. Contrast the ancient Greek and Roman systems of physical education as to aims and means.

4. Show the relation of the physical to the moral element in chivalric education.

5. Make a survey of the physical educational movement in the 19th century.

6. Make a survey of the physical educational movement in the 20th century.

7. Give a critical account of the playground movement in the United States.

8. "Health versus physical education." Discuss.

9. "Aims and ideals in physical education." Discuss.

10. Contrast the educative value of play and gymnastics.

11. Contrast the educative value of gymnastics and sports.

12. "Manual training as an agency for physical education." Discuss.

13. Compare physical education in England and Continental Europe.

14. "The influence of phy. `~al education on character formation." Discuss.

15. "The influence of physical education on intellectual education." Discuss.

16. "Physical education as an element in education for culture." Discuss.

17. "Physical education as an element in education for efficiency." Discuss.

18. "Physical education as an element in education for good citizenship." Discuss.

19. "The teacher's general preparation for physical education." Discuss.

20. "The preparation of the specialist in physical education." Discuss.

SUGGESTIONS FOR READING

Burgerstein, L., and Netolitzky, J. A., *Handbuch der Schulhygiene* (Jena, 1902).

Donaldson, H., *The Growth of the Brain* (New York, 1905).

Gulick, L., and Ayres, L., *Medical Inspection of Schools* (New York, 1908).

Halleck, R., *Education of the Central Nervous System* (New York, 1906).

Horne, H., *The Philosophy of Education* (New York, 1910).

Johnson, G., *Education by Plays and Games* (Boston, 1907).

Ladd, G., and Woodworth, R., *Physiological Psychology* (New York, 1911).

Mero, E., *American Playgrounds* (Boston, 1908).
Shaw, E., *School Hygiene* (New York, 1901).
Shields, T., *Philosophy of Education* (Washington, 1917).
Stevens, E., *Medical Supervision in Schools* (London, 1910).

CHAPTER VIII

Intellectual Education: Its Proximate Aim, Its Materials and Their Educative Values

Learning

The proximate aim of intellectual education is learning, which may be defined the process through which the individual acquires knowledge or skill or both, thereby undergoing certain modifications that we can designate as the development of ability or power. All learning, whether in or out of school, insofar as it is educational in character, should have this threefold purpose: knowledge or the assimilation of some intellectual content; skill or the ability to perform certain tasks or movements; and, above all, power or the capacity for independent thinking. Thus, given a lesson or a series of lessons on the division of fractions, the process of learning involves the knowledge of at least the essential elements of the operation, the ability to perform it, and, in connection with both knowledge and ability, some development of the power to judge and reason.[1]

All three elements are ever present in learning, though

---

[1] Some transfer of training is, of course, taken for granted here. On this question, see Castiello, J., *Geistesformung* (Berlin, 1934).

not in the same proportion or in the same degree. Barring the individual's native talents, the actual increase in intellectual power will depend upon the extent to which his faculties are called into play; the writing of an original composition or the solution of a problem evidently requires a more vigorous exercise of the intellect than the mere committing to memory of some list of words. Knowledge and skill are involved in all lessons, but at one time knowledge, at another time skill, will be predominant. In such subjects as geography and history, the learning process is chiefly one of grasping and assimilating some information; skill is involved only insofar as there are applications connected with the lesson or intellectual habits to be developed in the handling of the subject. On the other hand the mastery of the arts of reading or drawing, for instance, is, in the main, a matter of skill; at least insofar as the learner is concerned, in the early stages of the process, the only knowledge that is required is that of the symbols or conventions used.

Learning may be differentiated into formal and informal. In formal or classroom learning, the process takes place according to a preordained plan; the learner is expected to assimilate the subject matter that is presented to him. In informal learning, on the other hand, taking place through observation, experience, social intercourse, independent reading, and travel, the mind is free to select the subject matter and to take in as much or as little of it as it chooses. Whether formal or informal, however, learning implies the individual's self-activity; it is essentially an act of the free will, but it also implies the assistance of others. This coöperation between the learner and those who assist him, at once evident in the school, may be direct or indirect. The state or city government that provides school facilities; the school officials who organize the curriculum and supervise its administration; and the authors of books, plays, and films assist the learner, but their assistance is indirect, impersonal, whereas relation between learner and teacher is personal and direct. Here, we are, of course, concerned chiefly with formal learning.

Teaching

The concept of learning is closely related to that of teaching, which could be defined the actual, direct, presentation of an intellectual content for the purpose of having it assimilated by others. Just as the teacher does, the poet, writer, orator, and preacher present an intellectual content, but their intention, as a rule, is not to teach; their main purpose is to elevate, please, convince, or persuade. It is only exceptionally, as in the case of the preacher and the writer, that their intention is to have their subject matter assimilated by the reader or listener. For the teacher, on the other hand, this assimilation should ever be the primary aim, which, of course, does not preclude the element of interest in the teacher's work, but this element is only a means to an end.

The teaching process may assume any number of particular forms in the classroom, but they are all particular types of either the instruction or lecture method of teaching. Instruction could be defined as that form of teaching, below the university, in which the teacher sees to it that the pupil learns what is taught. The instructor is not satisfied with a mere presentation of the subject matter. He asks questions to ascertain whether or not the class understands the subject matter presented; he assigns and controls applications that will make the assimilation more thorough and lasting. The university professor, on the other hand, is justified in limiting his work, as a teacher, to lecturing on the subject, because he has to deal with students who can be held responsible for the assimilation of subject matter once it has been brought within their reach.

Learning and teaching from the viewpoint of the school presuppose a subject or pupil, a teacher, a purpose, a subject matter to be learned, and a certain way or method of learning it, together with the appropriate equipment. The nature of the individual to be educated and the purpose of his education have already been treated at some length, though in a general way, in the preceding chapters, and we shall have occasion again and again to return to those subjects in the following pages; the teacher's preparation and the question of method will receive separate treatment in subsequent chapters; for the present we are concerned with the fourth element enumerated above, that is, the subject matter to be learned.

Curriculum Construction

By subject matter or content of education is meant here all the intellectual materials used by the school for educative purposes. They are selected from what is sometimes referred to as the spiritual treasure of the race, that is, religion, language, literature, science, art, and philosophy, but they do not come directly to the pupil; before they reach him, they have received some sort of formation, first, from those entrusted with the organization and administration of the curriculum and secondly, from the teacher. Evidently this selection and organization of the materials of instruction cannot be made in a haphazard way; it is governed by a few general principles that apply not only to the curriculum as a whole, but to every course of study, every series of lessons, and particular lessons as well.

Stated in briefest form, those principles are the following:

The selection of the materials of instruction and the apportionment of emphasis among them should be determined by their educative value and the needs of the time and locality.

The selected materials must be closely related to the final end of all education.

They must be well correlated.

They should be carefully graded.

They must be so presented that they further their actual assimilation by the pupil.

Education being a preparation for life, it would seem logical to fit all the elements of life to the elements of the school curriculum, but the complexity of our civilization evidently precludes such a process; besides, there are many activities that can be learned more readily in actual life than in the school and, therefore, need not be included in the curriculum. 'The first step in curriculum construction should then be the selection of those elements of human life worth learning, in the school, because of their educative value. The second step should be the apportionment of emphasis among the selected subjects, or, what amounts to the same thing, the amount of time that should be allotted to each. And here again the criterion is to what extent, in what degree, will a particular study prepare the individual for the truly human life?

An inductive study of the whole environment with a view to determine with accuracy what should be included in the curriculum and what should be left out is evidently out of the question here. We must confine ourselves to the more modest task of examining those elements of human life that the wisdom of the race has selected as the most appropriate subject matter for schoolwork, and, by way of introduction to this task, it will be appropriate to formulate a few general considerations on the more commonly mentioned educative values of school studies.

Educational Values

Practically every subject prepares in some way for the study of one or more subjects. Some mastery of the traditional three "R's" is the prerequisite for all subsequent studies; arithmetic prepares for the study of algebra which, in turn, prepares for the study of analytic geometry and calculus. The intensive study of the biological sciences presupposes a knowledge of physics and chemistry. In general, all subjects in the elementary school prepare for the study of high-school subjects, the latter, in turn, preparing for college work. Thus most subjects, if not all, have in some measure a preparatory value.

A second value that a school subject may have is the practical value, in the sense that the knowledge of a given subject may help one, either directly or indirectly, to satisfy the material needs of life. Some knowledge of drawing will help the carpenter or mason in his trade; the knowledge of botany, zoology, and chemistry with its applications to agriculture may help the farmer and cattle breeder to make their work more remunerative. A high-school education is a very common prerequisite nowadays to secure office positions, and the members of the professions depend upon their liberal and technical preparation for a livelihood.

Knowledge has a practical value in a still wider sense. It contributes to making effective the whole machinery of our public life. Wise legislation, the efficient administration of the nation's political and economic interests, and the just interpretation of its laws require, on the part of legislative, executive, and judicial officers, a knowledge of history, economics, sociology, and political science; public health in a community depends in no small degree on the knowledge health officials have of the laws of bacteriology, hygiene, sanitation, pure food, and fresh water supply.

School subjects not only help as tools, to take up and carry on the study of other subjects, or achieve utilitarian purposes in life, but are also cultural. They help us develop and refine our mental capacities, they are means of self-improvement, of intellectual and aesthetic enjoyment. Culture has already been dealt with at some length in the treatment of educational aims and ideals and therefore need not detain us here beyond a few supplementary remarks. All studies are cultural insofar as they improve our psychical capacities and our outlook upon life. The extent to which culture is achieved will depend upon the way in which the school subjects are handled by the teacher, the mental attitude of the learner, and the amount of effort the learner puts forth in his studies. Some studies, however, like religion, language and literature, history, and philosophy are intrinsically more cultural, more humanizing than others, because they enlist the whole range of our mental faculties and deal with distinctly human interests. They should, on that account, occupy the first rank among school subjects.

Closely related to the cultural is the formal or disciplinary value which of late has been vigorously challenged by some educationists and no less vigorously defended by others. It is usually associated with the study of the formal subjects: grammar, mathematics, rhetoric, and logic. The defenders of this educational value maintain that the material of the formal subjects can be so selected and treated as to awaken the powers of the mind and secure mental training as no other subjects could.

The fifth and last in this short list of educational values is the moral value, corresponding to the moral educational aim. All studies, in fact all school activities, possess this value to the extent that they require effort on the part of the student, keep him busy in worthy occupations, and lead to the formation of good habits. There are four subjects, however—literature, history, civics, and, above all, religion— that possess the moral value in a far higher degree than other subjects. The characters portrayed in history and literature, if properly presented, cannot fail to have a wholesome influence on the student, either as an inspiration to a good life or as a warning as to the consequences of wrongdoing. Civics, if properly handled, can do much to develop in the student a sense of his social and political obligations. Of all subjects, however, religion has the greatest moral value, because it reaches deeper than any other subject in human nature and sets before the student the loftiest examples of the good life and the strongest motives to live it.

Essential School Subjects

Viewed from the standpoint of general education, school subjects have not all the same importance; some are essential; others, secondary elements of the curriculum. Those elements should be considered essential that, possessing the greatest educative value, cannot easily be learned without the aid of the teacher; they have formed, from time immemorial, the core of the academic content. On the other hand we should consider as secondary all school subjects that possess a lesser educative value than the preceding and can be mastered more or less easily outside the school. These secondary elements were introduced into the curriculum at a much later date than the essentials.

Language

Among the essential elements of the educational content, the first place next to religion [2] belongs to linguistic studies. Language is the natural means of social intercourse, the natural vehicle for the expression of our own thoughts and feelings and the assimilation of the thoughts and feelings of others, and the chief agency for the transmission of spiritual treasures from one generation to the next. Language is the most important agency for intellectual formation and culture. In fact, it would be more accurate to say that language makes possible intellectual formation and, therefore, culture. It facilitates attention by giving body to our thoughts which otherwise would remain vague, fleeting, and easily escape the mind's scrutiny. Language makes possible the processes of analysis, abstraction, and generalization. Without the aid of signs or symbols of some kind—and such are words—the mind could not in practice hold and consider separately the elements or properties that make up any object or thought.

It is, of course, possible, without the use of words, to reach the notion of something common to a number of individual objects, but the notion will remain obscure, indistinct, and will not be easily retained unless it receives a sort of body through some term attached to it. Still more difficult would

---

[2] See Chapter XIV.

be the processes of judging and reasoning, if they were to be carried on without the aid of words. Language, especially written language, gives thought a fixity, and permanency that permits us to recall it at will and transmit it to others. It is through the written language, mainly, that each new generation comes into the possession of the intellectual treasures accumulated by the generations that have preceded it. But language has another, no less important value. In the service of the orator, the preacher, the poet, the journalist, in fact all those who can wield it efficiently, it becomes a sharp weapon and an instrument of power. It was in this sense, that is, as an instrument of power, that the ancient Greeks and Romans, and the sixteenth-century humanists considered language; but they also regarded it as a personal ornament, an essential element of beautiful living, and therefore looked upon the ability to express one's thoughts and feelings in elegant, even poetical form as the choicest fruit of education. That this emphasis upon the choice and arrangement of words would lead to a neglect of the substance of speech, to verbosity, and artificiality, words that convey neither sense nor spirit was to be expected. Decadent Latin literature and the writings of sixteenth- and seventeenth-century "Ciceronians" contain ample evidence of this misguided emphasis upon form.

Modern "realism," on the other hand, considered it a waste of time and energy to pay any attention to the refinements of style as cultivated by the old school. Content and not form, it says, should be the one concern of teacher and pupil. The two views should be reconciled. The writer or speaker should have something to say. Language, back of which there is no thought or sentiment, is so much wasted breath. On the other hand, much of the value attached to our thoughts and sentiments and their influence upon others depend upon the way they are expressed, and it is evident that we cannot properly express our thoughts and sentiments unless we possess some command of words, phrases, and constructions, all of which is the subject of the science and art of language.

The linguistic element in the modern plan of school disciplines includes the study of the mother tongue and foreign languages. In elementary education, the mother tongue is represented by reading, writing, spelling, pronounciation, grammar, and composition; in secondary education, by grammar, rhetoric, prosody, and composition. In both the elementary and secondary school, the work in language culminates in literature. The study of foreign languages is commonly assigned to the secondary school, and, like the study of the mother tongue in the elementary school, it involves reading, writing, spelling, pronounciation, grammar, and composition. Rhetoric and prosody are sometimes added in the study of some foreign language, and here again linguistic study culminates in literature.

Learning the mechanics of reading and writing is the first step in elementary-school education and the indispensable prerequisite for all further progress in schoolwork. Beside this preparatory function, reading and writing, even at this elementary stage, have an important intellectual value of their own, because they require constant analysis and synthesis and call the attention of the child to something intangible through the visible symbols of language. Then, too, the repeated efforts that are required of the child in order to master the arts of reading and writing cannot fail, if only indirectly, to exert a wholesome influence upon his character. In former times, much attention was paid to the artistic aspect of the art of writing. Today, however, we prefer to insist upon clear, efficient penmanship, than upon calligraphy. Closely related to the arts of writing and reading is that of drawing. As a means of conveying thought, it is often more effective than either the spoken or written word, and it may be classed among the essentials of elementary and secondary education for the prospective carpenters, cabinetmakers, masons, stonecutters, and the like.

Grammar

Leaving aside theoretical, comparative, and historical grammar, which properly belong in the domain of the university, grammar has a twofold purpose in general education: to be a guide in the correct use of language and to be an aid in the interpretation of literary masterpieces. Of these two purposes, the first is, of course, the more important and, even when grammatical study has no other purpose than the correct use of the mother tongue in speech and in writing, its educative value is very great. Not a little sustained study and practice is required on the part of the pupil to master the words and constructions of the living speech and the rules governing its use. Nor should we consider grammar a purely formal subject; the vocabulary, systems of forms, phonetic laws, and constructions form an intellectual content of no mean importance. Besides, the mastery of this content is a key to the intelligent reading and appreciation of literary classics, an introduction to another conception of grammar that was formerly an integral part of linguistic studies.

The grammatical study of the written speech not only insures the grasping of the writer's meaning, which, in itself, is an intellectual gain, but it involves much mental training, because it calls into play, the processes of analysis and synthesis, comparison and contrast, judging and reasoning. In this respect language study may be likened to gymnastics, because it develops qualities similar to those we try to develop through systematic physical exercise, that is, habits of linguistic accuracy and mental vigor.

Another important result of the systematic study of language is language consciousness. The words, phrases, and constructions that have accumulated in the memory may be used, more or less unconsciously, through mere imitation of speech in our environment. Such is the way the child and uneducated man use language. We use language consciously when we look upon words and their relations as something objective, having a content of their own, independently of what we have actually in mind. The grammatical study of the mother tongue will undoubtedly develop in the pupil's mind a clarification of the language consciousness, because it compels him to stop and, as it were, watch his native language in actual operation. There is, however, a serious handicap in this method of achieving language consciousness. The mother tongue is so bound up with the pupil's nature and habits of speech that he will never succeed in considering it as something really objective. The study of foreign languages, on the other hand, frees thought from its dependence upon words. It shows the possibility of expressing the same thought in various ways and, at the same time, it leads to a better knowledge of the mother tongue.

A further important gain resulting from the study of language, both native and foreign, is the acquisition of the information that words necessarily convey. Even the young child that begins to use its mother tongue acquires, with a knowledge of words, a goodly stock of simple notions concerning persons and things about him. This original stock of ideas is constantly added to in the school, if the teacher lets no new term pass without its meaning being made clear to the class and if he makes it a practice to ascertain whether the words used by the pupil correspond, in the speaker's mind, to the notions they should convey.

In the elementary school, language study will, of course, be limited to the national language as it is actually used today. In the secondary school, it should be extended to at least one foreign idiom, and it could use with profit the comparative, historical method in order to help the student get an insight into the very genius of the languages that he studies—the "why" and "how" of their development into their present form. Above all, however, the study of language should be a matter of practice, oral practice, possibly even more than practice in reading and writing, practice in imitating carefully supervised and criticized good models.

Literature

Because of the universality of its domain, its strong appeal to the sentiments and the imagination, and the wealth of its thought materials, literature has ever held an important position in the curriculum. Drawing its materials from the whole world and assuming all manners of forms, it touches upon the inner life at every point. On the wings of fancy, it will carry us into the past or the future, or lift us into the realm of the spiritual, far away from the material world. Epic poetry unfolds before us its pageant of colorful descriptions and great characters; lyric poetry reveals the secrets of the inner life, its hopes and joys, its sorrows and illusions. The novel and short story lead us into all sorts of interesting situations in everyday life, while the oration shows us how the passions and will of man are moved. The drama arouses our sympathies and fears by showing us the close relation between cause and effect in human life. In the fairy tale, literature adapts itself to the world of the child, and, through the fable, it succeeds in enlisting even dumb nature in the service of moral education. Aside from religion there is, indeed, no subject in the curriculum that rivals literature in moral and aesthetic value, because there is none that can bring the child and the youth so completely under the influence of great deeds, noble feelings, and beautiful heroic types of manhood and womanhood.

But, in order to fulfill its mission of aesthetic and moral education, literature must be used primarily for literary purposes. Its appeal should ever be to the imagination and higher emotions and to the idealizing, epic, and dramatic tendencies. Too often, literature is made to serve some utilitarian purpose, to be an aid in the teaching of another subject, a means of illustrating some point in history, geography, or nature study. Literary masterpieces were not produced to help students in their spelling, grammar, history, or geography; they were intended by their authors to be the artistic expressions of the writer's reaction to some phase or problem of human life. They should be treated as such, and, furthermore, they should be read in their entirety. Extracts from a masterpiece never give an adequate view of the whole, and therefore they fail to lead the student to the proper appreciation of its value. Another error to be avoided in the teaching of literature is the overstressing of the historical and critical aspects of the subject. Literary criticism and the history of literature possess, of course, an educational content and value of their own which should be included in the language course, but they are, after all, only aids to the study of literature and should never obscure the main purpose of its use in the school, which is the understanding, appreciation, and enjoyment of literary masterpieces.

Classical Studies

All that has been said so far of the educative value of linguistic studies applies to all language courses, but in a very particular way to the language courses that include Latin and Greek. A thorough discussion of the educative value of Latin and Greek is, of course, out of the question here, but we can at least mention with brief comment some of the reasons why Latin and Greek were considered for centuries and are still considered by many educators as one of the best agencies for a liberal education. The first and perhaps more potent reason for the inclusion of Latin and Greek in a liberal course of studies is the close, intimate, cultural relationship of the modern Western world to ancient Greece and Rome. Leaving aside the special contributions made to our civilization by Christianity, its choicest elements came to us from ancient Greece through Rome and the Church. Our science, philosophy, literature, and art begin with the science, philosophy, literature, and art of ancient Greece, and her achievements in some of those fields as well as in national life may have been equaled but were never surpassed in the following ages. "The Greeks have succeeded," says a modern writer, "in establishing themselves as the models of a beautiful humanity, and the Spartans at Thermopylae, the Athenians at Marathon and Salamis, the death of Socrates, the imperial figure of Alexander the Great will probably continue to the end of time to be celebrated as the classical examples of self-sacrifice, heroism and the spirit of enterprise—not as though other ages had not produced instances of the same deeds and that at times with purer motives, but nowhere else has the greatness of these deeds found such eloquent and beautiful expression as with the Greeks; here the imagination need not remove the bitter shell before it can enjoy the sweet kernel within." [3]   With some variants, that statement applies to ancient Rome no less than to ancient Greece. Roman history also abounds in accounts of great, noble, inspiring deeds; Latin literature may lack the freshness, originality and variety of the Greek, but it does not suffer too much otherwise from a comparison with its model, and it has the additional merit of having contributed more directly to the rise and development of the Western languages and literatures. This influence of Latin on the modern European idioms is at once evident in the Romance dialects, but even languages like German, which outwardly seem to be free from that influence, had been Latinized in spirit, and one may wonder how it could have been otherwise, since the whole spiritual life of the West was that of the Latin Church for over a thousand years.

It is sometimes said that one may reap from a good translation of the ancient classics all the advantages that accrue from a study of the original. If it were only a question of gathering information, the translation of a classic would answer the purpose just as well as the original, but information gathering is only one of the minor aspects of the study of the classics, whether ancient or modern; its chief purpose is to introduce the young into the circle of the master minds

---

[3] Lotze, Mikrokosmus, III, p. 295 (*cf.* Willmann-Kirsch, *op. cit.*, Vol. II, p. 105 f.).

of the race, and this purpose will never be achieved by a translation. Any one acquainted with the originals and translations of English, French, German, or Italian literary masterpieces knows that a translation may be good as a translation, but it fails to convey the subtle spiritual qualities of the original.

Another reason for the high educative value of the study of the classics, especially Latin, is the logical training that it provides for the student. Greek possesses a flexibility and a wealth of words and etymological forms that make it an admirable instrument for the expression of fine distinctions and the greatest variety of relationships. Latin on the other hand, is more systematically organized. "An immanent logic is the characteristic of the Latin language, particularly of its grammar—both the law and the grammar of Rome have in them something of the intellectual drill regulations." [4] Whether it be the translating of Latin into the native idiom or the latter into Latin, or the writing of verse, or some prose composition, the process is always rigidly regulated by clear-cut rules and laws; it calls for a careful examination of words, their various meanings and their function in the sentence, as indicated by their endings; the student must ever bear in mind the relation that the different parts of speech have to one another; he must select the special relations that will bring such and such words together in a sentence in order to express the thought that is conveyed in the Latin text, or else to express in Latin some thought of his own or some text from his native language. Nor is this all. Latin grammar insists upon a close, and, as it were, tangible connection between sentences through the

---

[4] Willmann-Kirsch, op. cit., Vol. II, p. 104.

use of the appropriate particles, according to the order of importance among sentences. This intensive grammatical work carried on daily for years can result only in an excellent logical training. But it means more. The translation, if it is properly conducted, will accustom the student to divest thought of its verbal form, to think in terms of thought instead of in terms of words, and to reach that vision of reality which it is the purpose of all great writers to give us.

In the schools of ancient Greece, the linguistic element was limited to one language, Greek, which, through colonization, later on through the conquests of Alexander the Great, became and remained for centuries the most widely used language from Sicily to the Indus. Greek, however, never acquired in the West the prominent position it had obtained in the East, though for a time it was placed on a par with Latin in Roman schools and was quite commonly used by the better-educated classes of Roman society. In the Middle Ages most schools were one-language schools; the language taught, Latin, had now become a foreign idiom for the masses, but it was, as yet, the only channel of Western culture. The one noteworthy exception to this dominant position of Latin was in the education of the prospective knight, whose intellectual education was, on the whole, based on the knowledge of the Romance languages, particularly French, because they gave access to the lyric and epic poetry dealing with knightly life. With the Renaissance, Greek once more took its place by the side of Latin in Western schools, and a knowledge of Italian, or Spanish, or French, for political or social reasons, was quite commonly insisted upon among the aristocracy of the sixteenth and seventeenth centuries. By that time, the mother tongue was gaining recognition in the schools everywhere, but its position was still secondary to that of Latin or even French, without a knowledge of which no one could feel at ease in the higher circles of his own country.

No language course is complete today, which does not include at least two of the foreign modern languages. The demands of political and economic intercourse will naturally influence the selection of the foreign idioms and the importance attached to each, but French, German, Italian, and Spanish, more particularly the first three, are commonly offered by the school in the English-speaking world for general educative purposes. The time allotted to the study and the method of treatment varies with the specific aims in view. For one who intends to use the language merely as a tool in research work or in written business transactions, a satisfactory command of the language can be acquired in a comparatively short time. If, on the other hand, we want the student to reap the full benefit of the study of a foreign language and to become acquainted with the national culture whose medium it is, long years of study under competent teachers is the essential prerequisite.

Mathematics

Like language, mathematics has always occupied a prominent position in the school curriculum. One reason for the importance attached to mathematics is the practical value of the subject. In all the trades as well as in common, everyday life, there is a constant demand for the ability to add, subtract, multiply, divide, handle fractions and complex numbers, measure, and weigh. Beyond this everyday use of elementary mathematics by the average person, an extensive knowledge of higher mathematics is needed in many vocations that require the use of applied science, such as engineering and navigation. A wide knowledge of mathematics is also necessary today for the advanced study of science. Physics, astronomy, and physical geography have long been considered semimathematical sciences; mineralogy, chemistry, biology, and other natural sciences are increasingly becoming mathematical, which is also true in a lesser degree of the social sciences. History uses mathematics in questions of chronology; experimental and educational psychology use a number of mathematical formulas; statistics, a branch of mathematics, is extensively used by educational and social research workers.

Treating quantities as such, independently of all considerations concerning the origin, nature, and possible uses of things, mathematics gives us a knowledge of the relationships existing in the material world, now from the viewpoint of progression and number, now from that of form, or again from the viewpoint of a combination of both number and space. The assumptions of mathematics—though seemingly clear, evident propositions to the casual thinker—come at the bar of metaphysics for a good deal of discussion and demonstration, but the consideration of this aspect of the subject can be postponed until the student takes up the study of philosophy. The validity of the assumptions of mathematics can be taken for granted without in any way impairing the educative value of the subject in elementary and secondary schools.

Unlike philosophy and the natural sciences, mathematics does not depend for its apprehension upon the experience of the learner. It is concerned with abstractions that can be dealt with independently of reality and readily lend themselves to all sorts of combinations that call for vigorous mental activity. Imagination is given free play in the search for the relationships suggested by the data under consideration, and, at the same time, it is constantly called at the bar of reason which determines whether the suggested combination is sound and therefore a valid premise for further progress.

As remarked before, the immediate aim of intellectual education is essentially the development and discipline of mental power, of the capacity for independent thinking. The touchstone of this power is the ability to read aright any situation that may face us, and to discover the solution of the problems it may suggest. Mathematics is eminently adapted to that purpose. No other subject offers such a wealth and variety of problems that can be well graded according to the pupil's mental capacities and his acquaintance with the subject. Again, beside the educative value common to all problems in whatever subject, problems in mathematics have this particular merit: the solution is, so to say, checked up at every step; the student is taught, through the very process of learning, to be cautious in progress, to be accurate in his statements, and to reject any judgment that does not tally with the data of the problem. And herein lies the more important and more commonly mentioned educative value of mathematics. It develops the habit of looking for the reasons of things behind the screen of appearances, of asking for and finding out the answers to the "whys" that we meet everywhere in life.

We noted previously that the lower branches of mathematics possess a preparatory value with reference to the higher branches, and the knowledge of the subject as a whole is, on its material side, an excellent and indispensable prerequisite for the study of science in the university and technical school.   In a still higher sense, the study of mathematics affords the best preparation for the study of philosophy.   It is this propaedeutic value of mathematics for philosophy that accounts for the importance attached to the subject by the Pythagorean and Platonic schools in antiquity, by most medieval teachers, and by those modern educators who still believe that philosophy is the capstone of a liberal education.

Philosophy

The third one of the essential elements in the educational content, philosophy, has already been discussed at some length in the introduction.   There remains only to point out some of its values as a school subject and its relation to other elements in the course of study.   The main purpose of philosophy is to give us an intelligent view of reality as a whole.   Literature tries to give us such a view, but it usually deals with the world of sense, or else, when rising above the sensuous, its view of reality is colored and distorted by imagination and feeling, whereas philosophy views reality in the light of reason, free from the bondage of sense, fancy, or sentiment.   The sciences, also like philosophy, try to explain reality, but they are, each and everyone of them, interested only in one aspect of things and their explanation never goes far enough beneath the surface of appearances, whereas philosophy is ever in search of the ultimate reasons of things.   It is sometimes said that philosophy deals with abstraction.   That is true to this extent, that philosophy must proceed through abstraction in its search for truth.   When, however, philosophy allows itself to be unduly detained in the world of abstractions, it ceases to fulfill its mission, which is essentially the explanation of reality.

One of the most valuable lessons taught the student in
philosophy is the importance of order and the need of cau-
tion in reasoning.   Starting from principles, the validity of
which cannot be questioned, with well-defined terms and
limiting its study to one aspect of a question at a time, it
proceeds slowly and is never reluctant to retrace its steps, to
compel thought, as it were, to give an account of itself.   But
while thus giving proper attention to details, philosophy
never loses sight of the main issue, which is to make a unit
of the whole field of knowledge while determining the relative importance of its every branch and the relation of one
branch to another and to the whole.

The systematic study of philosophy comes as a capstone
to the course of study in the last two years of the college,
but the philosophical spirit, the interest in philosophical
speculation concerning the nature and relations of things,
appears long before the student reaches that stage in his
studies.   It is already evident in the first "why" and "what
for" of the child, which shows that, though still immersed
in the variety of phenonema surrounding him, he begins to
take an interest in the causal relations that he wants to
understand.   The real awakening, however, does not occur
until the beginning of the adolescent period, when the craving for factual knowledge yields to the desire for explanations.

Every subject will offer opportunities to develop and train
this speculative interest, thus preparing the student for the
systematic study of philosophy.   Without failing to do justice to other aims, language study can still be, as it was for
centuries, a sort of introduction to logic.   Literature, history,
civics, school life, and the larger life of the community offer
the thoughtful and well-prepared teacher a wealth of events,

situations, and problems that cannot be explained except through the aid of psychology, ethics, or politics, though the explanation need never be technical. Mathematics and the natural sciences, when properly taught, will provide a splendid training in vigorous intellectual activity while preparing for a synthetic survey of physical reality.

Religion closes the list of the most essential elements in the school curriculum. Because of its vital importance in education, as in life, it is the subject of a separate chapter.

Secondary School Subjects

The secondary elements in the school curriculum could be arranged in the following groups: social science; natural science; the fine arts (treated in the chapter on aesthetic education); and a fourth group, including gymnastics, manual training, and athletics which have already been discussed in the chapter on physical education. Aside from psychology, ethics, aesthetics, and political economy, which belong to the domain of philosophy, the social sciences that enter into the general course of study are geography, history, and civics.

The Social Sciences

Geography acquaints us with the earth as the scene of man's manifold activities, present and past. It helps us to understand and to explain facts by showing us where they are located and associating them with other facts suggested by the map. Geography has been called one of the eyes of history; chronology, the other. It is likewise closely related to other sciences: in physiography, with mathematics, geodesy, and astronomony; in physical, political, and commercial geography, with the natural sciences, politics, and economics. It derives its data from many quarters, but views them all from the fundamental standpoints of space and society.

History, formerly considered a branch of literature, is treated today as a science, "the science of the development of man in his activities as a social being." It is primarily interested in the life of civilized peoples, leaving to biology, ethnography, ethnology, and linguistics, the explanation of the life of savages and barbarians. It studies and explains the past on the basis of existing documents that it examines and appraises with the assistance of allied historical sciences. Formerly, history was chiefly concerned with the political life of nations and the doings of statesmen and generals, their wars, conquests, and treaties. Today the tendency of historians and writers of history textbooks seems to be to neglect political life and to insist upon the development of civilization, which is treated by many as one phase of a materialistic evolution, a product of biological characteristics, climate, products of the soil, and so on. Aside from the reservations that a materialistic treatment of civilization calls for, one may wonder if the complexity and impersonal character of the subject are not a serious handicap for its presentation and assimilation in the elementary, and, even, secondary school.

Though but an accessory subject, history is rich in educative values. It widens the student's intellectual horizon by showing him that the past no less than the present is a part of the community life in which he shares. It makes him realize the indebtedness of the present to past generations, thus helping him to make a correct appraisal of the achievements of the present. Like literature, it develops and deepens the social feeling, it quickens and trains the imagination, it conveys many a telling lesson in morality, and it is a school of patriotism. History also contributes to our knowledge of other subjects by showing us their evolution from simple beginnings to their present condition, and it is an excellent introduction to a few sciences like civics, the elementary science of sociopolitical relations. When properly presented, civics cannot fail to be an aid in the building up of a good, intelligent citizenry, but the nature of the subject is so complex that a direct presentation is bound to result in confusion. The best approach seems to be through history.

The Natural Sciences

The natural sciences (astronomy, physics, chemistry, biology, zoology, and so on) acquaint us with the material world above and around us. They satisfy the interest that prompts us to inquire into the nature of things, and, at the same time, when properly taught, they foster the interest in the beauty of creation. For some particularly gifted students the study of the natural sciences, even in their elementary form, may be the starting point for a brilliant scientific career. For all students the study of natural science, like the study of mathematics, develops habits of neatness, precision, thoroughness, and the habit of holding fast to the facts of a given situation. From the viewpoint of general education, physics and chemistry are today the most important of all the natural sciences, because of the many changes they have introduced into modern life. No man today could claim that he is well educated who is not more or less familiar, for instance, with the production and uses of electricity. Besides, a general knowledge of these subjects is a prerequisite for special studies preparing for industrial or commercial positions.

Topics for Further Study

1. "Children learn as animals do." Prove or disprove that statement.

2. "Animals cannot learn as children do." Prove or disprove that statement.

3. "We learn not from things but from the use of things." Discuss.

4. "Learning by doing." Contrast the traditional interpretation of this maxim with that of the "school of activity."

5. Differentiate experience from experiment.

6. Compare the relative values of experience and experimentation as sources of learning.

7. "The objective versus the subjective meaning of value." Discuss.

8. "All teaching and learning depend on actual experience." Discuss.

9. Give a list of the valuable phases of human life arranged in a decreasing hierarchy. Account for your arrangement.

10. Submit a tentative arrangement of (a) elementary-school curriculum, (b) high-school curriculum, (c) college curriculum corresponding to the preceding list.

11. "The teacher's personality is an essential element in the learner's environment." Discuss.

12. "Education in a democracy should provide a knowledge of the fundamentals of the social and political life." Discuss.

13. Discuss the value of history as an aid to self-knowledge.

14. Discuss the value of literature as an aid to self-knowledge.

15. Compare the educative values of the humanities and natural sciences.

16. State and comment on the pragmatic view of the school curriculum.

17. Discuss the relative importance of history as an elementary- and secondary-school subject.

18. "Grammar study as a preparation for the systematic study of logic." Discuss.

19. "Elementary- and high-school studies as a preparation for the systematic study of psychology and ethics." Discuss.

20. "Philosophy, the capstone of a sound liberal education." Discuss.

SUGGESTIONS FOR READING

Arbousse-Bastide, P., *Pour un Humanisme Nouveau* (Paris, 1930).

Bobbit, F., *How to Make a Curriculum* (Boston, 1924).

Charmot, F., *L'Humanisme et l'Humain* (Paris, 1934).

Dupanloup, F., *De l'Education* (Paris, 1851).

Herbart, J., *Outlines of Educational Doctrine* (New York, 1913).

Newman, J., *The Idea of a University* (New York, 1921).

Plato, *The Republic.*

Quintilian, *Institutes of Oratory.*

Ruediger, W., *The Principles of Education* (New York, 1910).

Snedden, D., *Foundations of Curricula* (New York, 1927).

Spalding, J., *Means and Ends in Education* (Chicago, 1895).

The Classical Investigation (Princeton, 1923).

The Classics in Education (London, Board of Education, 1923).

Willmann-Kirsch, *The Science of Education* (Beatty, 1921).

CHAPTER IX

Intellectual Education *(Continued)*

Relating Educational Content and Aim

The first step in curriculum construction is the selection of the materials of instruction, the second step is the apportionment of the time allotted to every subject, and, in both instances, the criterion is the educative value of the materials under consideration. The third step in the organization of the curriculum is the coördination of its materials with the final end of education, which is moral and religious. All studies and school activities should be so selected and so related to life as to arouse in the young, a deep, abiding love for the true, the beautiful, and the good, and their eternal fountainhead.

Religion, and we mean here Christianity, should occupy a central position in the curriculum, as it did for centuries everywhere in the West and still does today in Catholic education. All subjects should be taught in such a way as to reflect the views on man, life, and the whole universe which form the philosophy of Christian life. Religion, then, is not to be treated merely as one of the school subjects, like language, history, or geography, but as the very core of the curriculum, a trunk from which all the other subjects branch off.

The content of religious education includes acts of worship

and the doctrines of faith, Scriptural texts, Bible and Church history, the precepts of the moral law, and certain regulations of conduct—like fasting and abstinence—outside the sphere of the moral law. Instruction in these elements of the religious content naturally lends itself to direct connection with studies in language and literature, music, and general and national history. The Catechism is not only a digest of Christian theology, but the best little text ever devised for moral instruction; it also affords the teacher splendid opportunities for language practice. The Holy Scriptures, Bible and Church history contain a wealth of reading materials for all grades. The classical languages have come to us through the Church, and through her they have left their imprint on all Western languages and literatures. No account of ancient classical literature is complete which does not take into consideration the contributions made to it by the early Church Fathers. The history of the West for over a thousand years was the history of the Church; and the student of the plastic arts, music, and national literatures is constantly reminded of the cultural influence of Christianity. All subjects will serve the moral religious end of education if none but the best materials are used for instruction, if the student is trained to detect and appreciate the good and the beautiful whenever he meets it.

Foremost in the list of subjects next to religion come, of course, the national language, national legends and tales of heroism, the national literature and history, and the local and national traditions and customs, which reveal to the young the treasures of their spiritual environment and will not fail to arouse a deep, lasting interest in the family and national welfare if properly presented and connected with life. The study of general history, of the foreign languages and literatures, both ancient and modern, will introduce the young to the larger international environment, will show them that the good and the beautiful are not the monopoly of one time or race or nation. It will show them, too, the national indebtedness and contribution to foreign types of culture and will thus help to correct the one-sidedness and narrowness of the nationalistic type of culture. Even those subjects that seem to be ethically indifferent can be made to serve the moral end if the mastery of such subjects demands deep, concentrated effort on the part of the student.

Coördinating the Materials of Instruction

The fourth step in the organization of the curriculum is the bringing out of the relations existing between its several elements, in order to unify the process of instruction and make an organic whole of all the educational materials. This objective, inner connection of all the elements of knowledge, and, more particularly, of all school subjects, has ever been recognized by leading educational theorists. Plato applies it in his *Republic,* in working out a plan of education for the youth of his ideal state. It is insisted upon by Cicero in his *De Oratore,* and applied by St. Augustine in his *Doctrina Christiana.* St. Thomas, and with him all the Schoolmen, looked upon the whole body of knowledge as a sort of living organism that has its origin and reaches its full development in the Divine Intelligence. In modern times, as we shall see later on, the principle of coördination has been extensively applied in a number of ways.

Next to religion, philosophy is the one subject that, from its very nature, is best adapted to unite all the branches of knowledge. It is the logical, natural climax, the capstone of a sound system of general education, because it provides a general survey of the whole field of knowledge after its different parts have been examined. The student, however, should become aware of the interrelation of all the school subjects long before he takes up the study of philosophy—in fact, from the very beginning of school life.

Geography is one of the best associative subjects in elementary and secondary education. The student can easily form the habit of asking for the "where" in connection with the knowledge that he acquires and thus be led to connect its various elements. Home geography deals with the immediate environment of the child, general geography, with his more distant environment. The first one appeals chiefly to the senses, the second to imagination, and the combination of both will establish a close relation between the sensuous horizon of the child and that of his imagination. The connection between geography and the natural objects of our environment is at once natural and obvious and so is the relation between geography and history; this twofold relation, in turn, may be used to introduce the student to the natural sciences, economics, foreign languages, and literature.

Like geography, history can easily be used to bring out the interconnections between the elements of knowledge even though its associative value cannot be utilized at once in the school; time relations being more abstract than space relations are not at first easily realized by the child. The aim pursued here cannot, of course, be achieved by limiting instruction in history to the narration of military and political events; whenever the opportunity arises, the teacher should, without unduly widening the scope of his subject, call the attention of his class to the linguistic, literary, artistic, and scientific aspects of history.

The fact that language is the natural medium of instruction would point it out as an important link between the different branches of the curriculum. This demands that instruction in language, whether it be the mother tongue or a foreign idiom, be not limited to a matter of words and their arrangement in sentences and paragraphs. Content and form, thought and expression should ever proceed *pari passu*. Exercises in language, as pointed out long ago by Pestalozzi, can further aims other than mere correctness in expression. History, geography, arithmetic, natural science, and national and community life can supply an abundance of materials for those exercises, which will thus serve the threefold purpose of linguistic proficiency, assimilation of useful knowledge, and the realization by the student of the correlation of studies. On the other hand, accuracy and correctness in expression could and should ever be insisted upon in all subjects. Students too often entertain the mistaken notion that the proper use of language is the rule only in language lessons.

The mother tongue is, of course, the natural starting point and center of all language studies. The teaching of a foreign language should always be related to the native idiom through the comparative method, in order to bring out similarities and differences in phonology, vocabulary, syntax, and literature; also to show the indebtedness to foreign sources of the national language, national literature, and, in general, the national culture, thus again calling the attention of the student to the correlation of all the elements of knowledge. The study of authors, whether national or foreign, will prove particularly helpful in this respect, on condition, however, that it be realized that a classic is not only a masterpiece of expression but a source of information as well and that it be used from both viewpoints. Cæsar's *Gallic War,* for example, is at once a model of straightforward, simple, clear Latin prose and an interesting, precious historical document on Roman political and military life and peoples that were to become modern Western nations.

Mathematics, though seemingly ill-adapted to correlation purposes, can, nonetheless, be related to many other subjects as it was in the old medieval liberal arts course. The core of the quadrivium or science branch of the course consisted of arithmetic and geometry, closely related to the teaching of music and the materials gathered under the heading of astronomy. In the more advanced stage of scientific study today, the student soon realizes the interdependence of mathematics, physics, chemistry, mechanics, geography, and astronomy. In the early stages of school life the relation between mathematics and the other branches in the course of study is not obvious, and the student is apt to consider the subject as completely isolated in a little domain all of its own. It is not difficult, however, to bring out a number of relations between mathematics and other subjects and also the child's environment. The teaching of arithmetic can easily be related to little problems arising from the experiences of the child, or the teaching of geography, or the chronological side of history. Geometry is naturally related to drawing and geography through the construction of maps. A further means of relating mathematics, and the other sciences as well, to other branches of the curriculum is through their history. Without overstepping the limits of his subject, the teacher can, in connection with some theorems, formulas, properties of matter, and the symbols used today in mathematics, take his class on a brief excursion into the past, in order to show them the knowledge of the subject at such a time and in such a country, the extent to which the subject was taught in the school, the methods used and the progress since realized.

Various Organization Theories

Of the modern educational theorists, Herbart is perhaps the one most insistent upon the interconnections of the materials of instruction. His suggestions were taken up by his followers and led to various schemes of concentration and coördination of studies. A plan of coördination is one in which the materials of instruction are divided into groups; the most essential, or, at least, what is considered the most essential subject in each group is used as a core around which are arranged the other subjects; all groups are related at some point with one another. A plan of concentration is one grouping all the materials around a single core or subject which is considered as the most essential. Plans of coördination were generally adopted for the years above the primary grades, because it was found that no matter what the core, there would always be some subject that would not naturally fit into the scheme of concentration. On the other hand, concentration has been extensively applied to the primary grades, sometimes with language, sometimes with history, geography, or social activities, as a core. It was this concept of the correlation of studies which, by some followers of Herbart, has developed into the so-called culture epoch theory, at one time very popular in some quarters, but today of purely academic and historical interest. This culture epoch theory is part of a broader conception, the so-called theory of recapitulation, itself a progeny of the theory of evolution.

The recapitulation theory was developed in a twofold way: the psychophysiological and the cultural theory of recapitulation. Both theories take it for granted that the development of the individual is a repetition of the development of the race; ontogeny repeats philogeny. According to the psychophysiological theory of recapitulation, our physical and mental powers develop as they have developed in the race, independently of any training. The theory has been applied to the order of development of our mental faculties and instinctive tendencies. The race, it was assumed, having gone through three stages—intuitive, imaginative, and logical—so must the psychical development of the individual. During the intuitive stage, he depends chiefly, as the race did, on the faculty of sense perception for the acquisition of knowledge; in the next stage, on memory and imagination; and during the last one, he comes to depend more and more on his logical powers. In the application of the theory to the order of development of the instincts, it was asserted that all the instincts should be allowed to have their "fling" at the time of their development, lest they should reappear later on in some undesirable, distorted form. Teachers were advised to take this development of the instincts as some sort of index in the presentation of subject matter. Thus, the presence of the collecting instinct should tell them that now is the time to teach those branches in which the instinct can be called into play, as, for example, in botany.

According to the cultural theory of recapitulation, experience should be acquired by the individual in the order in which it was acquired by the race. Thus in religion, for instance, let the child be treated first like a little savage, then as a Jewish boy, and then as a Christian, since, it was asserted, these are the stages through which the race has passed in its religious development. It was this cultural theory of recapitulation that, in the hands of some of the followers of Herbart, led to various schemes of concentration and coördination of studies. In justice to the theory, let it be remarked that it contains an element of truth to which we shall return later on when dealing with the historical principle of grading.

It is not an easy matter to devise an arrangement of the whole curriculum that will do justice to the nature of the materials of instruction and, at the same time, satisfy the requirements of correlation, grading, and actual teaching. Some subjects, such as ethics, language, and religion, are of a decidedly ethical character. Others, like physics and chemistry, are essentially physical. That would suggest a twofold division of the materials of instruction into ethical and physical subjects. But then there are subjects like geography which belong to both fields. The problem would not be simplified if we divided the school subjects, as some do, into material and formal subjects. The sciences are both formal and material. Language contains a formal element in grammar, but literature, on the other hand, belongs to the material division. Mathematics is essentially formal, yet it contains a material element in the practical problems that are connected with it. And so it is throughout the whole range of studies.

Of the many plans for the organization of school subjects advocated in this country, we can mention only a few. There is, to begin with, the five-group classification suggested by William T. Harris—mathematics and physics; biology, including chiefly plant and animal life; literature and art; grammar and the scientific study of language leading to the study of logic and psychology; history and the study of social and political institutions. Nicholas Murray Butler, president of Columbia University, conceives education as a process of adjustment of the individual to his spiritual environment, and he divides this environment into five groups of subjects which he calls the five possessions of the race—scientific, literary, aesthetic, institutional, and religious—to which he later added a sixth group, the industrial. De Garmo, in his *Principles of Secondary Education,* divides the content of school education into three groups: the natural sciences, including mathematics, which pertain only to nature; humanities, including what primarily pertains to man, that is, language, literature, art, religion, and so on; and the economic sciences, including all the applications of the laws of nature for the material well-being of the race. Professor Herman H. Horne, in his *Philosophy of Education,* suggests an arrangement which corresponds to the three main faculties in man: intelligence, feeling, and will. The whole curriculum should be divided into science, arts, and volitions.

The country-wide movement for curriculum revision in the last two decades has brought out many other plans, some of a general character, but most of them concerned with the elementary-school, high-school, or college curriculum. A detailed, comparative study of those plans, more generally of the whole problem of curriculum organization, is, of course, the particular concern of the science of school administration. The problem comes within the purview of the philosophy of education only insofar as it is related to the question of the nature of knowledge and the general principles governing the presentation of the materials of instruction. From the viewpoint of the nature of knowledge, the problem can be briefly stated as follows: to organize the whole curriculum and every course of study in such a way as to bring out the objective relations existing between the elements of knowledge. From the viewpoint of the actual presentation of the materials of instruction, the solution of the problem depends on the teacher. He must feel at home in his own subject, be interested in all the branches taught in the school, and be ever ready to call the attention of the class to the points of contact between one subject and another.

Grading the Materials of Instruction

The next step in the organization of the curriculum is the arrangement of its materials into grades corresponding to the stages in mental growth and development. Nature and society have divided preadult life into four well defined periods: infancy and early childhood, childhood, boyhood, and youth. The mental characteristics of each period should evidently be the deciding factor in determining the kind of materials and the method to be used in intellectual education.

The main characteristic of infancy and early childhood is rapid physical and mental growth which should be furthered by allowing the child all the freedom of movement that is consistant with safe-guarding him against any untoward influence. The faculties of sense perception are fast reaching maturity; imagination is very active but draws little or no distinction between fact and fancy. Education at this stage is essentially a home affair, though the kindergarten may in some cases share in the responsibility. It is, in the main, free and informal and its chief concern is the training in obedience, the learning of the mother tongue and the beginnings of religious education.

The second period in preadult life, which corresponds to the primary and early grammar grades, is, in some respects, a mere continuation of the preceding. The acquisition of knowledge still depends mostly on the senses, now very alert and keen; the logical powers, though awakened, are still very weak, but the memory and the imagination are craving for constant exercise. It is also during this period that some of the instinctive tendencies come to maturity.

Religious education assumes now the formal character it should retain all through the period of school life. The child is now occupied with the mastery of the three "R's," prerequisite for further advancement in his studies. During the first years of this period, object lessons, simple exercises in drawing, nature study, constructive work, and vocal music, can be used to advantage to train the senses and develop the faculty of observation. Fairy tales, fables, legends, folklore, and national myths, will develop and train the young imagination. Home geography and biographical history also belong to the child's circle of interest and they prepare the widening of his intellectual horizon.

The next period in preadult life is one of deep physical and mental changes that transform the child into the boy and girl of the upper grammar grades and high school. There is now a superabundance of energy and a consciousness of strength; the spirit of independence begins to assert itself with a desire to know the reasons of things. Imagination is no less active than before, but the line between fact and fancy becomes clearer. New instinctive tendencies continue to assert themselves, among them the collecting instinct and the spirit of adventure. With the wider range of interest and stronger intellectual grasp in boyhood, there should go a corresponding widening of instruction and a more systematic appeal than heretofore to logical powers. Instruction in geography should now proceed from the study of the national environment to that of foreign countries. To the mother tongue should now be added the foreign languages; the systematic study of natural history should now take the place of object lessons in nature study. Tales of ,adventure and heroic deeds will respond to the boy's spirit of adventure.

Around the sixteenth year, a little earlier in the South than in the North, the period of adolescence begins. It is a time of great, rapid physical and mental expansion. By the eighteenth year, the girl has attained practically her full height and weight, but the boy still has to gain in these respects. The higher intellectual powers are fast increasing and craving for exercise, but imagination and feeling still play the leading role in decisions and the conception of reality. The most essential requisite in education during this period is the discipline of hard work, requiring an effort of the will bent on completing the task once begun. Instruction in all subjects is now concerned with the elaboration of the materials that have been gathered in the preceding periods. Heretofore, it has relied mostly on sense perception, imagination, and memory for the acquisition of knowledge. Its appeal should now be mostly to judgment and reasoning, and it should lead the student to a realization of the higher educational aims.

By way of summing up the foregoing outline, let us say that the sequence in the development of psychical powers is paralleled by a similar sequence or grading of studies in general school education, that is, the empirical, rational, and philosophical studies. To the first group of studies belong religion, language, drawing, music, geography, history and civics, elementary mathematics, and science insofar as the method of teaching those subjects is empirical, that is, concrete. They form the curriculum of the elementary- and early high-school grades. Mathematics, being essentially a rational subject, is one of the most important elements in the second group of studies. Religion, of course, belongs to this group as it does to the other two. Other subjects, like literature, history, geography and the physical sciences, belong to this group to the extent that they offer opportunities for the stressing of the rational aspect of the educative process. Philosophy closes the psychological series of subjects because, more than any other subject, it demands exercise in abstract thinking.

The grading of studies, as outlined in the foregoing paragraphs, is dictated by psychology and is therefore basic. Sometimes, however, it is desirable and possible to organize the materials of instruction both psychologically and historically. The historical principle of grading, so much insisted upon by Herbart and some of his followers, can be formulated in some such way as the following: Precedence in the sequence of studies should correspond to their precedence in historical development. Thus, in Herbart's plan of grading, the study of the Greek classics should come first, then that of Latin and then the study of modern languages and literature. The widest application of the historical principle of grading has been in the field of history and literature.

Topics for Further Study

1. Compare the naturalistic and Christian conception of the supreme end of education, drawing conclusions for curriculum organization.

2. Show the bearing of naturalistic or socialistic educational aims on curriculum organization.

3. Show the bearing of the cultural and efficiency aims, respectively, on the teaching of any high-school or college subject.

4. Give a detailed illustration of the teaching of national history for moral purposes.

5. Should history be taught primarily for moral purposes? Discuss.

6. Give a detailed illustration of the teaching of literature for moral purposes.

7. Should literature be taught primarily for moral purposes? Discuss.

8. Give a detailed illustration of the relation of the history of Christianity to either national or general history.

9. Give a detailed illustration of the relation of religion to Latin, Greek, or any modern literature.

10. "Philosophy as a coördinating, unifying subject." Discuss.

11. Illustrate the respective values of history or geography as coördinating subjects.

12. Give a detailed illustration of the comparative method of language teaching.

13. "Ontogeny repeats Philogeny." Discuss.

14. "Instincts should be allowed to have their 'fling' at the time of their development.' Discuss.

15. Compare critically any two plans for the organization of studies.

16. Show the bearing of a nationalistic philosophy of education on curriculum organization.

17. What are the merits and limitations of the historical principle of grading?

18. Give a detailed illustration of the application of the historical principle of grading.

19.   Discuss Plato's grading of subjects in the *Republic*.

20.   What is the modern trend in curriculum organization?
Discuss.

SUGGESTIONS FOR READING

Bobbit, F., *How to Make a Curriculum* (Boston, 1924).

Boutroux, E., *Science and Religion in Contemporary Philosophy* (London, 1909).

Brown, E., *The Making of our Middle Schools* (New York, 1905).

De Garmo, C., *Principles of Secondary Education* (New York, 1907).

De Hovre, F., *Le Catholicisme, ses Pédagogues, sa Pédagogie* (Bruxelles, 1930).

Foerster, F., *Politische Ethik und Politische Pædagogik* (Munchen, 1920).

Horne, H., *The Philosophy of Education* (New York, 1910).

Meriam, J., *Child Life and the Curriculum* (Yonkers, 1920).

Newman, J., *The Idea of a University* (New York, 1929).

Ruediger, W., *Principles of Education* (New York, 1910).

Snedden, D., *Foundations of Curricula* (New York, 1927).

Spalding, J., *Education and the Higher Life* (Chicago, 1922).

Willmann-Kirsch, *The Science of Education* (Beatty, 1921).

CHAPTER X

Intellectual Education (*Continued*)

The Meaning of Intelligence

In its most general sense, intelligence is the faculty of knowing. In the more common and more restricted sense of the term, it is the faculty of thinking, of knowing the universal and immaterial. In the latter sense, it is also referred to as reason, understanding. In that sense, too, intelligence is man's prerogative. Animals do not possess it in any degree; to say that animals are intelligent can mean only that they possess the capacity to know material objects through the senses. To man, as to the brute, knowledge comes through the senses, but it becomes human only through the activity of those intellectual powers that are man's prerogative.

The Stages in the Assimilation of Knowledge

The faculty of knowing, like the soul, of which it is but one aspect, always functions as a unit; all its operations are more or less simultaneous and copenetrate one another, but they can be classed into three groups, corresponding to a threefold aspect of knowledge from the viewpoint of the knowing subject: acquisition, conservation, and elaboration or transformation.

The faculties and processes of acquisition or perception are: sense perception, through which we are acquainted with the external, material world; inner perception or consciousness,[1] informing us of our mental states; reason, through which we apprehend such abstract notions as the true, the beautiful and the good, cause, effect, and substance.

The faculties and processes of conservation of knowledge are memory, imagination, and the association of ideas.

Abstraction, comparison, generalization, judgment, and reason are the processes and faculties of elaboration or transformation.

Before we pass on to a more detailed consideration of each group of intellectual capacities with their educational implications, it may not be out of order to insist once more upon the radical difference between sense and sensory knowledge on one hand, and intellect and intellectual knowledge on the other.

Through the senses, we perceive the particular, the material, and the contingent; through the understanding, the abstract and general. My senses tell me of a round or square object; my understanding is aware of roundness, squareness, extension, thickness, and depth—all abstract notions beyond the reach of the senses. The understanding perceives the various types of beings—that is, their intimate nature—independently of all circumstances of time, place, and form, which give them individuality. It reaches beyond the world of sensible things into that of absolute perfection which material objects never realize.

Sensory knowledge resolves itself into images, that is,

---

[1] For a lengthy discussion of this subject, see Rickaby, J., *First Principles of Knowledge,* pp. 340–347; or Maher, M., in the *Catholic Encyclopedia,* art. "Consciousness."

pictures or copies of sensations received and preserved through the memory and imagination. Intellectual knowledge consists essentially of ideas understood here to mean intellectual representations of things. Images refer to individual objects and their particular form, ideas to the essence of things, and the properties without which we cannot conceive them. Material objects are represented both by images and ideas, but they are understood only through ideas.

The Acquisition of Knowledge

Sense perception. As stated above, the intellectual faculties primarily concerned in the acquisition of knowledge are sense perception, inner perception, and reason. Our knowledge of the material world comes to us through the senses, but its real agent is perception, that is, sense or external perception. The senses—sight, hearing, touch, taste, and smell—do but supply sensations, the stuff out of which are made percepts, the constituents of our knowledge of material objects. Perception, in the modern sense of the term, though depending upon sensory data, is an essentially psychical process. It is, so to say, the mind's interpretation of the materials supplied by the senses. The senses will report, "white," "black," "round," and "green"; and the mind, through perception, says, "white paper," "black ink," "green apple."

Sensation, which is the most fundamental and primitive form of conscious life, is a process at once organic and psychical. It directly depends upon the organism, thus involving, besides the psychical element, several physical and physiological factors. There must be a material object, actually present, acting through some agent like sound and light waves upon a sense organ; there must also be some form of molecular disturbance in the substance of the nervous system transmitted through a sensory nerve to the cerebro-spinal mass, where it awakens the psychical phenomenon that we call sensation. The whole process can be summed up in the term *impression-sensation;* impression refers to the action of the external agent upon the organism, and it is a physico-physiological process; sensation, the outcome of that process, properly belongs to consciousness. Sensation, then, presupposes impression, but the two processes should not be confused as is the fashion today in many psychology textbooks.

Further psychological analysis reveals a number of properties of sensations: quality, intensity, duration, tone, and their hierarchy and informative character. Those properties of sensation are all more or less involved in the educative process, but the subject can be explained here only in briefest form.

From the standpoint of the general influence upon the whole of our sensitive life, the sense of touch occupies the first rank, the other senses more or less depending upon it. From the standpoint of organic well-being, touch and taste rank above all the other senses. Intellectually, that is, if we consider the amount of information the mind receives through each sense, touch again comes first, then follow sight, hearing, smell, and taste. In point of dignity, however, sight and hearing rank first; they are, par excellence, the aesthetic, social senses, the main channels for the expression of thought and the enjoyment of beauty, bearing in mind, of course, that the real agent of the expression and interpretation of thought, of the appreciation and enjoyment of beauty, is not sense but reason.

In what has been said so far and what may be said later of sense, sensation, and sense perception, it is assumed that there are realities outside and independently of our thought, that knowledge is not limited to a perception of mental states and relations between ideas, but includes as well the immediate or presentative perception of material reality. Leaving the discussion of these and kindred questions to metaphysics and epistemology, we now pass on to a brief consideration of the other two sources of the acquisition of knowledge, that is, inner perception and reason.

Inner perception. Inner perception or consciousness *(secum scire)* is understood here to mean the capacity through which the soul is aware of its own activities and cognizant of its powers and various states: sensations, recollections, sentiments, thoughts, and volitions. Those states of consciousness have not all the same degree of clarity or distinctness. There are those that we awaken or at least try to direct: remembrances, thoughts, reasonings, deliberations, decisions, of which we have a clear conception. There are other states of consciousness that are rather vague and fleeting, such as ideas we accept or inclinations we follow without giving either sufficient consideration. This would suggest a twofold classification of mental states, but the more common arrangement is a threefold one: conscious, semiconscious, and unconscious mental states.

The extent to which we are aware of our mental states depends mainly upon the three laws of intensity, attention, and habit. We fail to be conscious of a mental state when it is too weak; attention, though not changing the intrinsic strength or weakness of mental phenomena, focuses, so to say, the intellect upon these phenomena, thus making them clearer and more distinct; the continuity or repetition of the same mental state tends to deprive it of its emotive, effective quality, thus removing it from the field of consciousness. Those laws that express the conditions under which consciousness functions are of paramount importance in the teacher's work, as we shall have occasion again to remark later.

The object of consciousness is the self, the soul immediately perceived as a single, identical entity, in and with all its activities, an intelligent, free, responsible cause. The conscious self then cannot directly become aware of or be identified with the mental states of other selves or external objects or God. What we directly perceive is, first, some sensation, image, thought, desire, or volition that we refer to some internal or external cause; secondly, we perceive the share of the ego in producing, directing, or suppressing the phenomenon, provided, of course, the conditions or laws stated above are satisfied. If those conditions are not satisfied, the psychical phenomenon is but dimly or not at all perceived; it falls into the vast and mysterious region of the semiconscious and uneonscious self, whence it may unexpectedly reappear at any time.

Reason. Reason, intellect, understanding, intelligence, properly so-called, are the terms used to designate the thinking faculty, the power to understand things—more particularly, the faculty through which we know the general or universal—or again the faculty through which we know what is beyond the senses. Other names still are sometimes applied to reason, to designate a certain type of activity in which it is involved, or, what amounts here to the same thing, the standpoint from which we view it. Thus conscience, or practical reason, is the understanding functioning in matters of right and wrong; taste is reason at work in the field of the beautiful, tact is reason applied to social intercourse; common sense, the popular name of reason, is the sum total of those notions, beliefs, and experiences that are common to all men, the principles that reason at once perceives in the common run of things; it is the philosophy of everyday life, reason applied to the plain, simple facts of this workaday world. Another distinction is sometimes made between intuitive and discursive reason, or the immediate perception of truth and its apprehension following a process of reasoning.

The Contributions of Reason to the Acquisition of Knowledge

In the process of acquiring knowledge, reason provides primary ideas, like the notions of being, substance, cause, and effect, which knowledge implies and the first principles or analytical judgments attached to those notions. Both primary ideas and first principles possess certain characteristics of their own which it may be useful to enumerate here. They are:

Necessary, because we cannot think without them or conceive their opposite.

Eternal, in the sense that from all eternity they have existed in the Divine Intelligence.

Absolute, for they are not conditioned by time or space or any other circumstance.

Universal, because they are the common property of the race; they are applied by every normal person though not every one can formulate them.

Self-evident, needing no definition or demonstration; they are at once perceived by the intellect.

A priori; they are not reached through experience like the laws of physical science, though they are not antecedent to all experience; the intellect applies them on the occasion of the first experience.

Leaving aside the more elaborate classifications, we can list the essential relations of reality under the three principles of identity, causality, and finality—the three regulating principles of reason and knowledge.

The principle of identity or sameness is the expression of the fundamental truth that any being ever remains identical with itself, that what is, is. When negatively formulated, this truth is called the principle of contradiction: a thing cannot be and not be at the same time. Assuming the form of an alternative, this truth is referred to as the principle of excluded middle: "A door must be either closed or open." When applied to the thinking process, the principle of identity signifies that we avoid contradiction and its application is constant. Any good definition, for example, illustrates the application of the principle, since it is the expression of an identity between an idea or object and the explanation that is given of that idea or object, an agreement between subject and predicate. The widest and most systematic application of the principle is to be found in mathematics, particularly in equations. Its most obvious expression is the axiom, as for example, "the whole is greater than any one of its parts" or "two quantities that are each equal to a third quantity are equal to each other."

The principles of causality and finality are sometimes combined into the one principle of sufficient reason expressed thus: "There is nothing that exists without a reason as to the 'how' and the 'why' of its existence"; or else, "Nothing is made or begins to exist but by a cause"; or again, "Everything that exists has its *raison d'être*." It is through this *raison d'être* that anything that exists becomes intelligible for us, hence sufficient reason is sometimes referred to as the principle of intelligibility.

The two principles of identity or contradiction and sufficient reason or intelligibility are the very foundation of all knowledge. The principle of identity removes whatever would break the unity and harmony of knowledge. The principle of sufficient reason, on the other hand, enables us to explain the existence and relations of things and therefore to connect with one another, the elements of our knowledge.

The Origin of Primary Ideas and First Principles

How do we acquire the primary ideas and first principles? This question is but one of the subdivisions of the problem of the origin of ideas, a much debated question which properly belongs to the province of epistemology. According to some philosophers, our ideas are altogether derived from experience, be it the experience of the individual or that of the race; others suppose that we have some "innate" ideas, like those of justice, truth, or virtue, that we possess at birth previous to and independently of any experience; other philosophers claim that all our ideas are "innate," being awakened but not acquired on the occasion of experience; others still appeal to tradition, claiming that the first notions and principles were revealed by God to the first man and then passed on from generation to generation. The true answer is the empirico-rational, common sense explanation of the School. Experience and reason, sensations and intellectual operations coöperate in the origin of all our ideas.

The empirical formula that "There is nothing in the mind which was not before in the senses" is accepted by the Schoolmen, but is explained by them in a way entirely different from that of the empiricist. According to the latter, sensation is the sole cause of all our ideas; the scholastic interpretation is that sensation is but the starting point, the occasion of our ideas. Sensations supply the materials out of which ideas are evolved by the intellect, through processes of abstraction, comparison and generalization; so it is, for all ideas in general and for the primary ideas and principles in particular. The latter are not innate, any more than any other idea; in every normal individual they function, one might say, instinctively on the occasion of experience, because it is in the very nature of the intellect so to function as soon as it is awakened. All the "whys" of the child, for instance, imply the principle of causality, since the child is asking for the cause of something. When a child refuses to acknowledge a stranger as his mother he applies the principle of identity, although he would not understand it if it were expressed in its abstract form.

Educational Applications

Since intellectual life has its starting point in sense perception, the first step in intellectual education should be the development and training of the senses, educating the mind to an intelligent reading of the reports that are constantly pouring into it through the senses. Incidentally, it must be remembered that the efficient functioning of any sense depends upon the condition of the sense organ, which should be ascertained at the earliest possible stage in school life. If it is discovered, for instance, that the child is afflicted with defective eyesight, the case should be immediately referred to the eye specialist in order that the defect may be removed or at least remedied.

The senses have been likened to windows through which come to us the materials of our knowledge, but this gathering of information, though their chief function, is not the only one. When properly trained, the senses become the agents of intelligent observation and efficient scientific work, the agents too, of the appreciation of the beautiful which for us is always clothed in some sensible form.

The importance of the principle of sense appeal throughout the whole process of education, but especially in its early stage, has been one of the keynotes of educational theory and practice in the last two hundred years, and it is today an integral part of the A B C of the art of teaching.

Aside from the special exercises provided in the kindergarten for training in the perception of color, form, and the like, and the use of the equipment of the school in collections, tools, weights, measures, scales, and plane and solid geometry figures, there are certain agencies in the curriculum which make for sense training when they are properly utilized. Those agencies are penmanship, drawing, nature study, manual training, vocal music, and object lessons, that is, lessons concerning a given object. Very much the vogue a few years ago, the object lesson seems to have fallen today into disfavor, probably owing to the fact that it was too often used and abused to convey worthless, unrelated bits of information. To discard the object lesson because of the ill-usage or abuse of it would certainly be unfortunate. When properly handled, it will develop and discipline the capacity for intelligent observation, that is, the capacity to analyze, to compare, to judge and select, amidst a mass of unimportant details, the one element that really counts.

More important than any one of the above-mentioned agencies in the use and training of the senses, because of its constant availability and wide range of application, is the objective method of teaching. Insofar as the nature of the subject will allow, the teacher appeals to consciousness through the use of objects whenever that is possible, or, when objects are not available, through the use of pictures, diagrams, maps, charts, and, more particularly, through the use of the blackboard. One of the characteristics of a good teacher, it has been remarked, is the readiness to use chalk whenever the occasion will arise. A few words on the blackboard, a brief outline, a few lines by way of a diagram will at once bring clarity into a narration, description, or explanation that otherwise would remain obscure. The objective method of teaching is the readiest, most natural, and most general application of the principle of sense appeal, the natural consequence, as we have seen, of the very nature of the learning process. And the principle can be applied in all subjects and at all stages in school life.

In the perception of any object, the mind first receives some sort of general impression of the object as a whole, then, upon closer scrutiny, it perceives the several constituent parts of the object with their relations to one another and thus reaches a clearer, more adequate perception of the whole. What is true of the perception of any object is equally true of any lesson. If we would teach as the mind learns, we must begin the lesson with some general statement of its purpose, then take up in their natural sequence, the several points suggested by the nature of the subject, thus leading the class to a second, this time an adequate synthesis of the whole.

The nature of the new knowledge that we acquire does not merely depend upon the impression we receive from a given object or the information that is supplied by book or teacher. It is also conditioned by what is referred to in Herbartian terminology as the apperceiving mass, that is, the knowledge we already possess. We interpret any new experience according to what we know, and a new presentation is intelligible only when we can connect and classify it with something that we understand. The significance of this fact for the teacher is obvious. Before presenting any new subject to the class, he must make sure that they possess the knowledge needed for the assimilation of the new subject. If such knowledge is wanting it must be supplied before proceeding any further. It would be poor methodology, for example, and worse psychology to teach a lesson on the adjective to a class that had no previous lesson on the noun.

A clear, adequate perception of things is an important step in the acquisition of knowledge and therefore in intellectual education, but it is only a beginning, the foundation upon which will be raised the structure of our intellectual make-up through the activity of the higher intellectual faculties. Perception is concerned with facts, with the individual, and with actually present, concrete phenomena; knowledge, such as we should aim at, is concerned with the classification of facts, their meaning and relations and the general notions which underlie the particular data supplied by experience; it rises from the world of sense into that of ideas. Sense training and sense perception should, then, never be too prolonged, nor become too exclusive, even with young children; they possess, if only in a crude, rudimentary way, the power to reach the universal and to reason, and this power should be exercised on every possible occasion. Sense perception is not the end of education but merely a means to that end.

The Conservation of Knowledge

Imagination. The second stage in the assimilative process is the conservation of the knowledge that has been acquired and the arrangement of its elements into various combinations, which is the work of the imagination, the memory and association of ideas. Imagination may be defined "the faculty or mental capacity to make and combine images." An image could be described as a revived percept. Imagination is a representative faculty, whereas sense perception is presentative. Through the latter, we receive direct impressions, leading to percepts, from the objects that surround us. Imagination revives those percepts in the form of pictures and combines them in all sorts of ways. The very terms *imagination, image* would suggest that our revived percepts are visual, and so they are for the most part, but there are also images corresponding to the other senses and, in some cases, or with some individuals, they may be as vivid as visual images. Beethoven became deaf, but continued to compose and enjoy his compositions. From this viewpoint, there are as many types of imagination as there are senses: visual, auditory, tactile, motor, smell, and taste images. No less important from the teacher's viewpoint than these types of imagery are the stages in the development of the imagination in preadult life, corresponding, in the main, to childhood and youth, with a transitional stage in boyhood and girlhood. The imagination of the child is exuberant, fantastic, and draws little or no distinction between fact and fancy. In youth that distinction is made but reality is idealized and the future appears in roseate colors. The more common and more important distinction, however, is that suggested by our definition, that is, the distinction between reproductive imagination and constructive, commonly, though erroneously, called creative imagination.

Reproductive imagination is "the power of forming mental pictures of objects and events as they have been originally experienced." Constructive imagination, on the other hand, not only combines images, but, with the aid of the intellect, it modifies images and their combinations in order to give a sensuous, concrete form to thought. It is only in that restricted sense that imagination is creative. Receiving its materials (forms, colors, sounds) from nature and through the senses, imagination will faithfully reproduce an experience recalled by the memory, or else it will transform and arrange its materials into something that, better than actual reality, corresponds to the ideal the individual is aiming at.

Imagination plays an important part in literature, art, science, and social life, in general, in every form of activity. In literature and works of art, the imagination of the poet, musician, painter, sculptor, and architect is employed at times in producing as faithful a picture as possible of objects and happenings of real life. At other times, the aim of the poet or artist is the nobler one of giving expression to some thought, some type of beauty or excellence not to be met in common, everyday life; it is then that imagination needs reason's discriminative power in order to select and arrange the materials needed for the expression of aspirations toward an ideal and to reject the others. In scientific research, imagination will perceive between objects or phenomena relations beyond the reach of sense perception, and it will suggest hypotheses which may lead to important discoveries. Imagination enables us to identify ourselves with the difficulties, hardships, and sufferings of others, thus arousing or increasing our sympathy, esteem, or admiration. Imagination, again, enables us to visualize the goal of our activity, thus inducing us to renewed efforts to reach it. The activity of the imagination is also the chief source of wit and humor, as it is of illusions, hallucinations, dreams, and reverie, which at once suggests the necessity of keeping it under the control of reason, otherwise imagination will surely become *la folle du logis,* as Pascal calls it, a constant source of error. It will mislead judgment, warp our views of things and persons, feed our minds on all kinds of unrealities, and prove the chief source of our unhappiness.

Educational Applications

The foregoing outline of the nature and function of the imagination leads to a few practical conclusions for the teacher. Before appealing to the imagination of the class, he should make sure that they possess all the elements entering into the making of the picture he intends to evoke. Descriptions of rustic scenery, for example, will remain a dead letter for most city children until the teacher has supplied the necessary perceptual background, by means of pictures, diagrams, or definitions. All school subjects can be used profitably for the development and training of the imagination, but there are some like literature, history, and geography, which more readily than other subjects lend themselves to that purpose. Literary composition, especially, is one of the best school agencies for the development of the young imagination, provided, of course, that the young writers are allowed some freedom in the selection of their subjects and the method of treatment. The presence of different types of imagery facing the teacher in any class at once suggests that in teaching there be an appeal to as many senses as possible. Stages in the development of imagination call for corresponding adjustments in reading matter and composition: fairy tales, fables, legends in childhood; stories of adventure, romance, lyric and dramatic poetry in youth. Needless to add, the imagination should be fed only on what is pure and ennobling.

Memory and the association of ideas. Defined in briefest form, memory is the faculty of retaining, reproducing, and recognizing representations of past experiences. Memory is, of necessity, involved in all our mental processes. Even the simplest of comparisons presupposes memory, since the discovery of similarities and differences between two ideas requires that the first idea be still present while attention is concentrated on the second and vice versa. Like reproductive imagination, with which it has much affinity, memory is concerned with past psychical life, but its activity is of much wider scope; our reminiscences include not only images, but ideas and combinations of ideas as well.

Certain forms of memory activity have received special names, such as organic memory, visual memory, auditory intellectual memory, which call for some explanation. It is a fact of common, everyday experience, that we acquire the ability to perform unconsciously certain movements with an almost machinelike precision. When learning to perform those movements we were at first conscious of the process and had to attend to it, but, gradually, through repetition of the act, consciousness and attention were eliminated; the organism had retained the "knowledge," that is, the impression received, and it could reproduce it. The main difference between this "organic" memory and higher types of memory is this: Here the last stage, recognition, is absent. Another fact of common experience worth mentioning is that some persons remember best the things they have seen, others what they have heard; some have a good memory for words, others for figures, others still for facts. The success of the politician, it has been remarked, depends to a great extent upon his ability to remember names and faces.

Sensuous memory is concerned with the world of sense, intellectual memory with the world of ideas, the former depending chiefly upon the empirical relations of similarity, contrast, and continuity in time or space, the latter upon logical relations. Both, however, are closely related, because images and ideas constantly suggest and complete one another; at one time the image, at another time the idea will first appear in consciousness and suggest its intellectual or sensory counterpart. A further distinction worth mentioning is that between spontaneous and voluntary memory. It is expressed in the words remember and recollect. To remember does not necessarily imply volition, whereas to recollect conveys the notion of conscious effort in the act of the memory. All those distinctions are more or less useful in schoolwork, but they should not obscure for us the fact that in all kinds of reminiscences, throughout the whole series of phenomena in the functioning of the memory, the self that has known remains identical with the self that remembers or recollects.

Our definition of memory enumerates three stages in the complete act of reminiscence: retention, reproduction, and recognition. Retention or conservation of experiences, even though they are not realized in consciousness, is admitted as a fact, testified to by consciousness itself. Reproduction is the reappearance in consciousness of a mental state connected with a past event. This reappearance may be spontaneous or voluntary and it chiefly depends upon the association of ideas. Recognition, insofar as reminiscences are concerned, is an assertion that a mental phenomenon actually present was in consciousness before, and that assertion implies a belief both in the existence of that phenomenon in consciousness for some time past, and the identity of the self; it is also an assertion that what we have seen or heard was seen or heard at such a time and such a place. Recognition is the most characteristic difference between memory and imagination; the former localizes in time and place, which the latter does not. This threefold function of the memory suggests the qualities of the good memory: facility of acquisition, tenacity of retention, readiness in reproduction, and accuracy in recognition.

The conditions under which the memory functions are both physiological and psychological. The ability to remember is conditioned first of all by the native retentiveness of the nervous system, more generally by the general condition of the organism. Fatigue and illness impair our mental efficiency and more particularly the efficiency of the memory. To the diseased condition of the organism, especially of the nervous system, must be ascribed amnesia, the loss of memory, and its more particular form, aphasia, both of which may be total or partial.

The psychological conditions of the efficiency of memory are the vividness of the impressions received, their frequency, their recentness, and our mental associations. The vividness of the impressions depends upon the attractiveness of the stimuli producing them and the energy of our voluntary attention. Repetition is an essential condition for an efficient memory, as it is in the formation of habits, and it is evident that the shorter the time that has elapsed, and the fewer the intervening impressions, the better, clearer, more readily will reappear former mental states. The last mentioned of the psychological conditions or laws of memory, the association of ideas, needs a somewhat more lengthy exposition.

In the process of reminiscence our representations reappear in consciousness, not in a casual manner, but according to a general law known as the law of association of ideas which has been likened to the law of gravitation in the physical world. Any given mental state suggests one or more mental states or is suggested by them, just as any material body attracts and is attracted by other material bodies. All mental states are subject to this law; an image may suggest a thought, prompting a sentiment upon which may follow a resolution. The phrase "association of mental or psychical states" would then be more appropriate than "association of ideas."

Psychologists have reduced to a few principles the conditions under which this law functions, the conditions, that is, under which the process of reproduction of mental states takes place. The more important of these principles are the following:

The law of similarity, according to which mental states suggest or recall their like in past experience. A piece of music that we hear reminds us of a similar experience in the past.

The law of contrast, according to which mental states suggest their opposite in past experience; black suggests white; vice, virtue; peace, war.

The law of contiguity which can be enunciated thus: mental states connected with objects or events closely related in time or space have a tendency to recall one another in the same order; 1492 suggests Columbus; Russia, Poland.[2]

The association of images and ideas, insofar as the individual is concerned, essentially depends upon the order in which images and ideas have occurred, but it is important to note that the relations upon which the associations are founded may be objective or subjective. Objective relations are of three kinds: natural or logical, accidental or empirical, arbitrary or conventional. Natural or logical relations are those between cause and effect, means and end, principle and consequences, or whole and part, as, for instance, the relation between the location of New York City and its trade, guns and war, free will and responsibility. The accidental or empirical relations are those of contiguity in time and space as, for example, the relations between Charles I and Cromwell, Poland and Russia. Arbitrary or conventional relations, as the term readily suggests, are relations depending upon a mere convention, such as those between flag and country, dove and peace, laurel and victory. All those relations are objective, they belong primarily to the realities surrounding the individual and, therefore, to the subject matter of education; the extent to which they lead to associations of images and ideas in the individ-

---

[2] The tendency now seems to be to reduce these laws to one: the law of integration. What has been once experienced in a definite, unified setting or pattern will tend to reappear in its integrity. The pattern is placed in time and space and does not exclude intellectual elements.

ual's mind depends on native dispositions, voluntary atten-
.tion and the teaching process.

Association plays a very important part in other phases
of our psychical life than memory activity. It is intimately
related to habit formation. Any well-formed habit is made
up of a series of ideas or acts that will reappear in the same
order, because, through repetition, they have been closely
associated with one another. Association is an essential element in literary or artistic creative ability. The so-called
figures of speech are founded on association by similarity or
contrast; wit has been defined as the ability to express in
pithy sayings unexpected, amusing associations, and it has
also been remarked that the best style is the most suggestive,
the style that will arouse all sorts of associations in the reader
or hearer. The beauty and value of many an artistic masterpiece, as, for instance, the *Angelus* of Millet, does not lie as
much in its technique as in its power of awakening in us a
world of associations. The work of the scientist or scholar
could be described as a search for hidden associations among
the materials under investigation. It is in education, however, that association is most important and far-reaching.
Prejudices, superstitions, errors of all kinds can be traced
to wrong associations formed in childhood and youth.
Virtue is connected with a certain kind of association just
as vice is.

Educational applications. The foregoing account of the
conditions under which the memory functions points to a
few practical remarks on the question of how to improve it.
Retentiveness, as we have seen, depends for the most part
on the actual condition of the nervous system. Fatigue and
illness impair the organism and therefore the retentive
quality of our memory. On the other hand, whatever tends

to improve the condition of the organism will indirectly improve the effectiveness of our native retentiveness. The practical conclusion is obvious: before any trial of memory one should avoid brain fatigue; the best memory work is done in the morning after a sound night's sleep. On the psychological aspect of the question, let it be said, in the first place, that constant, intelligent exercise is the one great requisite for the improvement of the memory as it is for the development of every one of our latent capacities. Secondly, in memory work as in habit formation, well begun is half done. Let us then make the first impressions as vivid and clear and definite as possible, then repeat by means of drills or reviews as the subject may require. And, thirdly, think! Nothing should be committed to the memory which is not in some measure understood. To sequence of words should always correspond in the young learner's mind, a sequence of thoughts. All the elements of knowledge should be welded together by means of as many natural associations as possible.

The Elaboration of Knowledge

Abstraction and comparison. The elaboration of knowledge is achieved through the mental processes of abstraction, comparison, generalization, and judging and reasoning.

"To abstract" means here to consider an object, event, or mental state apart from all other objects, events, or mental states; or again any one element in a given object, event, or mental state, independently of all other elements. I abstract, when I consider the length of a table, the color of an orange, the date of the discovery of America, or the vividness of a perception, apart from all other features in the table, orange, discovery of America, or percept. We are abstracting in this very paragraph, since we attend to the mental process of abstraction, taken singly, independently of the whole stream of consciousness.

Abstraction, in the sense attached to the word here, begins with the dawn of psychical life, that is, with the awakening of the senses which have been aptly described as abstracting machines. Sight abstracts form, colors, movements; hearing abstracts sounds; smell abstracts odors; and the elements of reality thus singled out by the several senses are combined by sense perception into a synthesis, a percept, and referred to a concrete, individual object. Imagination, though removed one step further from concrete reality, since it deals with copies more or less faithful of percepts, is still concerned with individual objects. Reason alone reaches the species, the genus, that is, the general or the universal, through the process of abstraction, by dropping all individuating characteristics and combining the features common to all individuals of the same class into an abstract notion, a general idea expressing the genus or species. Let us note, however, that abstract notions are not necessarily general. The idea of the roundness of this particular orange is an abstract though not a general idea, but the idea "roundness" is both abstract and general. Nor should we confuse abstract notions or ideas with the ideas of things spiritual. My idea of such a soul is a concrete notion whereas the idea "soul" is both abstract and general.

Like attention, abstraction is one of the essential conditions of our intellectual activities. Illustrations of the use of abstraction are as many as the thousands of situations we meet in life. We cannot think, express ourselves, or deal with any question or situation without using abstraction. Every branch of knowledge starts with an abstraction, since it deals with but one aspect of reality, and we must, in the mastery of it, constantly resort to abstraction because our knowledge of the whole requires the mastery of each one of its elements.

This constant, necessary use of abstraction is not without some danger. It may happen, for instance, that we become so engrossed in the study of a certain aspect of things that we lose sight of all the other aspects, or else, we may forget that abstractions are but a product of our intellectual activity, that they are realized only in persons and things. The history of science and the history of revolutions abound in illustrations of this abuse of abstraction, so-called scientific principles that are but a cloak for our ignorance or empty phrases that catch the fancy of the masses.

The elaboration of knowledge beginning with abstraction proceeds through comparison to generalization. In comparison, the mind brings together percepts, images, and ideas, in order to discover their relations. The result is a judgment, an assertion of agreement or disagreement between the two terms of the comparison. To this mental process, we are indebted for the notions of superiority, inferiority, equality, and progress. Its systematic use in the comparative method has given rise to several new sciences.

Generalization. Abstraction and comparison prepare generalization, the process through which the mind extends the same idea to any number of beings or facts of the same class. Starting with the data of sense perception and imagination, the mind analyzes, abstracts, compares, eliminates what differentiates one individual object from another, and finally brings the remaining elements together into a synthesis, or concept, which will contain all the essential characteristics of the facts, objects, or persons corresponding to it, provided, of course, the process has been accurate and thorough. The notion thus reached possesses both extension and comprehension. The extension of a concept is the number of individual objects, facts, or persons it includes, whereas its comprehension is the number of elements, qualities, and properties it possesses. The greater the extension, the lesser the comprehension and vice versa, as it can readily be seen from some such series as the following: form, geometric figure, plane geometric figure, polygon, quadrilateral, rectangle, square; or animal, mammal, man, Aryan, European, English. These series also show us that there are various degrees of generalization, the more commonly mentioned being the species and the genus; the former has the greater, the latter the lesser comprehension.

Is there any reality corresponding to a concept or general idea? This question, which in the Middle Ages led to the controversy concerning universals, has since been taken up again under different names, because it raises vital issues in epistemology, metaphysics, theology, science, and everyday life as well. The nature and the scope of this brief survey precludes, of course, the treatment of this question here, and the reader is referred to treatises on epistemology or metaphysics or to the history of philosophy.

Judging and reasoning. To complete our survey of the elaboration of knowledge, there remain to be examined two of its agencies, judging and reasoning. To judge is to assert that a thing is or is not, that it has or has not a given quality, or, again, as stated before, that there is agreement or disagreement between two ideas. It is an analytic-synthetic process, examining separately, then connecting two ideas. When formulated, a judgment becomes a proposition or statement composed of a subject, a predicate, and a verb or copula. In this form, the judgment belongs to the province of logic. Its grammatical counterpart is the sentence. The close relation noted here between psychology, logic, and language is not an isolated case. We meet it at every step throughout the whole series of mental states, and we shall have occasion to examine it a little more extensively in the treatment of the process of teaching.

Judgments, like propositions, differ from one another in a number of ways. Some treatises on logic list as many as twenty different kinds of judgments: affirmative, negative, particular, general, contingent, *a priori, a posteriori,* and so on.

In judging, the intellect connects ideas; in reasoning, it connects judgments. To reason is to draw one judgment from one or more judgments. Both judging and reasoning can be viewed psychologically or logically. Psychology, with which we are here concerned, examines the nature of the reasoning process independently of the rules of correct thinking, and it reveals the fact that in its search after truth the intellect proceeds both downward or deductively and upward or inductively. In deductive reasoning the mind goes from the whole to its parts, from the general to the particular, from principle to consequences, from cause to effect, from law to fact. The process is founded on the general principle that what is true of a general proposition must be true of all the particular propositions it contains. Inductive reasoning, on the other hand, proceeds from the particular to the general, from the concrete to the abstract, from fact to law, from effect to cause, from consequence to principle. Induction is founded on the belief that the laws of nature are at once stable and general; it is the method mainly used in the natural sciences, whereas mathematics, for example, chiefly depends on deduction.

Educational Applications

Of the many practical suggestions that can be drawn from the preceding survey of the psychical processes involved in the elaboration of knowledge we shall retain the following:

In teaching, especially in the elementary school, whenever that is possible, let us proceed from the particular to the general, from the concrete to the abstract. If, for some reason or other, the process has to be reversed, illustrations should supplement and make clear the definition, rule, principle, or formula that has been explained.

Develop in the class the habit of conceptualizing the lesson, that is, of bringing all its details under a few well-related headings.

Use correlation, reviews, applications, as means both to clarify and enrich concepts.

Use every subject as a means to train the mind to judge and reason.

In teaching and recitation subordinate the importance of fact to its explanation.

Whenever possible, use the Socratic method. Allow freedom, initiative, in answers to questions and in the solution of problems; use variety in applications and emphasize judgment and reasoning in the assignment of lessons.

Topics for Further Study

1. "The soul always functions as a unit." Illustrate.
2. Explain the nature and purpose of epistemology.
3. Show with illustrations the relation of epistemology to the question of knowledge assimilation.
4. State with a brief comment thereon the positions of Thomistic epistemology.

5. State with a brief comment thereon the fundamental positions of pragmatic epistemology.

6. Show the relation of the conception of reality to the problem of knowledge.

7. State and criticize the sensationalistic conception of knowledge.

8. Compare critically the Platonic and Aristotelian conception of knowledge.

9. Differentiate memory from imagination.

10. Discuss the question of the innateness of ideas.

11. Discuss and illustrate the importance of imagination in science.

12. Discuss and illustrate the importance of imagination in literature or art.

13. "Memory retentiveness is at birth what it will be all through life." Prove or disprove that statement.

14. "Some political and social consequences of the abuse of abstraction." Discuss.

15. "The qualities of a good concept." Discuss.

16. "How to reach a good concept." Discuss.

17. "Is there any reality corresponding to a general idea?" Discuss.

18. State and comment on the fundamental positions of nominalism.

19. "The bearing of nominalism on the learning process." Discuss.

20. "Monism versus dualism as philosophies of learning." Discuss.

Suggestions for Reading

Bagley, W., *The Educative Process* (New York, 1905).

Bode, B., *Conflicting Psychologies of Learning* (New York, 1929).

Castiello, J., *A Humane Psychology of Education* (New York, 1936).

Colvin, S., *The Learning Process* (New York, 1921).

Dexter and Garlick, *Psychology in the Schoolroom* (London, 1913).

Garth, T., *Educational Psychology* (New York, 1937).

Horne, H., *Psychological Principles of Education* (New York, 1906).

James, W., *Talks to Teachers* (New York, 1914).

Maher, M., *Psychology* (London, 1915).

Mercier, D., *Les Origines de la Psychologie Contemporaine* (Louvain, 1915).

Willmann-Kirsch, *The Science of Education* (Beatty, 1921).

CHAPTER XI

Intellectual Education *(Continued)*

The Classroom

The teaching-learning process. In preceding chapters, there was examined a series of steps or principles that govern the general organization of the educational content, preparatory to its actual use in the school. The same principles apply to every special course of study, every series of lessons, and every particular lesson. In each and every case, the materials to be used must be carefully selected and related to the purposes of education; they must be well correlated and graded. The use of the materials of instruction in the actual processes of teaching and learning also raises once more the question of the psychical operations involved in learning taken up this time from the viewpoint of method and types of lessons.

We have seen that the psychical faculties involved in learning can be classed into three groups corresponding to a threefold stage in the learning process: acquisition, conservation, and elaboration. To these three terms, however, there should be added a fourth one, application, without which the description of the learning process is incomplete. Application or practice is admittedly the all-important factor in the acquisition of skill, and its importance in the assimilation of knowledge, though not paramount as in the acquisition of skill, should not be minimized either, because no spiritual content really becomes our own without practice of some kind. Acquisition or perception, conservation, elaboration, and application thus form the complete cycle of intellectual activities involved in the learning process.

For all practical purposes, however, the series can be reduced to three stages by combining the first two (acquisition and conservation) into one stage which we shall call *reception*. If we substitute for the word *elaboration* the term *understanding,* which better expresses the purpose of learning, we shall have the threefold series of stages in learning: reception, understanding, and application.

In all three stages, the teacher must assist the pupil in various ways. In the stage of reception, the teacher appeals directly to the senses by presenting the object to the class or by means of pictures, maps, charts, or diagrams, or else he appeals to the pupil's imagination and memory by means of narrations and descriptions. In the second stage of the learning process, the teacher analyzes the subject of the lesson into its component elements, compares, points out relations, and draws conclusions. In the third stage, that of application, an attempt is made to fix knowledge in the pupil's mind through appropriate exercises, and other applications are pointed out that may offer themselves later on. These stages or steps in learning and teaching are in the very nature of things, and they have been stated time and again by educational theorists. They correspond to the stages in mental development in the young: presentative, in infancy and early childhood, when the mind chiefly depends on sense perception for the acquisition of knowledge; representative, for the next six or seven years, when in addition to sense perception, the mind mostly depends upon imagination and memory; the logical stage in adolescence, when the mind more and more penetrates into the nature of things. As a final stage, corresponding to the third one above, we have the applications of knowledge in one's profession and in life.

The name of Herbart is often mentioned in connection with this question of stages in the assimilation of knowledge, but Herbart is not always clear or consistent. In his *Outlines of Educational Doctrine* he uses the terms *clearness, association, system,* and *method* to describe what he considers the four stages in the assimilation of knowledge, but these terms describe the work of the teacher rather than what takes place in the pupil's mind. The more common expression of Herbartianism on this subject mentions the following steps in the assimilation of knowledge or apperception: preparation, presentation, comparison, generalization, and application. Preparation is a sort of introduction to the real process of assimilation; the teacher states the aim of the lesson, tries to enlist the attention of the members of the class and discover whether they possess the knowledge needed for the apprehension of the new subject matter. In the stage of presentation, the subject matter of the new lesson is actually presented inductively to the class. In comparison, the old knowledge or apperceiving mass is connected with the new knowledge; in generalization, the class is led to the concept, general notion, involved in the lesson. As a final step in the teaching-learning process, the class is made to apply what has been learned, in as many ways as possible. This terminology, however, like Herbart's own, refers more to the teacher's task than the processes in the pupil's mind.

Lesson   Types

To the three stages mentioned above, reception, understanding, and application, there correspond particular types of instruction. Reception, we have seen, will vary according to the faculty that is chiefly appealed to in the presentation of the materials of instruction. The teacher may appeal to sense perception by showing the object or its graphic representation, or else he may appeal to imagination and memory by means of narration and description. The type of lesson in which this element predominates, we may call *presentative.*

Instruction of this type would find its application in a lesson or series of elementary or junior high school lessons on, say, the early American settler. The thoroughness of the presentation evidently would depend on the grade of the class, but, in any case, maps, diagrams, and pictures would be important helps to a presentation of the subject. Narration and description would be the chief modes of exposition, the teacher taking care to give, as a background to the settlements, the European conditions leading to these settlements. In the senior high school and, still more, the college, the treatment of this subject evidently calls for a type of instruction in which a far greater appeal is made to the reasoning powers of the student.

Elaboration or understanding may be concerned with the meaning of words or the relations inherent in the nature of things, whether material or spiritual. The types of instruction dealing with the meaning of words, more generally with the meaning of symbols, we may refer to as explanatory, whereas the term *developmental* would characterize lessons concerned with the relations existing between facts or ideas, that is, relations of cause to effect, of principle to consequences, of fact to law, of whole to its parts, or of means to end. Developmental instruction expands the subject before the class in such a way that its import will be grasped. Development may be inductive, proceeding, in the main, from the particular to the general, or it may be deductive, proceeding from the general to the particular.

Explanatory instruction would be used in lessons on a poem or prose selection, in general, on any text to be explained. The explanation would include, of course, remarks on the writer, the conditions under which he wrote, or the genesis of the selection—its purpose, the literary type to which it belongs; then would come the reading of the selection from beginning to end which will give a general idea of the subject preparatory to a detailed study. The sciences would supply any number of illustrations of the third type of instruction. The following proposition, for example, would afford a good illustration of development by deduction. "The area, generated by a straight line revolving around an axis in the same plane, is obtained by multiplying the projection of the line upon the axis, by the circumference whose radius is the perpendicular raised at the middle point of the straight line and limited by the axis." A consideration of the various positions that the revolving line may occupy with reference to the axis will naturally lead to the development of the formulas for the areas of the cylinder, cone, truncated cone, and sphere. A type of lesson combining both the inductive and deductive forms of development, which was very much in favor among teachers two or three decades ago, is the so-called method-whole, calling for the systematic use of the Herbartian steps in apperception.

As a form of instruction, application includes problems, experiments, composition, and writing—in general, all school exercises. Application is not so much a distinct lesson type as the necessary complement of each and every lesson. Longer lists of differentiated types of lessons, with appropriate applications to various subjects, will be found in treatises on method, where they properly belong. The threefold lesson type which has just been outlined is offered merely as a sort of synthesis of this phase of classroom work. This synthesis, however, calls for a final remark in order to be complete. The three lesson types do not exclude one another. Presentation, explanation, and development may find their place in one and the same lesson; the age of the pupils and the nature of the subject taught determine the type of instruction that will predominate.

Securing the Learner's Coöperation

The proper assimilation of knowledge implies not only an act of the intellect, but an act of the will as well. The pupil will thoroughly assimilate only what he is intent upon learning, and this fact brings us to a brief consideration of three closely related topics: curiosity, attention, and interest.

Curiosity. Curiosity has been defined, "an instinctive sensitiveness to novelty, prompting us to approach and examine any new element in our environment." It produces that concentration of intellectual activity we call attention, and it is accompanied by the feeling we call interest. It is this intimate psychological connection between curiosity, attention, and interest, which suggests the treatment of the three in one and the same chapter.

Novelty is the essential, though not the only characteristic feature of the stimulus that arouses curiosity; the intensity of the stimulus and the sensitiveness of the organism to it are other important factors. A loud sound is likely to arouse curiosity more readily than a dull one, and it is a well-known fact that different individuals, or the same individual at different times, do not respond in the same way to the same stimulus. Again, aside from the condition of the organism, previous experiences and the development of instincts and interests will prompt the individual to respond more readily to some stimuli than to others. Thus, when the competitive instinct is developed, the sight of baseball scores is sure to arouse the curiosity of an American boy. It is true that newness, the prime mover of curiosity, is continually destroyed by the very action of the instinct, but, then, the knowledge gained through familiarity with things becomes the basis for a fresh growth of curiosity, through the discovery of characteristics that were unnoticed before. Thus, the interest of the class once aroused in the geography of the State of New York will be kept alive by the presentation of new features of the subject: the rivers, mountains, lakes, and natural products; its cities, industry and trade; its commercial relations with other states and foreign countries.

Curiosity, then, is an incentive to the acquisition of knowledge in at least two distinct ways: first, through new stimuli which arouse it when the individual's environment is changed or enlarged; second, through the discovery of new characteristics in objects which have become familiar, and their relations to other objects. In infancy and early childhood, when everything in this workaday world is new, the growth of curiosity is, in the main, of the first kind, whereas in the succeeding stages of intellectual development it is rather of the second type. A fairly good index of this growth of curiosity is supplied by the questions of children.

At first and for some time the constantly recurring question is, "What is that?"; the child is mainly interested in naming objects and occurrences which it notices in surroundings; later on, questions—such as "What is that for?" and "How do you do that?"—become more and more common, showing us that the child is now interested in the use and manipulation of objects; still later, children's questions betray a growing desire to inquire into the causes of things, a sure sign of the dawning of reason.

Like imitation, curiosity is one of the surest of the teacher's aids, provided, of course, it be used aright, not as a means of interesting, of amusing the class, but as an incentive to effort, to hard work, which is the price which every one of us has to pay for an education that is worth the name.

Attention. Attention, in the true sense of the term, can be defined, "the active use of all our intellectual capacities." The difference between the passive and the active use of our senses, for instance, is well illustrated in the following and like terms, the equivalent of which we find in other languages: to hear and to listen, to see and to look at. To hear and to see express a mere receptive, passive state of mind; to listen and to look at, on the other hand, express the active use of the senses of hearing and sight; in other words, the terms *to listen* and *to look at* mean that a new element, attention, that is, intellectual concentration, has been added to the mental states expressed by the terms *to hear* and *to see.*

Attention is not an intellectual faculty, nor an intellectual process, but a concomitant of each and every one of our intellectual processes, the condition of its vigorous, efficient functioning. Our percepts, images, and thoughts become clear and distinct to the extent that they are attended to. Thus, for example, a teacher becomes aware of some whispering in the classroom; she listens, "attends to," the cause of the disturbance; discovers its location, and may finally succeed in singling out the offender. Let it also be remarked that we should not identify attention with the will either. Attention is not will, but intellectual, cognitive energy supported and backed up by the will. Thus, for example, when engaged in the solution of a problem, the attitude of the mind is not, for instance, "I wish to have more problems," but "I wish to understand and to find the solution, and I will give this question my closest attention."

Attention has been likened to a lens which, so to say, focuses intellectual activity, and this focusing may be directed upon any object, whether material or spiritual, external to the self or internal; it may be some article of furniture, a piece of machinery, some question to be examined, some task to be performed, or one's own thoughts or feelings or those of others. In every case, the process is fundamentally the same: the mind concentrates its cognitive energy upon some object to the exclusion of others, the better to study that object. Attention has also been described as a process, both physical and psychical, of an adaptation of the ego to some situation, some object. Sometimes this physical adaptation is remarkably striking, as for example in the case of children listening to a fascinating story, or a crowd watching an exciting baseball game; not only the expression of the eyes and features, but the attitude of the whole body in such cases betrays the intensity of mental concentration. For the teacher, this physical adaptation is a very valuable index of the mental attitude of the class. Wandering eyes and listless faces are sure signs that the attention of the class is away from the lesson.

Attention has received various names that differentiate

its degrees of intensity or its objects. Observation is attention concentrated upon material objects; we observe a plant, an insect, a piece of machinery, or the setting of the sun. Reflection is attention turned within, the reverting of the mind to a thought, a question which has already occupied it. Application is a continued, persevering attention; meditation is a deep, prolonged reflection; contemplation, a kind of meditation in which the mind is, as it were, held spellbound by the beauty or sublimity of some object. In ecstasy, the highest stage of attention, the mind is in such a state of rapture and exaltation that it is beyond the reach of ordinary impression.

Attention is either voluntary or involuntary, according to its exciting cause. Involuntary attention, sometimes referred to as spontaneous, automatic, is, as the term would suggest, attention without any particular effort of the will. Its stimulus usually is external, as a loud noise, a bright light, an interesting story, though the stimulus may be internal as well. Voluntary attention, on the other hand, is attention resulting from an effort, an act of the will. From a number of objects that may claim our attention, the mind selects one, as the more desirable or useful, and "attends to it." Thus, I may be tempted to continue an interesting conversation, the reading of a fascinating novel, or to go out for a stroll, but the thought of some letter that is to be dispatched immediately will make me forego all else and "attend to" the more useful, desirable, if less attractive, object.

The conditions under which attention functions are sometimes referred to as the laws of attention. Briefly stated, those laws are the following: Involuntary attention depends chiefly on the attractiveness of the stimulus, which, in turn, depends on a number of factors: the strength of the stimulus, its duration, its novelty, and the feelings it arouses in us. Voluntary attention, on the other hand, depends upon the amount of mental energy that we can put forth at any given time, the intrinsic attractiveness of the subject attended to and the motives back of our attention, that is, the associations we detect between the object attended to and other objects that appear to us as desirable. Thus, for example, the thought of an impending examination is likely to intensify attention to the study of geometry though otherwise the subject might be an uninteresting one. Attention whether voluntary or involuntary is variable. "It flows in waves rather than in a constant level stream and soon grows feeble unless revived by a new effort or a change of subject." [1]

Attention should not be confused with certain morbid states in which the mind seems to be at a standstill, unable to get away from a certain thought or series of thoughts. The terms *fixed idea, fascination, obsession, monomania,* and *insanity* describe various degrees of this hypertrophy of attention. At the other pole of this abnormal condition stands atrophy of attention, or the inability of the mind to concentrate on any one of a series of mental states, either because they are too weak or follow one another too rapidly. We are all subject to a certain kind of this atrophy of attention when we are tired or ill.

Attention influences both feeling and intellect. It may intensify feeling or it may have the opposite effect. Thus the pleasure we derive from a beautiful melody is increased by the attention we give it; grief may become unbearable

---

[1] Maher, M., *Psychology,* p. 348, Longmans, Green & Co. London, 1915.

for the same reason. Conversely, attention may indirectly make us for a time unaware of physical pain; soldiers have been seen unmindful of their wounds in the heat of battle. Far more important from the teacher's viewpoint, however, is the influence of attention upon the intellect. Attention is not knowledge or intellectual insight, but it is their most essential prerequisite. Knowledge, insofar as it is our own possession and a well-organized, serviceable body of information, is a structure that must be erected through our own efforts: the active, energetic use of our intellect, that is, through attention, which makes for clear, distinct and well-related notions. The greater the attention, the deeper we go into the nature of things. Perhaps it is not going too far to say that the chief difference between the intellectual capacity of one person and that of another lies in their respective capacities for attention, for the patient, steady, energetic use of the intellect.

To say, with Buffon, that genius is a capacity for patience, that is, for attention (*le génie est une longue patience*), would be an overstatement of the case. There are factors other than the power for intellectual concentration in the make-up of genius, but the capacity for intellectual concentration is certainly one of its outstanding characteristics. Newton, on being asked how he succeeded in discovering the law of gravitation, is reported as having said, "By constantly thinking of it." And Pasteur's biographers tell us that his discoveries were in a large measure the fruit of his tireless capacity for returning to the same problem until he had found a satisfactory solution.

Interest. Attention is a mental attitude, the focusing of intellectual activity upon some object, and this focusing is, of necessity, transitory. Interest, on the other hand, is a feeling, the "tone" of pleasure or pain which accompanies activity or attaches to any object, and that feeling may be a passing one or it may be permanent. ˙I may be interested in some object, say a picture, even though at present I do not attend to it nor will for a long time. Again, we are, or may become interested in many things, and those manifold interests vary with age and surroundings. Children, at first, are chiefly interested in themselves and the little world of concrete realities which surround them, insofar as they minister to their present needs or whims and fancies. Interest in others, in institutions, in the past or in the future, develops only by degrees.

From the viewpoint of education, interest is direct or indirect. We are all, or have been at one time or another, interested in listening to or reading tales of wonder, in relating our own experiences, in asking questions, in building, and in collecting all kinds of objects. All those and like inclinations may be called direct, educational interests. They contain the germ of what may, under proper conditions and guidance, develop into genuine educative activities. When, on the other hand, children are interested in their schoolwork through fear of punishment, or for the sake of a good mark, promotion, or a position to be secured, we have to deal with indirect educative interest.

The teacher's office, with regard to interest, is a twofold one. He should endeavor, in the first place, to develop in the child as many of the higher interests as possible; interest in literature, in art and science, in good conduct, in the family and the community, in religion and all it means for the individual and society. In the second place, whenever that is feasible, the teacher should connect classroom work with the experiences and actual interests of the child, in order to induce him to put forth genuine effort and give to the task in hand the best that is in him.

Educational Applications

The foregoing considerations on the nature of curiosity, attention, and interest will help us answer the question that is our primary concern here: How can we secure attention in the classroom? Many suggestions have been made in answer to that question, but they can all be brought under the following heads.

First, we should remove so far as it can be done, all causes of inattention: distracting sights or sounds; poor ventilation, temperature, lighting conditions, or seating conditions; defective eyesight or hearing; the use, by the teacher, of a tone of voice that is too high or too low; or the use of language beyond the grasp of the class.

Second, matter and method should be adapted to the intellectual capacity of the class. Mathematical geography, for instance, would be out of place in the elementary grades, when the child is not as yet sufficiently developed mentally to understand and to be interested in that aspect of the subject. Likewise, a learned discourse on the properties of matter would be out of season below the college, though children, even of the lower grades, would understand and enjoy elementary experimental physics.

Third, avoid monotony. "Tedium was born of uniformity," says a French literary critic, which is as true of teaching as it is of writing. Variety in subject matter is provided for by the school authorities in the arrangement of the curriculum, but the teacher's initiative and resourcefulness have practically free scope in the presentation of the subject matter and conduct of the recitation. There are all kinds of devices to which he can resort in order to bring zest and interest in what at first sight looks like downright drudgery. The whole lesson, or part of it, might be connected with interesting stories read by the child; comparisons and contrasts will bring out new points of view in subjects already explained; some humorous remark or anecdote will enliven the lesson when the class seems to grow weary; the order of recitation might be changed; the teaching of the new lesson today might precede the recitation and tomorrow follow it.

Fourth, use motivation, that is, connect schoolwork with the child's experience, thus showing the utility and immediate practical application of what he is learning at school.

Fifth, appeal to the senses through the use of objects, pictures, maps, and diagrams.

Sixth, let the teacher show a genuine interest in the lesson. The fire of enthusiasm is contagious; if we show a genuine interest in our work, we may be sure that the class will eventually catch our spirit.

Those and similar suggestions would help the teacher in awakening interest in the subject matter, in securing for a time, at least, the attention of the class. But interest in the subject matter may be on the wane, it may even die out, and there are not a few school activities which are repellent to the young, tasks for which the skill even of the best teachers could not arouse a spark of interest, if they are to be performed for their own sake. What is then to be done? What will induce the pupil to put forth the effort that will carry him through the uninteresting task? The answer is appeal to the mediate, indirect interest: marks, prizes, a word of praise, desire for promotion, and, if need be, the stern voice of authority—duty to be done because it is duty. With the coming of the period of adolescence, new interests, those of a higher character, will be added to the earlier ones: a growing realization of the meaning of life, of its aims and ideals, and a willingness to undertake the arduous, disagreeable preparation for one's chosen field of activity.

The problem of attention then, so far as the teacher is concerned, essentially resolves itself into this: to get hold of those interests which are strong enough to tide the class over the dreary land of drudgery, which they are sure to come to in the study of every subject. But there is another and far more important aspect of this question. The education of the capacity for attention, voluntary attention, of course, is nothing else, after all, than the education of the will from a certain viewpoint. To say of a man that he controls his attention amounts to the same thing as to say that such a man can keep steadily before his mind the claims of important though perhaps uninviting matter, the claims of duty in spite of the allurements of pleasure, of the craving of sense and gust of passion. A few of us perhaps possess such a control by nature; for most of us, it is the reward of long, painful struggle, the reward of repeated acts of free will and self-denial.

The Objective Aspect of the Learning Process

We have been concerned so far in this chapter with the subjective, psychological element in the actual teaching-learning process. This element, as we know, is of prime importance in elementary and early high-school work. The fact that the pupil is still immature, intellectually, in that stage must be the determining factor in the selection of the proper method of teaching. There are, of course, other factors to be taken into consideration. The training and personality of the teacher, the objectives assigned to classroom work, and the educational philosophy of the school administration are bound to affect the nature and the methods of classroom work. A more important factor, however, is the nature of the subject taught, which becomes the essential element in methodology beyond the elementary and early high-school grades.

From this standpoint, methodology is but an application to learning and teaching of the science of logic. Obviously, then, a knowledge of logic, both formal and material, no less than a knowledge of psychology is a prerequisite for the study of method. All teachers, particularly high-school and college teachers, should be familiar with such topics as truth, evidence, certitude, error and its causes, the various forms of judgment and reasoning, the general principles governing method and their application to the study and teaching of language and literature, history, mathematics, and the natural and moral sciences. The detailed treatment of those and related subjects evidently belongs to treatises on logic, epistemology, and method. In the remaining pages of this chapter, we shall confine ourselves to a few remarks on analysis and synthesis, the most important of the logical factors entering into the actual teaching-learning process.

Analysis and Synthesis

In its search after truth, the mind proceeds from the known to the unknown, but the road is not uniform. The mind may go from facts, notions, and consequences it perceives to the cause or, principle, which it doesn't know and from which flow these facts, notions, and consequences; that is analysis.   Or else the mind may proceed from a definition, a law, or a principle which it knows and try to reach the consequences flowing from the definition, law, or principle; that is synthesis.   All the particular methods used in the discovery, the exposition, or demonstration of truth are but particular applications of these two general methods. Observation and experimentation are methods of analysis. Analogy, classification, and hypothesis are methods of synthesis.   Our first perception of any object is a synthesis; then, through observation, the mind distinguishes parts and relations and reaches a better, more satisfactory perception of the object.   The mind, in other words, starts from a vague synthesis, then, through analysis, comes to a clear, adequate synthesis.   The meaning of the two terms is suggested by their etymology.   The root meaning of analysis is to tear apart, to let loose; that of synthesis is to bring together, to build up.   Hence, according to its etymology, analysis is a process of decomposing a whole into its parts, whereas synthesis is the method of bringing together all the parts of a whole.   Those definitions would particularly well apply to chemical analysis and synthesis.   More generally analysis can be described as a regressive process through which the mind goes from a given object to its antecedents, from what is conditioned to the condition, from effect to cause, from consequence to principle.   Synthesis is the opposite method of going from the condition to what is conditioned, from principle to consequences, from cause to effect.

The first pair of the above definitions would apply to the use of analysis and synthesis in the experimental sciences like physics, chemistry, and biology, whereas the other pair describe their use in the rational sciences like mathematics and logic. The physicist, for instance, uses analysis when, through a prism, he breaks up white light into rays of colored light, and synthesis, when he brings together all the elements of white light. The mathematician uses the analytic method when proving the validity or falsity of a given proposition through a series of other propositions leading to some principle, whose validity or falsity is admitted; he uses synthesis when, starting from some proposition accepted as valid, he draws from it a series of consequences leading to the proposition to be demonstrated. The following terms are practically synonymous with analysis: dividing, distinguishing, discriminating, discerning, and abstracting; whereas connecting, unifying, systematizing, and generalizing convey the same notion as synthesis. The immediate purpose of analysis is clarity, a better insight into the nature of the object under consideration, resulting from the examination of its constituent elements, in order to discover their nature, their relation with one another and to the whole. The purpose and result of synthesis should be to get a unified view of the parts examined in detail through analysis; gathering, so to say, all the threads together around one central point; and forming a clear, adequate percept of something, or a clear, adequate concept, rule, definition, or law that can be applied to particular cases. In teaching, analysis and synthesis should be used to reach some specific conclusion, as for example, the meaning of some sentence that is not clear upon first reading. In teaching, again, analysis and synthesis should not go on indefinitely, but stop when their particular purpose has been accomplished. Both methods have their place in every branch of knowledge, every situation in life, but the application will naturally vary from one field of investigation to another. Chemical analysis is one thing, physical analysis another, anatomical analysis still another; the lawyer, the physician, the businessman, the orator, the writer—all apply it, but in different ways. Likewise, analysis has its place in the teaching of every subject, but the application varies with the subject and so it is, of course, with synthesis. The inductive method is analytical because it uses observation and experimentation, whereas the deductive method is synthetical, because it starts from a consideration of the whole, some principle, definition, or general statement, before it passes to a consideration of its parts.

The process of investigation, exposition, or reasoning in any case should be analytico-synthetic. Analysis without synthesis will give us a knowledge of unconnected parts; synthesis alone will give us a knowledge of the whole that will be superficial, vague, even imaginary. The value of any analysis depends upon the corresponding synthesis and vice versa. So it is in general and, particularly, in teaching. But it may happen that in any given case one or the other method will prevail. The synthetic method is commonly used to expound, to prove, to demonstrate something known to the speaker or writer. It is the method commonly used in textbooks. The analytical method, on the other hand, is one of investigation; it is used to discover something unknown or supposed to be unknown. Hence, the teacher uses it when, instead of expounding the subject in a dogmatic way, he leads the class to its discovery by means of questions, hints, or directions. Thus, for example, in the teaching of the multiplication, the synthetic method will proceed from a statement of the rule to its application, whereas the analytic method would proceed from a number of applications to a formulation of the rule they illustrate. Thus again, the well-known proposition concerning the relation between the side of the regular hexagon and the radius of the circumscribed circle would be taught synthetically by stating the proposition in the form of a theorem to be demonstrated and, analytically, by stating the same proposition in the form of the problem: to inscribe a regular hexagon in a given circle.

Analysis and synthesis are sometimes confused with induction and deduction. The difference between analysis and synthesis, on the one hand, and induction and deduction on the other, is this: that the latter are merely particular applications of the former; in other words, analysis and synthesis are more comprehensive than induction and deduction. And there is this other difference; induction and deduction have but one purpose: to reach a general notion in the case of induction and to deduce from such a notion what it contains in the case of deduction. Analysis and synthesis, on the other hand, may have all kinds of purposes and be used in all kinds of situations. I may analyze a word to know how to spell it, a political situation to know how to vote, a business proposition to know whether it is worth while; and so it is with synthesis.

Educational Application

A summary. By way of summing up this rather lengthy discussion of intellectual education, we shall say that from the viewpoint of the school, the whole process resolves itself into series or chains of so many lessons on different subjects. And just as the strength and usefulness of a chain depends on the strength of every link in that chain, so the value of every lesson series—that is, the issue of intellectual education —will depend on whether each and every lesson in the series is a good lesson. Leaving to methodology the detailed examination of the essential characteristics of a good lesson, we shall remark here only that they can all be brought under one or the other of the following heads: preparation, teaching, apprehension, retention, application, or supervision. A good lesson, then, is one that has been well prepared, well taught, well apprehended and retained, and well applied and supervised. Of the six qualifications, three—apprehension, retention, application—concern the pupil, and three—preparation, teaching, supervision—concern the teacher.

Each of those qualifications is essential for the success of the teaching-learning process, but the first one, preparation, is particularly important; it is not asserting too much to say that the value of each and every lesson and, therefore, of intellectual education depends upon the daily, careful, conscientious preparation of lessons by the teacher. Even granting that the professional education of the teacher has been of the best, there is no other way for him than this daily preparation to gain that mastery of subject matter and method that gives poise, and self-confidence, which enables one to teach with clarity, zest, and interest, thus enlisting and holding the attention of the class.

Topics for Further Study

1. "Observe, suppose, verify." Discuss this expression of the inductive process in scientific investigation.

2. Compare critically the preceding formula with the Baconian conception of induction.

3. Contrast the use of induction in scientific investigation with its use in teaching.

4. Discuss "application" as an interpretation of "learning by doing."

5. Discuss fully the respective merits of interest and effort in intellectual education.

6. Discuss motivation as an incentive to study.

7. "Intellectual education is a work of authority." Prove or disprove that statement.

8. "Intellectual education is a work of free will." Discuss.

9. Discuss the respective merits of the direct and indirect interest in studies.

10. Discuss fully, the moral aspect of intellectual education.

11. From the viewpoint of the philosophy of education, account for the differences in classroom methods in the 17th- and 20th-century schools.

12. State and comment on the factors determining classroom methods in the elementary school.

13. State and comment on the factors determining classroom methods in high school.

14. State and comment on the factors determining classroom methods in college.

15. "The value of any synthesis depends upon the value of the corresponding analysis." Discuss and illustrate.

16. Discuss the Socratic method (a) as practiced by Socrates; (b) as used in the classrooms today.

17. Contrast the merits and limitations of the Socratic and catechetical methods. Illustrate.

18. State and comment on various conceptions of self-activity actually applied in (a) elementary schools; (b) high schools; (c) college.

19. "Hand work as an aid in intellectual education." Discuss.

20. "Independent thinking should be the goal of intellectual education." Discuss.

SUGGESTIONS FOR READING

Bagley, W., *The Educative Process* (New York, 1905).

Bode, B., *Conflicting Psychologies of Learning* (New York, 1929).

Dexter and Garlick, *Psychology in the Schoolroom* (London, 1913).

Donnelly, F., *Principles of Jesuit Education in Practice* (New York, 1934).

Garrison and Garrison, *Fundamentals of Psychology in Secondary Education* (New York, 1938).

Gray, W., *Psychology of Elementary School Subjects* (New York, 1938).

Horne, H., *Psychological Principles of Education* (New York, 1906).

Maher, M., *Psychology* (London, 1915).

Nutt, H., *Principles of Teaching High School Pupils* (New York, 1922).

Willmann-Kirsch, *The Science of Education* (Beatty, 1921).

CHAPTER XII

Aesthetic Education

The Feelings

The second group of psychical phenomena in our general classification is commonly treated under the generic term *feeling,* understood here to mean: (a) the pleasurable or painful tone of our psychical activities, that is, pleasure and pain, or feeling reduced to its lowest constituents; (b) the complex psychical phenomena including with pleasure or pain, sensations, images, and tendencies to action. In this second sense, *feeling* is commonly referred to as *emotion* or *sentiment.*

Pleasure and Pain

The nature and conditions of pleasure and pain were long ago thoroughly examined and explained by Aristotle. In substance, his explanation is the following: pleasure is the natural accompaniment of the normal activity of our faculties. Pain is the result of restrained, excessive, or misdirected activity. Pleasure, activity, life—all three are inseparably linked to one another. Activity is the essence of life; and, the more spontaneous, the healthier the activity, the better the life and the greater the pleasure of living. External objects affect us agreeably when they elicit the proper kind and degree of activity in the sense organs and mind. Sunlight, bright colors, and a melody normally affect us more agreeably than darkness, dull colors, and silence, because of the greater activity they arouse in ear and eye. Solitary confinement and enforced inaction are painful and may prove injurious to health if prolonged too long; we suffer from our inability to solve a problem mostly because the mind is then, so to say, at a standstill, cannot function properly. Play and sports are pleasant because they afford the free, spontaneous exercise of our physical and mental energy. So it is in a minor degree with gymnastics and, generally, with any kind of exercise—either physical or mental—that corresponds to our capacity. But activity is pleasant only to a point. When any kind of activity is indulged in too often or prolonged beyond a certain point at any given time, it becomes painful or at least ceases to enlist the interest and zest it arouses under normal condition. This fact, that any type of activity becomes painful or fails to stimulate interest when carried on to excess, partly explains the attraction of novelty and accounts for the need of change in occupation. Relief from fatigue does not necessarily mean inaction. Any occupation calling into play unused nerve centers, while providing a new outlet for our activity, will allow those centers to recuperate whose nervous energy has been exhausted.

The Emotions

As remarked before, the emotions are complex psychical phenomena into which enter, with the pleasure-pain factor, certain cognitive or appetitive elements. They can be classified in a number of ways, but the best one, from the educational viewpoint, seems to be the classification suggested by the genetic development of the emotions: egoistic emotions; social emotions; and intellectual, aesthetic, moral and religious sentiments.

The Egoistic Emotions

Because they spring from the self-preservative instinct, the egoistic emotions are the first to develop, and they assume a variety of forms such as self-esteem, self-worth, self-complacency, self-respect, self-reliance, self-confidence, and the sense for power. In its inordinate form, the self-regarding emotion becomes pride, the craving for undue superiority, and vanity—an inordinate desire for fame. Remorse, or the sorrow and self-condemnation following past actions, and shame, arising from a realization of the contempt of others, are two painful forms of the self-regarding feeling. Ordinarily classed with the same feeling are fear, a purely painful emotion, and anger, which may be partly pleasant. Both are very closely related to the self-preservative instinct. In its extreme form, fear becomes cowardice; anger, one of the most exciting of emotions, assumes a number of forms: revenge, antipathy, hatred, envy, jealousy, and malevolence. Emulation, rivalry, and competition are considered by some psychologists as other aspects of anger.

The Social Emotions

The social or altruistic emotions are rooted in the social instinct, the tendency attracting man toward his fellow beings, and they can be classified into three groups:

Emotions that have man, in general, for their object, like sympathy, the love of mankind.

Emotions concerning certain social groups like the nation and the family,

Selective emotions that have certain individuals as their object.

The most general form of the social emotions seems to be sympathy, the capacity to understand and enter into the feelings of others. It has been described as a sort of substitution of other selves for our own self. Sympathy and its opposite, antipathy, play, in the moral order, a part analogous to that of attraction and repulsion in physical nature. A special form of sympathy is benevolence, a disposition to do good to others; and this disposition may lead to beneficence. A classical illustration of this disposition is the parable of the good Samaritan.

Because the family is the most natural of all social groups, the essential condition and first form of social life, the family or domestic emotions may be considered the prototype and model of all social feelings. That man cannot fail to be a good citizen who is or has been a good son, a good brother, a good husband, and a good father; and Christianity teaches us to think of the whole human race as one family, of God as our common Father, and of all men as our brethren. The particular character of family emotions is naturally determined by the nature of the relation to one another of the members of the family circle: conjugal love; parental, filial, and brotherly love.

The words *patriotism, fatherland,* and *mother tongue* remind us of the close relation between the family and the nation, and we can say that national, patriotic feelings are but a sort of extension of the family emotions. The nation is the family "writ large," and love of country is nothing else than love of oneself and one's own in the national family. Aside from the family and the nation, there are various social groups or classes that give rise to certain emotions that may be all referred to by the generic name of *esprit de corps,* probably deepest among the members of the same army or army units.

The two forms of the selective social feeling are friendship and love. Real friendship is first of all founded on mutual esteem, and it is a feeling in which self interest has no share. A friend is a sort of *alter ego* whom we love for the sake of loving, of showing our devotion to him. Of love, so many vulgar caricatures of which appear in modern novels, there is probably no better description than that given in the fifth chapter of the third book of the *Imitation of Christ.*

The Sentiments

The third and last group in our classification of complex feelings includes the highest, most spiritual, and most impersonal of emotions: the intellectual sentiment or love of the true, the aesthetic sentiment or love of the beautiful, the moral sentiment or love of the good, and the religious sentiment or the love of God which combines them all. The development of the intellectual sentiment in the child is treated in some detail in Chapter V and that section of Chapter XI, dealing with curiosity and attention. We shall remark only here that the thirst for knowledge, the search for the true—being the natural object of the intellect—nothing short of the acquisition and possession of knowledge will satisfy it. The joy of knowing, of having discovered something new, is constantly exhibited in the life of the child. The "Eureka" of Archimedes is an historical illustration of the joy of the savant or scientist in reaching the goal of his efforts.

The moral sentiment, referred to under a variety of names that are not all very accurate, is a complex feeling made up of several elements that can all be summed up in the phrase "love of the good" and, therefore, hatred of evil. It is inseparably linked with human voluntary action. It is not, as is sometimes asserted, the essential element of conscience, but its necessary complement.

The religious sentiment, which, in some form or other, we find among all races and at all times, prompts us to attribute to a Supreme Being the intelligence that conceived the whole universe and the power that created it, and it induces us to try to know Him, revere, fear, love and serve Him.

The Aesthetic Sentiment

Like the preceding, the aesthetic sentiment has been variously, if not always appropriately described. It involves a number of forms, chiefly those of the sublime, the beautiful, the pretty, the graceful, the harmonious, and it commonly arises from sight and hearing impressions. As the aesthetic sentiment gains in refinement and purity, it becomes more impersonal, more spiritual and makes us shrink from what is coarse and vulgar.

When we look at certain works of art, or listen to certain melodies, we experience a certain kind of pleasure which we describe by saying that we like these melodies or works of art, that they are beautiful. The same kind of pleasure was experienced by the artist at work on the melody, or painting, or statue. He produced it such as we have it now, because it pleased him, because he found it beautiful. Now the question is: What prompts us to pronounce a certain thing beautiful? It is this question that aesthetics tries to answer.

Aesthetics

We have seen that reality appears to us under the three-fold aspect of the true, the object of the cognitive faculty; of the good, the object of the appetitive faculty; and the beautiful, the object of the aesthetic faculty. We also have seen that pleasure is the natural accompaniment of all normal activity. Thus intellectual activity is accompanied by intellectual pleasure, the joy of knowing, of grasping truth, and the degree, the quality of that joy in any particular case is determined by the extent, the degree, and the quality of our knowledge. Similarly, aesthetic pleasure is the natural accompaniment of the contemplation of any beautiful object; and the extent, the degree of the pleasure, is determined not only by the individual's capacity for aesthetic appreciation and enjoyment, but also by the extent and degree the object is the embodiment of reality, that is, of truth. This intimate relation of beauty to truth is brought out in the following definition of the beautiful attributed to Plato: *"that it is the splendor of the true,"* whether truth reveals itself directly to the intellect, or comes to us through the senses, in the garb of some sensible object. The beautiful and the true, then, are but two aspects of one and the same thing: reality in its relations to man. When we consider reality as the object of knowledge we refer to it as the true; when we think of it as the source of aesthetic pleasure we call it the beautiful.

The essential characteristic of the beautiful is that it pleases; *Pulchra sunt quae visa placent,"* says St. Thomas. And the pleasure aroused by the beautiful is due partly to the action of the senses, especially sight and hearing, partly to the action of the imagination, but chiefly to that of the intellect. Taste, the aesthetic faculty, is fundamentally rational; it is intellect at work in the field of the beautiful.

Of the many qualities we may look for in beautiful objects the one most generally accepted as fundamental is unity amid variety. The lack of variety is painful and so is the lack of unity. Other qualities of the beautiful, whether in nature or in art, or in the "suprasensible" world, are but particular expressions of those fundamental qualities. One of the most interesting applications of this general principle is utility, the fitness of any work of art, or any part of it to the particular purpose for which it is intended. It is this quality that mainly differentiates pure Gothic architecture in the 13th century from the "flamboyant" type in the 14th and 15th. This quality of fitness or utility is suggestive of a distinction between absolute and relative beauty. An object charming in itself, as a beautiful Gothic cathedral taken as a whole, would illustrate absolute beauty, whereas a pillar in that cathedral would illustrate relative beauty because of its association with, or rather fitness in, the plan of the whole building. Another important psychical factor in the appreciation and enjoyment of beauty is disinterestedness. The aesthetic sentiment will vanish as soon as there is a desire to possess the beautiful object.

The Science of Aesthetics

Before the seventeenth century. As a science, aesthetics is of comparatively recent origin, but its object, beauty, has been for a long time a matter of philosophical speculation. Socrates, we are told, raised the question of the relation of the beautiful and the good; both, he believed, answered some useful purpose, though that purpose might not be immediate. According to him, too, art consists essentially in an imitation of nature. When the imitation is successful, it will give pleasure.

Plato's views on beauty and art are formulated in several of his *Dialogues,* especially the *Symposium;* they form an integral part of his system of ideas, or general conception of reality. According to him, the artist should seek his inspiration and models not so much in the world of phenomena as in himself, and, above all, in the world of ideas. Proportion, harmony, and unity are the qualities emphasized by Plato as the essential elements of beauty. Aristotle's opinions on the subject are to be found mainly in his *Poetics* and *Rhetoric* though suggestions on the subject are scattered in other works of his, especially his metaphysics. He distinguished the good, which is always to be found in action, from the beautiful, which may be found in motionless beings; the two, however, are closely related. They are two aspects of being. According to him the essential qualities of the beautiful are order, symmetry, definiteness, and a certain magnitude. The fine arts are imitative, and their immediate object is pleasure.

The neo-Platonic Plotinus revived in an exaggerated form the views of Plato on beauty. He claimed that the use of intellectual notions as models would lead the artist to more beautiful creations than the material objects in his surroundings. Another name worth mentioning in connection with Greek speculation on the nature of the beautiful is that of Longinus, a Greek rhetorician of the 3rd century A. D. He has been credited with the authorship of the treatise on the Sublime, the inspiration of which is highly idealistic. It is concerned with style, sublimity in style, or rather the essential elements of an impressive style. Horace's *Ars Poetica* and some passages in Cicero's writings, though of a decidedly more practical character than the preceding, might be added to the list of noteworthy opinions on aesthetics in ancient times.

References to the nature of the beautiful can be found in early Christian, Medieval, and Renaissance literature, as, for example, St. Thomas' remark quoted above, but we have to reach the 17th century to meet again any systematic treatment of the subject. We must forego a detailed exposition here of the many theories of the beautiful and art that have been offered in modern times and be satisfied with stating in a general way, the essential characteristics of the more important schools of thinkers on this subject: the German, the French, and the English schools.

In modern times. For the German school the question of aesthetics is one of the problems of metaphysics. It is from that viewpoint that it is treated more or less thoroughly by Baumgarten, Kant, Schelling, Hegel, Schopenhauer, Herbart, the theories of the last four taking their start from the speculations of Kant. In addition to the discussions of the question of aesthetics by philosophers we have in the German school those of literary men like Lessing, Winckelmann, Goethe, and Schiller, and the contributions to the same discussions by scientists like Fechner. French speculations on beauty begin with literary criticism in the 16th, 17th, and 18th century. Of the many writers connected with this phase of aesthetics in France, we should mention in the 17th century, Malherbe, Boileau, Fontenelle, and Charles Perrault, the author of the Fairy Tales and the champion of modern times in the quarrel on the respective merits of ancient and modern writers. In the

18th century we meet, among others, the names of Voltaire and Diderot. In the 19th century the question of aesthetics was treated in a systematic way by several French philosophers more or less influenced by the German school. The better known of those French philosophers are V. Cousin, E. Jouffroy, and J. C. Lévêque. The general trend of the French school is spiritualistic, though some exceptions could be cited, as, for instance, H. Taine whose conception of art is decidedly realistic. English writers on the subject of aesthetics are commonly referred to as intuitionalists who admit the existence of objective beauty, or psychologists who are concerned only with the analysis of the aesthetic sentiment. Burke, Ruskin, Reynolds, Hogarth, among others, belong to the first class, whereas Hamilton, Reid, Bain, and Spencer belong to the second.

The Fine Arts

We shall close this all too brief excursion into the domain of aesthetics with a few remarks on the fine arts. Stated in the most general way, the purpose of any one of the fine arts is the creation or, let us rather say, production of things beautiful, the embodiment of truth in some sensible, beautiful form. The essence of art and its final end should ever be spiritual. Its appeal to the senses is but a means to that end. The poem, melody, statue, or painting that does nothing else besides stir up and satisfy our senses is a parody of art.

The artist may be concerned with the characteristic rendering of some object or person as in novels and plays, the expression of sentiments as in music and lyric poetry, or the symbolic translation of some abstract notion, as, for instance, when prayer is shown in the figure of a young girl kneeling, her hands clasped and head bowed. In any case, the artist's work should be an imitation of nature, an intelligent and beautiful interpretation, through poem, play, music, painting, or statue, of nature's mysterious language. And the great law of art is that it should please, but never at the expense of the true and the good.

Educational Applications

Apart from the schools of ancient Greece, very little was done by the school, until recent times, to develop the pupils' aesthetic sense. Literature, which has ever been an important element in the curriculum of the secondary school, was too commonly used to illustrate rules in grammar, logic, or rhetoric, or to convey some useful, interesting bits of information; seldom was its aesthetic quality emphasized. Music had been one of the medieval liberal arts, but the treatment of the subject had been scientific rather than aesthetic. The nearest approach to a recognition by the school of the value of the aesthetic element in education was the staging of plays, a common enough occurrence in post-Renaissance times, and the singing of religious hymns, quite common in the German elementary schools in modern times, as it had been in some medieval schools. It is only within the last fifty years that the aesthetic element has gradually come into its own in the schools. Its importance in general education has been pointed out from several viewpoints, especially the following. The aesthetic sentiment is no less a part of human consciousness than the intellectual, moral, or religious sentiment. To neglect cultivating it is to fall short of our purpose in education, which should be the complete development of the individual's consciousness, preparing him for an intelligent, humane adjustment to his surroundings. The individual whose sense of beauty has been neglectèd will fail to adjust himself to the whole of his envoriment, of which art is an integral part. Another value of the beautiful, very much insisted upon by the ancient Greeks, is the ethical value. Without going so far as to identfy the good and the beautiful, it can be asserted that we have taken a long step in moral education, when we have succeeded in showing vice in its true colors—as something ugly and repellent—and virtue likewise in its true character of beauty. Of late, the recreative value of the fine arts has been much emphasized, because of the increased leisure time that the machine places at the disposal of man.

How can we develop the aesthetic sentiment in the schools? Leaving to treatises on the teaching of literature and the fine arts the details of the answer to this question, we would say:

First, use the influence of example, imitation, surroundings. With the possible exception of moral training there is no phase of education where that influence is more vital, more telling, than in the cultivation of the aesthetic sentiment.

Second, make as large a place as possible in the curriculum for all the fine arts, and use them for aesthetic, not for scientific or utilitarian purposes.

Third, in all that the pupils do or say, insist upon a certain perfection in what is said or done, the sense of excellence, the finishing touch in all that they undertake.

And by way of concluding this brief survey of the field

of aesthetics, let us remember that beauty and the cult of beauty can be "a school of unselfishness." The aesthetic sentiment is "unselfish" par excellence.

TOPICS FOR FURTHER STUDY

1. Differentiate the beautiful from (a) the true, (b) the good, (c) the useful. Illustrate.
2. Differentiate the useful from the fine arts.
3. Submit a classification of the fine arts arranged in an ascending scale. Account for your arrangement.
4. "Works of art are the product of the imagination." Discuss.
5. "Works of art are the product of imitation." Discuss.
6. Make a comparative study of the definitions of aesthetics given in this chapter.
7. "The beautiful and the true are but one and the same thing." Discuss.
8. "Taste is fundamentally rational." Discuss.
9. Compare medieval and Renaissance art at their best.
10. Discuss the influence of religion on literature.
11. Discuss the influence of religion on the plastic arts.
12. Discuss the influence of religion on music.
13. "Art for art's sake." Discuss.
14. Contrast Plato's and Aristotle's views on the beautiful.
15. Show the relation of aesthetics to metaphysics.
16. Contrast the realistic and idealistic conceptions of art.
17. State and comment on the naturalistic conception of art.
18. Discuss the educational value of the staging of plays.
19. Discuss the importance of environment in aesthetic education.
20. "Aesthetic education takes place through all school activities." Discuss.

SUGGESTIONS FOR READING

Aristotle, *Poetics*.
Bosanquet, B., *History of Aesthetics* (London, 1892).
Cousin, V., *Du Vrai, du Beau et du Bien* (Paris, 1853).

Gietmann, G., *Grundrisz der Stilistik, Poetik und Aesthetik* (Freiburg, 1897).

Hegel, G., *Vorlesungen über die Aesthetik* (Berlin, 1838).

Horne, H., *Psychological Principles of Education* (New York, 1906).

Lessing, G., *Laocoon* (tr.) (Paris, 1880).

Lévêque, C., *La Science du Beau* (Paris, 1861).

Longhaye, G., *Théorie des Belles-Lettres* (Paris, 1885).

Plato, *Phaedrus.*

Plato, *Republic.*

Plato, *Symposium.*

Ruskin, J., *Modern Painters* (London, 1849).

Taine, H., *Philosophie de l'Art* (Paris, 1895).

CHAPTER XIII

Moral Education

The Problem Stated

The general aim of moral education is right conduct, action in conformity with the standards and ideals of sound morality. Our present inquiry should then include, in the first place, a brief consideration of moral standards and ideals.

The mainspring of human behavior is the will, understood here to correspond to the scholastic term, *appetitive faculty,* with its connotation of tendencies, dispositions, desires, emotions, passions, and volitions. The second important item in our study will thus be the will, the different types of action it originates, and the principles that should guide parent and teacher in dealing with the child's will.

Moral education is influenced by heredity, that is, certain organic characteristics which come to us from our forebears with predispositions for certain types of behavior. Moral education is influenced further by the direct environment of the individual, that is, the economic, social, and religious conditions amidst which he is born and spends the formative years of his life. Heredity and environment will thus be the next two important items in this inquiry.

If we add to the preceding the agencies of moral education in the school, the preparation it requires of the teacher, and a brief consideration of the importance of the moral aim, we complete the list of the more important topics in the general survey of moral education.

Heredity and the pre-eminence of the moral aim have already been discussed in preceding chapters, and the teacher's qualifications for an efficient coöperation in moral education will be examined in connection with the teacher's professional preparation. In this chapter, we shall then be concerned with the following aspects of our problem:

Moral standards and ideals.
The will.
Environment.
The agencies for moral education in the school.

The Moral Standard

As stated above in a slightly different form, the general aim of moral education is to prepare for the good life, to teach the child and the youth to live up to the standards of sound morality; and the question at once arises: What are these moral standards? That might have been an idle question a few generations back, but in this age of skepticism, it is a most pertinent one. For the Christian educator, there is but one answer to the question. It flows from a few fundamental truths that once were taught in every school in the West:

God is the origin, the end and Supreme Ruler of all things;
Man has an immortal soul endowed with reason and free will;

He has been created to know God, to love and serve Him, thereby to attain to that perfect happiness for which he has an unquenchable desire that can never be satisfied in this life;

But man comes into this world with Adam's inheritance, "fallen from an original estate, but redeemed by Christ and restored to the supernatural condition of adopted son of God." [1]

The standard of the good life, the moral law, is a God-given plan for the ordination of man's life, and because it is the expression of a Supreme Ruler's wisdom and will, this plan has characteristics of its own that it may not be amiss to state here.

It is universal, embracing all persons, all times, and places.

It is immutable, admitting of no change, though the knowledge of it may vary from individual to individual.

It is absolute, admitting of no condition, no prescription or dispensation; we may obtain a dispensation from the laws of the State or those of the Church, but never from the Ten Commandments.

The moral law is evident, in the sense that, upon reaching the age of reason, any normal person possesses an intuitive knowledge of what is right and wrong.

It is obligatory, binding the will, though not compelling it.

It is autonomous, deriving its authority from our reason and ultimately from the divine law.

It is inviolable in the sense that it ever remains the same in spite of all violations.

The standard of morality and therefore of moral educa-

---

[1] Pius XI, *Encyclical on Christian Education.*

tion is the moral law, in the sense in which it has just been explained. Its ideal is virtue, the habit of doing good for the love of the Author of all goodness. Virtue, then, is not for its own sake as the ancient Stoics contended it to be. It is not the mere knowledge of what is right, as taught by Socrates and his great disciple, Plato. As the root meaning of the term would suggest, virtue is strength, it is courage, perseverance, self-control, self-sacrifice, and self-denial, as we see it exemplified in the lives of countless Christian heroes that have tried to follow in the footsteps of the Divine Founder of Christianity.

The Will

The term *will*, let it be stated again, is used here in a very comprehensive though somewhat loose sense, to convey the same meaning as the scholastic term *appetite,* or *appetitive faculty,* the soul's natural inclinations, its aptitude for desires, aversions, and volitions. In this broad sense, the will expresses itself in a variety of movements or actions that can be classified in some such way as the following:

Instinctive action prompted by some instinctive tendency, such as fear, anger, imitation.

Habitual action, the outcome of habit formation.

Voluntary or deliberate action, which follows deliberation and choice.

Instinctive Action

Instinct can be defined as an innate tendency to feel or act in a certain way without any prevision of the cause or aim of such feeling or action. Like habit, instinct is primarily an inclination, a disposition to act in a certain way, but whereas the habitual disposition is acquired, instinct is inborn; it antedates all training. The bird needs no schooling to know how to build its nest, the beaver its dam, or the spider to weave its web. Instinct, of itself, is a blind, impelling force such as we see it manifested among animals and sometimes men, as when we speak of murder committed under the influence of blind fury. To act instinctively, then, is to act, as stated in our definition, without any prevision, that is, knowledge, understanding of the cause or purpose of the action. As soon as there is prevision, we have instinct supplemented by intelligence.

Instinct is universal in the sense that it assumes the same forms in all the members of the same genus or species.

Instinct is special; it is concerned with a particular series of movements leading to a particular end. Each species of spider, for instance, weaves its web in a particular way; the swallow does not build a nest, but a swallow's nest.

Instinct is infallible in the sense that it perfectly adapts means to end. It has been remarked that beavers build dykes as though they had studied engineering, that, in storing away their honey, bees proceed as though they had mastered the problem of maxima and minima. However, there may be deviations from the normal line, failures on the part of the animal to reach the end toward which it is working. The functioning of instincts in the animal as in man depends on sensation, and its senses may lead the animal astray. Certain flies deposit their eggs on flesh in a state of putrefaction so that the larvae will find at birth the food they need. Flies of this type, it has been observed, will sometimes deposit their eggs on leaves whose odor is very akin to that of putrid flesh, the consequence being, evidently, that the larvae are starved.

Instinct is immutable, though variations may occur in its functioning, due chiefly to the intervention of man. The barking of the dog and the trotting of the horse are illustrations of such variations owing to domestication. A beast of prey feeding upon a new kind of prey, because it fails to find its usual quarry, would be a variation imposed upon the animal by its natural surroundings. Those variations, however, never wander far from the normal and cannot be taken as evidence of progress. The basic tendency ever remains the same. The behavior of bees, for instance, is to-day substantially what it was in the days of Virgil.

The foregoing remarks apply to instinct as such, that is, instinct as we find it among the animals. In man, instinct comes under the influence of intelligence and will; from being blind and fatal, it becomes an incentive to the higher types of activity, a powerful agency in education and progress. Curiosity and imitation, for example, are shared in common by man and the animal. With the latter, they are merely means of adaptation to physical surroundings, of preserving animal life as it is. In man, curiosity is an incentive to scientific research and discovery, a means of learning and improving the environment; imitation leads us on in the footsteps of the great leaders of the race.

Various classifications of instinctive tendencies have been suggested, none of which is above criticism of some kind. The following has been adopted as best answering the purposes of the philosophy of education, but it should not, any more than any other arrangement, convey the notion of water-tight compartments. No human act is exclusively the result of any single type of instinctive tendency. Aside from the influence of free will, human behavior in any particular instance is the result in varying degree of several instinctive tendencies. We shall here distinguish five different types of those tendencies:

The individualistic or self-preservative instincts, such as fear and the tendency to run away from danger, prompting the individual to act primarily for his own sake; they subsist all through life, but they are particularly strong in infancy and childhood when the main business in life is to get for the self as many good things as possible.

The parental instinct prompting the individual to act for the good of the species.

The social instinct manifesting itself in the tendency to seek the companionship of others, in the impulse to feel as others do, in the tendency to please others, and in the tendency to act in harmony with them and for a common good.

The adaptive instinct at once evident in play, curiosity, and imitation; it prompts and helps adjustment to surroundings.

Instinctive tendencies resulting from various combinations of the foregoing, like the collecting, aesthetic, expressive instincts.

Educational Applications

Some of the more important tendencies have already been dealt with in previous chapters. Others will come up later for some comment. At present, we are concerned with the practical, but general question: What should be the teacher's policy in dealing with instinctive tendencies? Our definition and analysis of instinct at once suggest the answer to that question. Do not try to extirpate, because it would be of no avail—since instinct is part of our nature; rather try to regulate and direct, to bring instinct under the control of reason and will; repress at once, any undesirable trait that the instinctive tendency may develop, lest it become a deep-rooted habit. Repression or inhibition, as it is more commonly designated, can be accomplished through fear of immediate punishment of any kind, if the undesirable tendency is but transitory. Punishment, however, will fail to achieve its purpose if the tendency is a strong one; once the sense of fear has vanished, the tendency will reappear as strong as ever. A more effective way of securing inhibition is the substitution of some worthy form of the instinctive tendency for the undesirable one. The method is well illustrated in the following passage from James's *Talks to Teachers:*

Pride and pugnacity have often been considered unworthy passions to appeal to in the young. But in their more refined and noble forms, they play a great part in the schoolroom and in education generally, being in some characters most potent spurs to effort. Pugnacity need not be thought of merely in the form of physical combativeness. It can be taken in the sense of a general unwillingness to be beaten by any kind of difficulty. It is what makes us feel "stumped" and challenged by arduous achievements and is essential to a spirited and enterprising character. . . . The fighting impulse must often be appealed to. Make the pupil feel ashamed of being scared at fractions, of being "downed" by the law of falling bodies; rouse his pugnacity and pride and he will rush at the difficult places with a sort of inner wrath at himself that is one of his best moral faculties. A victory scored under such conditions becomes a turning-point and crisis of his character.[2]

Punishment and substitution undoubtedly will help the teacher to deal with the undesirable tendencies into which

---

[2] James, W., *Talks to Teachers,* pp. 54, 55. Henry Holt and Company, New York, 1914.

instincts may develop, but the true solution of the problem lies in the habit of self-control, which the teacher should take every opportunity to develop and strengthen. This aspect of the question will be dealt with in the paragraphs on habit and free will.

Imitation

Of all the native inclinations that contribute to the shaping of personality, none has a greater educational value than imitation, the tendency to reproduce the thought or act of another. In the early forms of the tendency, the stimulus to imitate is usually the perception of some act or series of acts; later, however, images and ideas become more and more frequent as stimuli and guides in reproducing. Psychologists have distinguished five stages or types in the development of the instinct: reflex, spontaneous, dramatic, voluntary, and idealistic.

Reflex imitation, a purely physiological form of the tendency, is the first one to appear and the only one present in early life. Smiling, laughing, yawning, crying are the more common expressions of this type of imitation. Though somewhat obscured later, it remains all through life an important form of suggestion, accounting partly for the readiness with which we catch the spirit or atmosphere of a social gathering. Like the previous type, spontaneous imitation is more or less unconscious, but its scope is much wider. Children will try to reproduce anything attracting their attention in their surroundings. At first the stimulus to reproduce, in this as in the preceding type, is the perception of some act or object, but gradually the tendency appears in response to memory stimuli as well. Dramatic imitation, otherwise very similar to spontaneous imitation, differs from it in this, that it contains an element of originality. Imagination now suggests to the child his own way of imitating, whereas in spontaneous imitation, he tried to give a mere reproduction, a copy, of what has been perceived. In voluntary imitation, the tendency to reproduce is brought under the influence of reason and will. The child imitates for a purpose and is mostly concerned with the "how" of reproduction, as when he watches the movements of the teacher in the writing of some word and then tries to repeat them to the best of his ability. In idealistic imitation, the tendency reaches its highest development. It is now no longer an attempt to repeat any one act or series of acts, as in the previous types of imitation, but an attempt to acquire certain qualities, to live up to certain standards of conduct that we notice and admire in some characters in history, on the stage, or in our environment. Of these several forms of imitation, the last two are by far the most important, and, with the advance in years, they gradually become the predominant forms of imitation, but the others, though overshadowed, remain present throughout life.

Educational Applications

The influence of example and imitation could hardly be overestimated, whether we consider it in society as a whole, or in the life of the individual. It accounts in a large measure for the transmission from generation to generation of forms of government, types of culture, systems of education; it helps us understand the spread of fashions, new ideas, new conceptions of life; it is, in a large measure, responsible for the behavior of the mob, for financial panics, and for much of what happens in times of revolution. Imitation is one of the most potent educative forces in the life of the individual. All through the entire process of learning, but particularly in his attempts to master the mother tongue, the child chiefly depends on the example of parent and teacher. Peculiarities in pronunciation, spelling, and construction that appear in the language of the boy or girl could be traced back, in most instances, to that early influence. Far more telling, however, is the influence of imitation and example in moral education. "A man is known by the company he keeps" is the proverbial and true expression of this influence on character. Example, whether good or bad, will make a far deeper impression than precept, especially if it be the example of persons that the child or adolescent loves, admires, or respects.

The lesson to be drawn for parent and teacher from this brief study of imitation is at least threefold:

In the first place, to realize the importance, and paramount educative value of example and imitation.

Secondly, to bear in mind that the child will preferably imitate whatever strikes his imagination and is in any way interesting, whether morally good, bad, or indifferent; hence the duty of parent and teacher to supervise the child's readings, surroundings and associations.

Thirdly, we should present virtue in striking personalities about the child, in the heroes of story, biography, or history; we should show vice in its true colors; above all, we should be for the child and adolescent, at any rate try to be, living models of all that we wish them to become.

Habitual Action

The second form of activity to be considered in this chapter is that which is the result of habit formation. Habit can be defined as a tendency to feel, think, or act, in a certain way, acquired through a continuation or repetition of the same feeling, or thought, or act. Habit is not feeling, thought, or action, but a disposition to feel, think, or act, and, at the same time, an aptitude or facility to feel, think, or act in a certain way that is increased by repetition. Thus, through habit, we acquire a facility to use a foreign language and at the same time, a disposition to speak it when among people who use it.

In the formation of any habit, we find two forces opposed to each other: the resistance of the organism to the new mode of activity, and a power that is increased by every act we perform to overcome the obstacle. Through repetition, the power gradually increases and the resistance decreases, and the time comes when the action, at first difficult, even painful to perform, has become automatic. Thus, in learning how to write, the child is called upon to make and co-ordinate a long series of efforts in order to understand the teacher's explanations, and then to perform the appropriate movements of fingers, hand, and arm. The task would evidently be hopeless if conditions always remained what they were at the start, but every effort lessens the resistance to be overcome and increases the ease and accuracy of movement, until, finally, the child can write without any appreciable difficulty.

Habit is sometimes defined in a most general way, as an aptitude to reproduce modifications once acquired, and, in that sense, we find it everywhere in nature. The tree grows the way it is bent; a sheet of paper will easily fold as it did before; our clothes become the "habit" of our body. This general aptitude to form habits is limited only by the fundamental laws that govern the existence of the thing, animal, or person concerned. No living organism, for instance, could form the habit of doing without food; after repeating the same act for some time, no further gain is made in rapidity and accuracy of movement, because of fatigue.

Habit begins with the first act, for there is no reason why there should be any change in the organism after two or three or one hundred acts, if there was no change after one. And habit occupies some sort of a middle ground between free will and instinct. It commonly starts from a deliberate act and, through repetition, tends to become instinctive, just as instinct, under the influence of intelligence and will, is raised to a higher level of action. Habit should be distinguished from custom, the usages of the time or country to which we conform ourselves. Habit is personal and may become a necessity, which is never the case with customs.

Habit is one in that it encompasses the whole person and ever retains the same basic characteristics, but it assumes as many forms as there are types of activities. We may, to begin with, distinguish between passive and active habits. In the formation of a passive habit the organism becomes less and less responsive to external stimuli, as, for example, when a person living in a busy thoroughfare becomes, after a while, unaware of its noises. An active habit, on the other hand, is the result of the repetition of the same act, as in piano playing, typewriting, or skating. The cause of the difference between what is referred to here as passive and active habits lies in attention which is practically nil in the formation of passive habits but always present, sometimes with great intensity, in the formation of active habits. Let it also be remarked that the same sense may form both passive and active habits. Our ear may become so accustomed to the din of traffic that we notice it only when it ceases, and, on the other hand, the ear of a musician will acquire, through habit, the ability to detect even slight differences in musical notes.

Organic habits are either adaptations of the organism to certain modes of living—as becoming accustomed to new climatic conditions—or else aptitudes to perform certain acts —as walking, speaking, dancing, or fencing. Intellectual habits are the way we think, the point of view we usually take on any subject. A lawyer is likely to view things from an angle that is different from that of a physician or business-man. Superstition and prejudice can be partly explained on the ground of intellectual habits, which also account for the skill of the specialist in any field. Moral habits are the bent we give to our will in accordance with or against the dictates of reason. Temperance, kindness, fairness, patience, and many other virtues or their opposite are mainly the result of habit formation. Finally, there could be listed under the generic name of aesthetic habits such tendencies as neat-ness, order, harmony; and beauty in thought, speech, and manners which must be partly accounted for by habit formation.

Habit, then, encompasses the whole person. All our capacities develop through habit along certain lines, and edu-cation is, in the main, a process of habit formation at a time when the organism is plastic and all our faculties can be easily bent one way or another.

The basis of habit is at once physiological and psychical. "The organism grows to the mode in which it is exer-cised." [3] Although there is going on in the living organism a constant process of waste and reconstruction, yet, in spite

---

[3] Carpenter, W., *Mental Physiology*, p. 340.

of ceaseless changes, the organism registers all the impressions it receives and they become deeper with every repetition. The formation of habit from this standpoint means the breaking up of the resistance of the organism along certain lines, the establishment of what we may, for lack of a better simile, describe as short cuts between different parts of the organism. The process may be illustrated from what takes place in the mastery of the art of writing. The teacher explains and illustrates before the class the position and movements of the whole body, the arm, the hand, and the finger, and the impressions received by the child through the eye and ear are carried along the sensory side of the nervous system to various areas in the brain, where they are transmitted through the motor nerves to the muscles in arm, hand, and finger. For a long time, the process is a conscious one, necessitating the use of the brain centers involved in actual thinking, but, gradually, by dint of repetition, the use of such centers is eliminated, and the sensory impression passes directly from the sensory to the motor nerves.

From a purely psychological viewpoint the basis and real cause of habit formation is the sum total of all our faculties and native dispositions. Thus, in the mind's capacity to remember, to form concepts, to judge, and to reason, we have the basis and cause of intellectual habits; in our disposition to respond to and appreciate beauty lies the foundation of aesthetic habits; in the tendency to act according to rule, the foundation of moral habits. The formation of habit, however, both from the organic and psychological viewpoint, is conditioned by the frequency, duration, and intensity of the organic or psychical experience, as also by the law of contiguity, the tendency of mental states that have appeared at the same time or in succession to reappear in the same order.

The passive, feeling side of our nature becomes blunted through habit. Thus, through habit, we become unaware of street noises, we grow accustomed to the severity of the climate and privations. Thus too, sensuous pleasures will vanish when indulged in too often; the capacity to enjoy may even disappear as is the case with the blasé. But the desire for such pleasures remains, and it has been strengthened through habit, constantly requiring new and stronger stimuli. And so it happens that when we fail to use our will to curb the senses, we have to use it in their service. On the other hand, those sensations that intelligence and will spiritualize become keener, more distinct and refined through repetition. Thus, through habit, the eye of the painter becomes very sensitive to differences in color; the ear of the musician, to differences in sound. Likewise, the higher emotions become stronger and more refined through habit. Taste, which is rather crude among uncultured people, develops through practice; the moral sentiment is fortified through constant associations with reason and will.

The active side of our nature is fortified through habit. Experience tells us that the influence of habit increases with every act. Repetition of the act increases the ease, rapidity, and accuracy with which it is performed. It is through repeated experiences that we learn how to walk, swim, or write; that we learn how to teach and think; through repeated voluntary acts, that we develop a strong will.

Habit formation is the condition of progress in every line of human endeavor. Habit, so to say, accumulates and preserves what our efforts have produced. Without habit, art, science, speech, education, and even morality are inconceivable, for none of those would be possible if every day we had to make the same effort, to go through the same struggle and find ourselves no better off at the end than the beginning of the day. As we repeat the same act, however, reflection and effort go on decreasing. Habit, we might say, lessens the expense and increases the receipt; it plays in our life the part that capital and labor do in economics; it creates an aptitude, a facility to do things which may be likened to a capital bearing interest. Virtue, for example, is such a capital; it is accumulated moral vigor.

Habit influences the whole of our life, but more particularly our actions, because all our actions more or less involve the coöperation of all our capacities; and all actions, whether morally good or bad or indifferent, come under the sway of habit carrying with them some degree of responsibility. The extent of this responsibility varies, of course, from one person to another, but the following rule may be laid down: Whenever there is freedom at the beginning of a habit and knowledge of the nature of the act to be performed, then we are responsible for what follows. There is, however, no irresistible habit; what one free act has done, another can undo. If it is true to say that the will is the mother of habit, it is no less true to say that habit fortifies the will. Willing, in the truly human sense of the term, can become a habit; character, a good moral character, is nothing more than the will to do what is right, become habitual through repeated acts of self-discipline, self-denial, and self-sacrifice.

Habit is a second nature. The tendency to reproduce habitual acts increases with the facility to perform them. At the origin an effort is required for the performance of the act, but once it has become habitual an effort is needed not to perform it. It has become second nature, a nature of our own making for which we were responsible from its very inception.   Any new act may be the first link of a long chain that may lead us heavenward or drag us into the mire.   The maxims that "We reap what we have sown," that "Vice carries with it its own punishment," and "Virtue is its own reward" are particularly applicable to habit formation. With the doing of any good or bad act arises the disposition to do other acts of the same kind.   Man is, in a sense, "the architect of his own soul."

Educational Applications

Many rules, so-called laws, have been formulated for the formation of habit.   They can all be summed up in the following suggestions: Enlist the whole person, intellect, feeling, and will in the service of the habit to be formed. The nature of that habit, its importance, and more important stages must be known, and their value realized.   Each and every incentive to the formation of the habit should be summoned to its support.   Above all, there must be a strong, never flagging will to go through the process—no matter what the cost may be to our ease and comfort—acting upon every opportunity, without ever. allowing any exception. Any exception means a snapping of the chain we are trying to forge, a falling back upon the starting point with a lessened chance of success.   As to the bad habits that should be broken, the only remedy lies in the formation of good ones, but much time and perseverance may be required.   To attempt to overcome and root out at once all bad habits is to court failure and discouragement.   The better policy is to proceed piece meal, to be satisfied with a series of small victories, because a positive gain, however small it may be, increases our self-confidence and strengthens our will.

Voluntary Action

In the true but restricted sense of the term, the will is the faculty of acting with reflection and freedom, the faculty to decide upon any course of action after deliberation.

The will expresses itself in volitions or voluntary acts, which presupposes freedom or full possession of one's self and includes the following elements: (a) the conception of the act or acts to be done; (b) deliberation as to what course of action should be taken; (c) choice or decision; (d) the carrying out of the decision, that is, the act itself.

Freedom or self-possession is the prerequisite for any voluntary act. We are self-possessed when we enjoy the free use of our faculties, when we are not subjected to any unconquerable force either internal or external. We are not free in infancy, or in sleep, or when we are under the influence of passion or drugs.

The voluntary act begins with the idea of what is to be done: the nature of the act, its importance and consequences, the means to be used and the actual process we must go through in performing this act.

In deliberation, we examine and weigh the pros and cons of the act and the motives, of whatever kind, that solicit the will. Those motives may be supplied by the intellect, the feelings, or the instincts. There may be reasons for or against a certain course of action, there may be desires or passions urging us to act in a certain way. In deliberation we also consider the means to be used in the performance of the act and its consequences, and it will often happen that these consequences become the real motives of our decision. Obviously, whenever that is possible, we should proportion the time of our deliberation to the importance of the decision to be taken, but it sometimes happens that we must act on the spur of the moment. In such a case, the habit of self-control, lucidity of mind, strength of character will save us from hesitation. In passing, attention may be called to the view people commonly take as to what is done on the spur of the moment. If the action is praiseworthy, the absence of reflection, of premeditation will increase its worth, but it will diminish the guilt if the action is blameworthy.

In choice or decision we have the essence of volition. So long as the will has not given its consent, the act is only in the stage of preparation; but once the will says "yes" or "no," the volition is virtually complete, even though execution does not follow. The actual carrying out of the decision reached is but its complement. The intrinsic worth of the volition lies in the decision. To carry it out merely increases the merit or guilt of the doer. It is the undue importance attached to this last stage in the volition, at the expense of its prime mover, that is, the intention, which has given rise to such maxims as "The end justifies the means" and "That is right which works."

From the foregoing remarks, it follows that the characteristics of the will in deliberate action are the following:

Reflection, evidenced in deliberation.
Freedom, the essential element in decision.
Efficiency, which the wisdom of the race has expressed in the maxim, "Where there is a will there is a way."
Responsibility, depending upon knowledge and freedom.

The will should be carefully distinguished from reason. The two were confused by Socrates and Plato in the maxim, "Knowledge is virtue"; if a man knows what is right, they taught, he will forthwith do it; vice is the consequence of ignorance, of a defective education. Descartes and his followers are guilty of the same error when they confuse assent, an act of the intellect, and consent, an act of the free will. Undoubtedly, there is a very close relationship between reason and will. We cannot want what we do not know; the practice of virtue presupposes the knowledge of it. Reason enlightens the will which of itself is blind; it supplies the will with the best motives of action, it teaches us what is right and what is wrong. In that sense and to that extent we can say that knowledge is virtue. Knowledge of the good is one of the conditions of the practice of the good but it is not the real cause of that practice. There are millions of men who know full well what is right, who can discourse at length on its nature and yet do wrong. To identify knowledge and virtue is to lose sight of the fact that ignorance is but one of the causes of evil doing; it is to overlook passion, bad example, evil habits, lack of decision, and lack of energy in the face of the effort that the practice of right requires. It is true, however, that in the long run, through the habit of effort, the habit of conquering one's easygoing tendencies, the time may come when the mere knowledge of the right course of action will mean immediate right doing.

The will, such as we consider it here, in its restricted, higher and essentially human form, should be distinguished from instinct—the nature of which has already been explained—and from likes and dislikes. We often have to do things that we do not like, and, on the other hand, from a sense of duty, we are led to like things which we are not otherwise much disposed to do. The will should also be distinguished from desire. The will is not a predominant, absolute desire, as a certain school of philosophers teaches. Desire might be identified with tendency, inclination, since tendencies express themselves in desires, but we could hardly identify will and desire. At times, the will conquers desire; at other times, it will intensify it. If will and desire were identical they would exhibit the same characteristics and vary in the same proportion.

A brief comparison, however, while bringing out a few similarities, makes it evident that there are several essential differences between will and desire. In common, everyday language we often say, "I would like," not to express a volition, but a mere desire. Like will, desire calls for action; there is no desire that has not some influence on the will, no volition that does not imply some desire, for we cannot conceive a person willing something that is not desirable in some respect. Desire then, like the idea, the conception of what is to be done, is one of the conditions of the voluntary act. But desire is fatal. It arises in us without our asking; it is blind, lacks deliberation. The morality of a desire depends on thought and will which foster, curb, or follow it. Will is free; it is thoughtful activity. If it proceeds in the same direction as desire, the cause of the action is not desire, but the consent that the will has given and could refrain from giving. Guilt, if there is any attached to the desire, does not arise from the desire itself, but from the consent of the will which has yielded or is responsible for the awakening of the desire. Furthermore, will and desire often are in inverse ratio to each other: the stronger the will, the weaker the desire; or vice versa. Will and desire have not the same extension. Desire extends far beyond the reaches of the will; in fact it knows no bounds, reaching even into the realm of the impossible. Never so with the will. We strive after what is within our power. We may desire fair weather, but we cannot say that we will have it.

Much has been said on the paramount importance of the will, its influence upon every phase of our life. It can all be summed up in the remark that the doctrine of the good will is the very core of Christian philosophy and Christian education. "Not everyone that sayeth to Me, Lord, Lord, shall enter into the kingdom of heaven; but he that doeth the will of My Father, who is in heaven; he shall enter the kingdom of heaven." [4]

The Child's Environment

As soon as life begins, the child is literally immersed in his environment, and it is no exaggeration to say that success in his education, particularly the moral phase of it, will in a very large measure depend upon the impressions he receives from all the forces at work in his surroundings. Heredity, so much emphasized by theorists of the naturalistic school, never has, in the formation of character, an influence approaching that of the environment. Recent studies have conclusively shown, as the Christian educator knew all along, that poor heredity will not necessarily lead to a bad character and that good heredity is no guarantee of a good character. The influence of atavism may be neutralized by the influence of healthy surroundings just as a poor environment may bring to naught the influence of the best native dispositions. It is only when heredity and environment are alike, instead of working at cross purposes, that the result can be predicted with any degree of certainty, but even then, the telling factor is not heredity, but environment.

---

[4] *Matt.*, vii, 21.

All the character building forces that surround the child belong to one or the other of the following agencies: the home, the school, the Church, or economic and social agencies. First, in point of time and importance, comes the home. For the first six or seven years of his life, at a time when he is most impressionable, the child knows no other influence than that of family life. Unconsciously but surely, through the intimate contacts established in community life, through the power of example, suggestion, and imitation, the child assimilates the family philosophy of life, and he forms habits. When he enters school his personality has already been fashioned for good or evil. The influence of the family circle will, of course, continue to be felt during the period of schooling, but other influences will appear that will strengthen or weaken it. As years roll by, the environment of the child, boy, girl, and adolescent is constantly widening. Contacts are established with friends and family relations, with playmates at school, clubs, and other societies of a more or less dubious character, with public and circulating libraries, the press, the theater, and the cinema. Finally, there is the influence of the Church, mentioned last because it is smallest with the vast majority of the United States school population. It has been computed that, from the beginning of school life to the age of seventeen, close to forty-eight per cent of the time is given to sleep, meals, and otherwise caring for the body; that even making allowance for home study, hours in the library, vacation school, and gymnasium class, the school cannot claim much more than twenty per cent of ten years in the life of most children. The rest of the time is taken up by activities out of the school and home. If parents fail in their duty to supervise these activities and to provide a wholesome home atmosphere for the child, it is evident that the moral influence of the school must be of little avail.

Moral Education in the School

We have seen that the end of moral education, the good life, is the resultant of a good moral character which is essentially a matter of will training, developing the habit of acting freely, in conformity with the dictates of the moral law. We have seen, also, that the will is not only solicited by motives supplied by the intellect, reasons for or against a certain course of action, but also by feelings, like and dislikes, and instinctive tendencies. In dealing with the subject of moral education in the school, we should then consider: First, the question of habit formation; second, the incentives to right conduct; and, thirdly, moral instruction.

Habit Formation

The question of habit formation has already been treated in a general way and there remains only to make a few remarks on the application to school life of what has been said on this subject. School life is, in some respects, very similar to the larger community life, and it offers many opportunities for will training, for the formation of those habits which make for efficiency and success in the business world, in social and civic life. We shall here consider very briefly, a few of the more important of such habits, referring the reader to treatises on school and classroom management for a detailed treatment of the subject. There is, to begin with, the habit of regularity which means that attendance at school has become a governing purpose to which all else must be subordinated. Closely related to regularity is punctuality, to be on time at school morning and afternoon, meeting promptly and faithfully every school requirement. The formation of these two habits calls for persistent efforts to overcome obstacles, to resist whims and wishes, temptations to dally and loiter, which cannot fail to strengthen the young will. The habit of cleanliness—not only on one's person, but in one's thoughts, speech, and actions—has been rightly ranked next to godliness. Accuracy in thought, word, and deed is another important school habit. Involving, as it does, the constant, vigorous use of attention, it is very valuable in will training and, in some measure, is also a check on the tendency to falsehood. Of all school habits, however, there is none half as important as the great cardinal virtue of obedience, which is the very foundation of the moral order. Obedience may be secured through fear, whether of punishment or the loss of some reward; it may be dictated by the love of praise or a sensitiveness to blame. True obedience, however, is the free, cheerful subjection of the individual to lawful authority, whatever it may be, because it is the authority of the law, of the Divine Will. This brings us to a consideration of the incentives to conduct.

Incentives to Conduct

By incentive or motive is meant here anything that induces the individual to put forth effort, anything that is an impulse to action. Incentives are commonly divided into *natural* and *artificial*. Natural or higher motives of activity are the immediate, natural results of the effort put forth by the individual. Thus, skill in the use of numbers is the immediate, natural result of practice in figuring; therefore a desire for skill in figuring would be a natural incentive to the study of arithmetic. On the other hand, when there is no such immediate, natural relation between aim and activity, the incentive is said to be artificial. Thus, in the above illustration, if the learner is aiming at some prize instead of skill, he is inspired in his efforts by an artificial incentive. It cannot be denied that the latter motives, especially prizes, are efficient means of securing certain ends. But they readily lend themselves to abuse and injustice, and they may have a baneful effect upon character. They appeal to instinctive tendencies like emulation and the love of praise, which easily turn into all absorbing passions closely related to malevolent feelings. Another serious objection to the use of the prize motive is that it reaches only a few members of the class, the bright and overambitious pupils, who need least this kind of incentive; the other pupils soon discover that they stand no chance of winning, and they lose all interest in the competition. Privileges and immunities, as a rule, are better incentives to scholastic achievement and good behavior than prizes, but they too suffer from serious drawbacks—one of which is the penalizing of faithful, painstaking members of the class who lag behind the other pupils through no fault of their own. But the most serious objection to the use of privileges and immunities, as it is to the use of prizes, is that it cannot result in the building up of a strong character. Good as a means to obtain some specific end, those artificial motives of conduct should never become the rule in moral education, not only because they are, of necessity, absent from most situations in life, but also and mainly because of their utilitarian character. Natural or higher motives of conduct, on the other hand, bear an intimate relation to good conduct; they are the springs of right action all through life and therefore should be made the incentives of good behavior in the school, in order that the child may carry them with him in life. Of those incentives to right conduct, the highest and most important is evidently the sense of our duties to ourselves, to our neighbor, to society—all of them flowing from our duties to our Lord and Maker. When this sense of duty has its inspiration in the love of God, it becomes the purest, noblest, and strongest motive to right conduct.

There now remains to consider, a little more in detail, an incentive that formerly was one of the characteristics of school life everywhere, that is, the sense of fear which was appealed to, not only to secure good behavior, but also as an incentive to study. To say, as some do today with Pestalozzi, that fear has no place in school life is going from one extreme to another; as long as human nature is what it is, fear will have its place in school life as it has in the larger community life. It will act as a restraint from wrongdoing, which is the first step on the path of duty; "The fear of the Lord is the beginning of wisdom" is as true and wholesome a maxim today as it was thousands of years ago. Fear, however, is a poor incentive to intellectual activity. It may induce the child to perform the task assigned to him, but the intellectual gain that may be realized through this method will be negligible. Intellectual education should ever be a work of free will.

The question of the fear "incentive" leads us on to the related topic of punishment and its use in the school. That there is and ever will be occasion for punishment in school no one would seriously deny. The question, then, is not whether or not punishment should be used in the school, but to what purpose it should be used and what characteristics it should possess. The purpose of punishment becomes at once evident by considering the essential function of the school, which is to make children, boys and girls, morally better. There may be other purposes for punishment in civil and military life, but in the school, as in the family, it should have one purpose: to prevent wrongdoing, to secure obedience to law. Of the characteristics punishment should possess in order to be effective, the following seem to be the most important:

In the first place, there should be certainty of punishment for all infractions of the rule. Whenever transgressions are fitfully punished, would-be transgressors will take their chances and infractions will abound.

In the second place, punishment should be just, neither too great nor too light, but in due proportion to the nature of the offense and the circumstances under which it has taken place.

. In the third place, there should be, so far as possible, a natural, obvious relation between offense and punishment. This is not the place to discuss the doctrine of moral education through the discipline of natural consequences. Let it be remarked only that, with all due regard for its limitations, the method is one of the most effective in the administration of punishment.

Moral Instruction

Recent investigations have shown that, while there is a general recognition of the importance and need of moral instruction, there is also great divergence of views as to the subject matter of the course and the method to be used. In general, however, school practices in this matter belong to one or the other of the following types. In some schools the virtues are taught and studied much in the same way as history or geography, and this systematic instruction is completed by pointing out specific applications in life. In other schools instead of starting with some definitions of honesty, generosity and the like, moral instruction will start from and stress concrete experiences selected from home, school, or community life past or present, and from these illustrations deduce the principles that the child is expected to carry with him through life. Some schools identify character with civic education, while others draw a line of demarcation between the two. Whatever the method is, the purpose should be the same everywhere: to clarify in the pupils' mind the notion of right and wrong, train the moral judgment, and develop and train the sense of duty. Needless to say, the teacher should not only have a clear conception of what is to be taught and how to teach it, but a deep-rooted conviction that he is teaching the true moral code and, in so doing, is assisting in the building up of a good moral character.

Topics for Further Study

1. Discuss the concept "law."
2. Enumerate the various types of law (natural, positive, and so on), stating the essential characteristics of each.
3. Differentiate the natural law from the laws of nature.
4. Discuss the importance of the moral aim in education.
5. Contrast the respective importance of heredity and environment in moral education.
6. "The moral law is immutable." Discuss.
7. "The moral law is absolute." Discuss.
8. "The moral law is obligatory." Discuss.
9. "The moral law is autonomous." Discuss.
10. Show, with illustrations, the importance of imitation in the transmission of types of culture.
11. Show, with illustrations, the importance of imitation in the transmission of types of education.

12. Show, with illustrations, the importance of imitation in artistic creation.

13. Show, with illustrations, the importance of imitation in literary compositions.

14. Show, with illustrations, the importance of imitation in social and political life.

15. "General versus specific habits." Discuss.

16. "The will is free." Discuss.

17. "Free will versus heredity." Discuss.

18. "Free will versus environment." Discuss.

19. "Free will versus determinism." Discuss.

20. "Free will versus fatalism." Discuss.

21. "Obedience is the great school virtue." Discuss.

22. Show the paramount importance of religion in moral education.

23. Discuss the concept "duty."

24. Discuss the concept "virtue."

25. Make a comparative study of the various methods in moral instruction.

Suggestions for Reading

Allers, R., *The Psychology of Character* (New York, 1933).

Bryant, S., *Moral and Religious Education* (New York, 1920).

Character Education, U.S. Bureau of Education Bulletin (1926).

Coe, G., *Education in Religion and Morals* (New York, 1904).

Engelman, J., *Moral Education in School and Home* (Boston, 1918).

Foerster, F., *The Art of Living* (tr.) (London, 1910).

Gillett, M., *The Education of Character* (New York, 1914).

Holmes, A., *Principles of Character Making* (Philadelphia, 1913).

Horne, H., *Psychological Principles of Education* (New York, 1906).

Jastrow, J., *Character and Temperament* (New York, 1915).

Maher, M., *Psychology* (London, 1915).

McGunn, J., *The Making of Character* (New York, 1913).

Pierce, E., *The Philosophy of Character* (Cambridge, 1924).

Ross, E., *Christian Ethics* (New York, 1924).

CHAPTER XIV

Religious Education

Its Nature and Purpose

This most important phase of general education will be treated here from the Catholic viewpoint, and the following extract may serve as an appropriate introduction to the survey.

Religious education, as we know it, is the characteristic feature of the Catholic school, but not equally clear to all of us perhaps, is the nature of this religious education. To many, if not most people, religious education means that so many hours are devoted every week to some sort of dogmatic instruction, explaining to a class, according to their intellectual capacity, the teachings of the Church on the Creator and his creatures, man's nature, his position in the universe, his origin and destiny, his duties to his Lord and Maker: . . . Instruction of this kind is and should be, of course, a part of Catholic education, because Christianity is a doctrine, or rather, a system of doctrines, that needs exposition and explanation. But Christianity is something else than an appeal to the intellect, something more vital than doctrinal subject matter calling for explanation. ⌊Christianity is first of all and most essentially, a Person and a history; . . . it is the history of the Son of Man and Son of God. Christianity, the word itself tells us that much at least—is Christ, in His Person, in His Life and teachings.⌋ The Christian is the disciple whose intelligence and will gladly surrender to Christ through faith and love, who shares abundantly in the life of his Master. And so it is that the one purpose of religious education in Catholic schools is to teach Christ, to reveal Him to the mind and heart of the child, of the boy and girl, to win them over to Him, to make of them followers of Christ. And so it is too, that religious education in the Catholic school is not, cannot be limited to a course on religious doctrines; the influence of the Christian religion should extend to every situation in school life, it should be felt in the teaching of every subject, because that religion should be the very life of the Christian.[1]

Religious Education in the Church

Religious education is, of course, first of all and essentially, a concern of the Church. She received her charter from the risen Christ.

And Jesus, coming, spoke to them, saying: "All power is given to me in Heaven and in earth.

"Going therefore, teach ye all nations; baptizing them in the name of the Father, and of the Son, and of the Holy Ghost.

"Teaching them to observe all things whatsoever I have commanded you: and behold I am with you all days, even to the consummation of the world."[2]

The better part of universal history for the last nineteen hundred years is an eloquent record of the Church's achievements in carrying out Christ's mandate, "to go and teach all nations." We enjoy today the fruitage of this age-long, never-ending mission of the Church. The best elements in our civilization are a direct contribution of Christianity, or else they are a legacy of the Greco-Roman world reaching us through the Church.

This educative mission of the Church possesses character-

---

[1] Marique, P. J., *History of Christian Education*, Vol. III, p. 249ff. Fordham University Press, New York, 1932.

[2] *Matt.*, xxviii, 18–20.

istics of its own which distinguish it from the work of other educative agencies. It is Catholic, that is, universal in the fullest, highest sense of the term. It welcomes every truth, every form of beauty and goodness from whatever quarter because all truth and beauty and goodness is from God. It transcends all limitations in time or space. The educational function of the home is limited to the members of the family; that of the ordinary schools to the rising generation; that of the state to the young of the nation. But the Church knows no such limitations; her mission is for all time and to the whole human race without any distinction as to sex, or age, or wealth, or intelligence, or learning, or nationality.

The Church carries on this Catholic, educative mission through many channels. She educates first and foremost through the example of the life of her Founder and the lives of her Saints; she educates through the administration of her Sacraments, her music, her liturgy, her buildings and their wonderful symbolism; she educates through all the activities of parish life. She educates through missions at home and abroad, in thousands of elementary and secondary schools, in colleges and universities; she educates through the decrees of her councils and through her congregations.

This educative mission of the Church is Catholic in this further sense that it embraces the whole man. School work is too often confined to the intellect. It fails to arouse the appropriate feelings, to reach the will, and therefore it is barren of any real educative influence. The Church reaches the whole man—sense, memory, imagination, feelings, intellect, and especially the will. A good will is the keynote of all her teaching as it was of the teaching of Christ, and it is particularly at this point that her education is intimately connected not only with moral training but with life and all its activities. And here, too, let us note it in passing, we have one of the most striking paradoxes in the history of Christianity. The same Church that appears to make little of this life, to be concerned only with man's happiness in the hereafter, is also concerned with all of man's activities as a source of happiness in this life.

Deserving careful study on the part of educators are the methods used by the Church in the fulfillment of her educative mission. All through her history, the Church has applied those essential principles of education presented to-day to prospective teachers as nineteenth- or twentieth-century novelties: appeal to the senses; going from the concrete to the abstract; appeal to imagination; reaching the will through intellect and feeling; using all native tendencies, particularly the imitative tendency.

Religious Education in the Home

Religious education is pre-eminently a concern of the home because, first, the home is the first and most natural educative agency; more particularly, because the home is the most effective teacher of religion. The Church and the school each has its goodly share of responsibility in religious education, but they can achieve little without home co-operation. A wholesome religious atmosphere should surround the whole family life, and the home should provide some degree of religious instruction. The formal, systematic teaching of religion belongs to the Church, but she expects the hearty coöperation of parents, more especially of the mother, not only because the father is removed from the family circle for the greater part of the day, but also because the mother's ways and knowledge of her children are best suited to this kind of instruction. With a keener insight into the intellectual capacity of her children, she knows best how to adapt the teaching of each religious truth to the understanding of the child.

In this way, in the "school of the mother's knee," the child will learn how to pray and be acquainted with the most essential religious truths. Of great assistance to parents in religious instruction will be appropriate religious literature: illustrated catechism, Bible history, Church history and lives of the Saints, religious magazines, periodicals and newspapers. Religious education, however, would be a failure if it stopped there because the essence of religion is not knowledge, but love of God, love of our neighbor translated into good works for the love of God. Religious instruction, then, should lead to religious deeds: visiting the sick, helping the needy, defending the weak, contributing in some way or other to the missions, practicing self-denial and self-sacrifice.

Religious Education in the School

Religious education is a concern of the school. On this point there used to be universal agreement before the nineteenth century, but the last 150 years have witnessed the gradual elimination of religion from the state schools of many lands. The Catholic Church, on the other hand, has ever considered religion, and she considers it today, as the very core of the whole educational content, and because of this conviction she insists upon the maintenance of a distinctly Catholic school system whenever religion is excluded from the public school. Typical of her position in this matter is the legislation of the Third Plenary Council of Baltimore in 1884.

1. Near each church, a parochial school, if it does not yet exist, is to be erected within two years from the promulgation of this Council and is to be maintained in perpetuum unless the bishop, on account of grave difficulties, judges that a postponement be allowed.

2. A priest, who, by his grave negligence, prevents the erection of a school within this time or its maintenance, or who, after repeated admonitions of the bishop does not attend to the matter, deserves removal from that church.

3. A mission or a parish which so neglects to assist a priest in erecting or maintaining a school, that by reason of this supine negligence the school is rendered impossible, should be reprehended by the bishop and, by the most efficacious and prudent means possible, induced to contribute the necessary support.

4. All Catholic parents are bound to send their children to the parochial schools, unless either at home or in other Catholic schools they may sufficiently and evidently provide for the Christian education of their children, or unless it be lawful to send them to other schools on account of a sufficient cause, approved by the bishop, and with opportune cautions and remedies. As to what is a Catholic school, it is left to the judgment of the Ordinary to define.

The following extract from the Pastoral Letter issued by the Hierarchy of the United States in 1919 will make clearer still the Catholic conception of education in general and particularly the place and function of the school in that conception.

The Church in our country is obliged, for the sake of principle, to maintain a system of education distinct and separate from other systems. It is supported by the voluntary contributions of Catholics who, at the same time, contribute as required by law, to the maintenance of the public schools. It engages in the service of education a body of teachers who consecrate their lives to this high calling; and it prepares, without expense to the state, a considerable number of Americans to live worthily as citizens of the Republic.

Our system is based on certain convictions that grow stronger as we observe the testing of all education, not simply by calm theoretic discussion, but by the crucial experience of recent events. It should not have required the pitiless searching of war to determine the value of any theory or system, but since that rude test has been so drastically applied and with such unmistakable results, we judge it opportune to restate the principles which serve as the basis of Catholic education.

First: The right of the child to receive education and the correlative duty of providing it are established in the fact that man has a soul created by God and endowed with capacities which need to be developed, for the good of the individual and the good of society. In its highest meaning, therefore, education is a coöperation by human agencies with the Creator for the attainment of His purpose in regard to the individual who is to be educated, and in regard to the social order of which he is a member. Neither self-realization alone nor social service alone is the end of education, but rather these two in accordance with God's design, which gives to each of them its proportionate value. Hence it follows that education is essentially and inevitably a moral activity in the sense that it undertakes to satisfy certain claims through the fulfillment of certain obligations. This is true independently of the manner and means which constitute the actual process; and it remains true, whether recognized or disregarded in educational practice, whether this practice include the teaching of morality, or exclude it, or try to maintain a neutral position.

Second: Since the child is endowed with physical, intellectual and moral capacities, all these must be developed harmoniously. An education that quickens the intelligence and enriches the mind with knowledge, but fails to develop the will and direct it to the practice of virtue, may produce scholars, but it cannot produce good men. The exclusion of moral training from the educative process is more dangerous in proportion to the thoroughness with which the intellectual powers are developed, because it gives the impression that morality is of little importance, and thus sends the pupil into life with a false idea, which is not easily corrected.

Third: Since the duties we owe our Creator take precedence of all other duties, moral training must accord the first place to religion, that is, to the knowledge of God and His law, and must cultivate a spirit of obedience to His commands. The performance, sincere and complete, of religious duties, insures the fulfillment of other obligations.

Fourth: Moral and religious training is most efficacious when it is joined with instruction in other kinds of knowledge. It should so permeate these that its influence will be felt in every circumstance of life, and be strengthened as the mind advances to a fuller acquaintance with nature and a riper experience with the realities of human existence.

Fifth: An education that unites intellectual, moral and religious elements is the best training for citizenship. It inculcates a sense of responsibility, a respect for authority and a considerateness for the rights of others which are the necessary foundations of civic virtue—more necessary where, as in a democracy, the citizen, enjoying a larger freedom, has a greater obligation to govern himself. We are convinced that, as religion and morality are essential to right living and to the public welfare, both should be included in the work of education.

In order that the educative agencies may coöperate to the best effect, it is important to understand and safeguard their respective functions and rights. The office of the Church instituted by Christ is to "teach all nations," teaching them to observe whatsoever He commanded. This commission authorizes the Church to teach the truths of salvation to every human being, whether adult or child, rich or poor, private citizen or public official.

In the home with its limited sphere but intimate relations, the parent has both the right and the duty to educate his children; and he has both, not by any concession from an earthly power, but in virtue of a divine ordinance. Parenthood, because it means coöperation with God's design for the perpetuation of human kind, involves responsibility, and therefore implies a corresponding right to prepare for complete living those whom the parent brings into the world.

The school supplements and extends the educational function of the home. With its larger facilities and through the agency of teachers properly trained for the purpose, it accomplishes in a more effectual way the task of education for which the parent, as a rule, has neither the time, the means, nor the requisite qualifications. But the school cannot deprive the parent of his right nor absolve him from his duty, in the matter of educating his children. It may properly supply for certain deficiencies of the home in the way of physical training and cultivation of manners; and it must, by its discipline as well as by explicit instructions, imbue its pupils with habits of virtue. But it should not, through any of its ministrations, lead the parent to believe that having placed his children in school, he is freed from responsibility, nor should it weaken the ties which attach the child to parent and home. . . .

Since the child is a member not only of the family but also of the larger social group, his education must prepare him to fulfill his obligations to society. The community has the right to insist that those who as members share in its benefits shall possess the necessary qualifications. The school, therefore, whether private or public as regards maintenance and control, is an agency for social welfare, and as such, it bears responsibility to the whole civic body.

Topics for Further Study

1. "Man is by nature, a social religious being." Discuss.
2. "Religion encompasses the whole of human nature." Discuss.
3. Discuss the religious origins of civilization and culture.
4. "Religion alone can supply the motives which, under all circumstances, can deter from wrong doing." Discuss.
5. Discuss the intellectual value of religious instruction.
6. Discuss the influence of religion on the imagination and emotions.

7. Discuss the influence of religion on (a) taste and tact, (b) the will.

8. Discuss the educative value of Sacred Literature.

9. "Church history is the most important branch of historical science." Discuss.

10. "The little Catechism is a compendium of the Christian philosophy of life." Discuss.

11. "As a science, religion is on a par with the highest of the branches of philosophy." Discuss.

12. Discuss the historical method of presentation in religious instruction.

13. "The purpose of religious education in Christian schools is to teach Christ." Discuss.

14. Enumerate a few of the great contributions of Christianity to education, with a brief comment on each.

15. "The Medieval Cathedral has been described as a book in stone." Explain.

16. Describe the educative importance of missionary work.

17. "Religion is the core of the whole educational content." Explain.

18. What is meant by a religious atmosphere in the school?

19. Discuss the importance of the teacher's personality in religious education.

20. Discuss the educative value of any two Catholic dogmas.

21. Discuss the educative value of (a) the Sacraments, (b) the Catholic Liturgy.

22. "Education is essentially religious." Discuss.

23. "I am the Way, the Truth, and the Life." Discuss the bearing of these words on Christian education.

24. Show the relation between faith and culture.

25. Show the vital relation of religious education to every other aspect of the educative process.

Suggestions for Reading

Castiello, J., *A Humane Psychology of Education* (New York, 1936).

Coe, G., *Education in Religion and Morals* (New York, 1904).

Dupanloup, F., *De l'Education* (Paris, 1851).

Foerster, F., *Christentum und Paedagogik* (Munchen, 1930).

Horne, H., *Psychological Principles of Education* (New York, 1906).

Publications of the National Catholic Educational Association.

Shields, Th., *The Philosophy of Education* (Washington, 1917).

Spalding, J., *Education and the Higher Life* (Chicago, 1922).

Spalding, J., *Means and Ends of Education* (Chicago, 1895).

Willmann-Kirsch, *The Science of Education* (Beatty, 1921).

CHAPTER XV

The System of Education

Educative Agencies

In the process of acquiring an education, the individual is assisted by external agencies which instruct, direct, and train him. The family, his playmates, the school and the book, insofar as they contribute to intellectual or moral development and discipline, are educative agencies. In fact, any object, person or group of persons, or institution is a potential educative agency, since it may influence the individual for good or evil. Usually, however, the term is restricted to those institutions which, from their very nature, are devoted, partly at least, to education and are conditioned upon collective activity. The home is an illustration of what is commonly meant by the term educative agency because one of its functions is education, which is carried on collectively by all members of the family.

All educative agencies of whatever kind, combined into one whole, form the system of education. The core of that system is the group of institutions whose explicit function is instruction and discipline, and we shall call it the school system. The two terms, system of education and school system, are often used indiscriminately, but they should not be thought of as synonymous. The system of education includes many agencies, such as the home, the Church, the newspaper, social intercourse, travel, that do not belong to the school system.

Educative agencies may be divided into formal and informal agencies. A formal educative agency is one whose "raison d'être" is education, whereas an informal agency is one that educates only incidentally, as a sort of by-product of its activity. According to these definitions, there are, strictly speaking, only two formal educative agencies: the school, and the apprenticeship system. Education, however, both formal and informal, forms such a large part of the activity of the home, the Church, and the State, that these institutions may be classed as formal educative agencies. An exhaustive list of informal agencies is evidently out of the question because every fact or institution in our environment contributes its own share, large or small, to the shaping of our personality. The more potent of informal educative agencies today are probably social intercourse, the library, the press, the factory and the professions, the radio, the theater, literary and scientific societies, and travel.

The Home

The importance of the home as an educative agency naturally follows from its importance as a social institution. In point of time, the family has precedence over all other social groups, both in the life of the race and the life of the individual. Families there were and must have been before there could be any nation, or school, or Church; and in the natural course of events the individual is a member of the family before he is a member of any other social group. Not only is the family the oldest of all social institutions, but it is also the most essential, the basis of society. The social unit is not, as some theorists claim, the individual, since the individual owes his existence to others; nor is it the nation, or the Church, or the profession, or the school, since they all ultimately depend on the vitality of family life. Of the many causes of the fall of the Roman state, not the least one was the decline of the family, which even the vitality and purity of the young Church could not restore to its pristine vigor.

It is through the family that man legitimately receives the essential elements of his personality; in the family atmosphere, and particularly under the influence of the mother, they first grow and develop. Other agencies than the home contribute to the fashioning of our personality, but their influence is not felt until comparatively late in childhood or youth, and it is exerted only at intervals, whereas the home influence begins with life and remains unbroken for years. The Church, the school, the state, the occupation can only help in developing the potential man that the home sends to them—the potential man who is now a child or youth bearing the indelible mark of heredity and an influence that has been constant and encompassing during the most susceptible years of preadult life.

It is evident that the home can perform its social mission of "man making" only when the conditions of a normal, healthy, happy family life are satisfied. Leaving to moralists, sociologists, and social workers the task of examining the detail of those conditions, we shall confine ourselves to stating the first and most essential condition for normal family life—that the home be founded on its ancient charter: "Therefore now they are not two, but one flesh. What therefore God hath joined together, let no man put asunder." Aside from all other considerations, the breaking of the family by divorce or otherwise means the defeat of the natural purpose of home creation—the procreation and education of children. And the surest guarantee of the stability and sanctity of family life is religion, which alone will enable the two partners to go through life, its joys and sorrows, with a deep sense of their responsibility to each other, to their children, and to society.

The first stage in the long process of preparation for independent life is marked by the utter physical and mental helplessness of the child. Education during that stage is chiefly a physical process because the chief business of infancy and early childhood is physical growth, requiring an abundance of fresh air, sunlight, pure and wholesome food, play, and sleep. Nevertheless, it is also during that stage that intellectual and moral education has its beginning. The process is somewhat subconscious at first, a kind of extension of physical life into the field of the spiritual. But with the advancing years, the impressions which the child receives from home life become more conscious, more distinct, more purposeful; and these impressions have ever been depended upon as one of the main factors in social stability and social reconstruction.

Among primitive people family life is the main agency for learning the language, the manners, customs, traditions of the tribe. Among civilized peoples, where the process of education is consciously furthered by a number of agencies, home environment will also have its sway; and, for good or evil, it will be the starting point and foundation of all subsequent education. It is in the home that the child learns the mother tongue which is, next to religion, the most precious gift of one generation to the next. Language is at once the mirror of the nation's thought processes and the vehicle of its spiritual treasures. In the field of conduct, the most important factor in family life is example, because the child is naturally inclined to imitate the sayings and doings of others and, more particularly, of those it loves.

Other agencies will, in the course of time, add their own contributions to the education of the individual, but the home is and should ever remain the great educational agency. It is then to the best interests of the state, no less than those of the individual, to safeguard the stability of the home and to uphold the authority of parents. If a situation should arise, as it sometimes does, when the state must come to the assistance of children, that assistance should, whenever possible, come through the parents and not over their heads.

Everywhere before the nineteenth century, the home was not only the social but the economic unit as well. The family produced much of what it consumed, and it practiced, besides, some industry upon which its sustenance depended. The possibilities of such a home for an all-round preparation for life were evidently very great. The child grew up in constant contact with the elder members of the family, and in their company received much valuable instruction on practical life. Home life provided an abundance of little tasks well suited to the child's strength and calling for ingenuity, resourcefulness, and perseverance. There was no make-believe in this childwork such as there is bound to be in present day school shop or school garden work. The child knew that he was actually contributing his own share to the family welfare, and his interest in the work was genuine. Besides, the responsibility placed upon him could not fail to strengthen his will and develop his character. Nor should we forget the deep and lasting influence upon the child of the thoroughly religious atmosphere in which he grew in and out of home. Under those circumstances, the school could very well confine itself to formal instruction in religion and the elementary school arts.

The industrial home is today a thing of the past, though agriculture and in some places a few trades are still taught in the home. The industrial revolution of the last 150 years has substituted factory for home production, taking away from the home the elder members of the family for the greater part of the day. In the city home, at least, there is today very little manual work for Johnny to do, though there may be a trifle more for his sister. The splendid sensory motor training and first hand acquaintance with the realities of life which the child acquired in the home have gone with the passing of the industrial home, and they have left in elementary education a great gap which the school is today doing its best to fill.

The home is no longer the economic unit, but it is still the social unit. It still retains its function of social reconstruction through engendering, rearing, and education; and, being free from the processes of industrial life, it can devote its energies to securing a higher intellectual, moral, and religious life. In the pre-Industrial Revolution days, when the home industry kept all the members of the family together, the responsibility for the education of children fell equally upon husband and wife. In present economic conditions, however, when the father is removed from the family circle for the greater part of the day, the larger share of that responsibility naturally falls to the mother, and her training should fit her to meet the requirements of this new situation.

The school education of girls, therefore, should have as one of its aims the development of the future mother and homemaker. Training in the domestic arts is only a minor part of this preparation. The future mother should be a woman of wide intellectual and aesthetic interests in order that she may always preserve a degree of culture and refinement in the home; she must be acquainted with the social and economic conditions of her environment in order to understand the cares and hardships of the family breadwinner, to assist her children in the wise selection of their vocation and the avoidance of the pitfalls they are sure to meet along their path in life; she must obviously be familiar with the essentials of child anatomy, physiology, and psychology but, above all else, she must be the guardian of the purity of the family life and the sacred fire of religion. The father, of course, has his own share of responsibility in the education of his children; but, being less in the home than the mother, his task is mainly one of supervision, of advice and support, his higher authority asserting itself only when there is danger that the maternal sentiment will have the better of reason.

The School

The origins of the school have been traced by anthropologists to those rites of primitive life which they call "puberty rites" or "initiation ceremonies" because they took place at the time when the boys of the tribe, upon reaching the period of adolescence, were initiated into full community membership. From their elders the boys then received instruction in the lore of the tribe, its religious ceremonies, its traditions and customs, their obligations and responsibilities as members of the tribe. A corresponding "initiation" for girls took place under the direction of the older women of the tribe. Those "initiation rites" and the instruction that

went with them formed the theoretical or "school" education of the savage. It contained, though in a very rudimentary form, the essential elements of any school: a teacher,
pupils, and a body of knowledge to be imparted. Practical
education was received in the family circle, as it has been
ever since, everywhere, until very recent times.

In the early stage of primitive life the same person was at
once head of the family, teacher, and priest; but, as life
reached a higher plane and became more complex, the need
was felt for a specialization of offices. The father, as head
of the family, remained responsible for the practical education of the child and the performance of all religious rites
connected with the hearth, but the more special, higher
functions of teacher and priest passed onto a special class.
Such is in substance the "anthropological" account of the
prehistoric school, surmised by "analogy" from the practices
of present-day primitive races.

What history tells us on this question of the origin of the
school is both plain and most significant. In all civilizations, intellectual aesthetic education starts off by being a
preparation for divine cult and a better knowledge of things
divine, that is, of God. Thus it appears in the civilizations
of the ancient East, in ancient India, Babylonia, Persia,
Egypt, Phoenicia, and Palestine. The educational systems
of those countries, though not identical, had in common the
following features.

The sacred literature of the nation had been committed to
writing and had become the chief, if not the sole, element in
the content of higher education; and the mastery of the arts
of reading and writing was then, of necessity, as it is today,
the first prerequisite for a higher education. Teachers
usually belonged to the priestly class, who thus controlled

not only education but, to some extent, the government of the nation. The masses received their practical education in the home or through some kind of apprenticeship system; they might be admitted into the elementary schools, but a higher education was the privilege of the upper classes. Strict adherence to the past, to the ways of doing things by their forebears, was the rule in all school work as it was in political, social, and economic life. Memory training, not independent thinking, was the aim of instruction, and correct acting, not right doing, was the purpose of moral education. In some respects, however, Chinese, Chaldean, Egyptian, and Jewish education departed from those general characteristics. In China, at least in theory, the higher schools were open to all and the control of education, as well as that of the government, was in the hands of a bureaucracy recruited through a system of examinations; but the length and consequent onerousness of the period of preparation made it prohibitive for the masses. In Egypt and Chaldea the content of education included, in addition to sacred literature, an important scientific element.

Among the Jews education was from the very beginning essentially moral and religious, and the family was its center. It was the duty of the parents to instruct their children in the history of the nation and the law, and to train them in the practice of some useful art. Formal schooling appears for the first time in Jewish history with the schools of the Prophets founded by Samuel, but the beginning of a national school system really dates from the establishment of the synagogues after the Babylonian captivity. There were gradually established both elementary schools in which were taught the arts of reading, writing, and arithmetic, and higher schools for a deeper study of the law and national literature. The essential feature of Jewish education, wherein lay its most characteristic difference from other types of Oriental education, was its emphasis upon the value of religious and moral personality. Each individual was taught that he was, like the whole nation, the object of the loving care of the Lord.

It is in ancient Greece that for the first time in history we come across the term *school* as well as the first type of Western schools. The word itself, which today means an institution for collective formal education, originally expressed the very opposite of its present day connotation; it signified not work but leisure, a time free from employment. Then, quite naturally, the word came to mean a time for free intellectual occupation which, of course, conveyed the concept of an exchange of ideas. Still later on, leisure came to be thought of as a time or gathering for the treatment of intellectual matters, either informally as in social intercourse or formally as in the process of actual teaching and learning.

Thus, quite naturally, the term *school (schole, schola)*, came to be used in the course of time to designate the places, in the neighborhood of some gymnasium, where the sons of the well-to-do gathered around some philosopher. By a further, natural extension of its meaning, the word *school* was applied to a lecture or class period—in general, to any place or time devoted to mental activity, to the service of the Muses. In the language of the early Church the term meant primarily religious instruction. It was in that sense that a Council of Constantinople decreed in 681 that parish priests should establish schools in towns and cities. The monasteries were sometimes referred to as *scholae Christi* besides being called *gymnasia* or places of spiritual exercise aiming at Christian perfection. In medieval times we see the term *school* applied to those who respond to the prayers of the priest, to their preparation in *scholae cantorum,* to guilds, whose full-fledged members were called "masters," to a series of university lectures. Thus gradually the word assumed its modern meaning as an institution of learning.

Ancient Greece shows us two distinct types of education, the Spartan and the Athenian. We are concerned here only with the second, since the school, in our sense of the term, never was an important educational agency in the first. Schools in Athens differed from modern schools in several ways. They were private institutions, preparing the sons of well-to-do citizens for the life of men of leisure. Once he had mastered the arts of reading, writing, and computation in the school of the grammatist, the boy attended simultaneously two other institutions. To the music teacher he went for instruction in music and literature, to the palestra for physical education. His secondary school education came to an end by the time he reached the age of sixteen, when his formal education as a prospective citizen began under closer state supervision.

In the fifth and following centuries B.C., there appeared in Greece new school subjects growing out of the work of the early Greek philosophers—Thales and Pythagoras, among others, the Sophists, Socrates, Plato, Aristotle, Isocrates, and the scientists and scholars of the Alexandrian period. Thus, gradually grammar, rhetoric, dialectic, and mathematics, together with other sciences, and philosophy found their way into the school curriculum. It was also during that period that school education in Greece became differentiated sharply into elementary, secondary, and higher. Elementary education was limited to instruction in reading, writing, and reckoning. Secondary education included instruction in music, grammar, literature, drawing, and a smattering of science; higher education was devoted to the study of rhetoric, science, and philosophy.

In the fifth and fourth centuries before the Christian era Athens was the undisputed center of Greek culture and education, but with the spread of Hellenism following Alexander's conquest rival centers arose in the East, particularly at Alexandria, which could boast of the largest library in ancient times and a "university" that, of all such ancient institutions, came nearest to the modern conception of a university as a research center. It was also in Alexandria that the course of study known in medieval times as the seven liberal arts was first elaborated; in Alexandria, too, the first Christian institution of higher learning, the catechetical school, was established.

In Rome the school did not appear until the fifth century B.C. and even then, as its name (*ludus,* play) would suggest, it was not an essential part of the Roman educational system. By the beginning of the first century B.C., however, Rome had adopted and made its own the Greek school system.

When dealing with early Christian education it is well to bear in mind that once it had left Palestine, Christianity found itself in a thoroughly pagan, if highly cultured, society. There were schools aplenty in the Roman Empire but their spirit, aim, course of study were in many respects a challenge to everything held dear by the Christian. If Christianity were to hold its conquests and make new ones, it was necessary to establish Christian schools.

The earliest Christian schools are usually referred to as *catechumenal,* because they were established to instruct the catechumens or candidates for baptism in the doctrines of the Church. Parish schools for the teaching of reading, writing, and the singing of psalms also appeared at an early date and soon became quite common in East and West. Higher Christian education gradually evolved from the catechumenal school when the study of language, literature, science, and philosophy was made a preparation for a more advanced study of the doctrines of Christianity. The institutions where this higher instruction was given were known first as catechetical and later as episcopal, cathedral, or bishop's schools.

The social reconstruction of the West after the barbarian invasions was, in the main, the work of the Catholic Church; and one of her chief agencies was the splendid educational system that grew under her tutelage from the sixth to the fourteenth centuries. Beginning with a few monastic schools, by the close of the middle ages in the fourteenth century the system had developed into a vast network of educational institutions covering the whole of Europe, with the exception only of Russia and some of the Balkan states. At that time there were scattered all through Europe no less than forty-five universities and thousands of elementary and secondary schools of various names and origins. The boy who looked forward to a full academic career would learn the rudiments of Latin at some local school; he would then repair to a secondary school where he would take up the study of the liberal arts.

The full arts course, however, was seldom offered in a secondary school in the fourteenth century; usually, after he had gained sufficient proficiency in Latin, the student had to enter a university where he would matriculate in the faculty of arts and, in due course of time, would be prepared to register as a regular student in theology, law, or medicine.

The language of the schools was, of course, Latin, but here and there in the larger cities there were already appearing vernacular or semi-vernacular schools established for business purposes. There was no compulsory school attendance law, but all the institutions were open to everyone; in fact, again and again in medieval history we come across the names of the sons of poor peasants or poor artisans who had risen to the highest positions in Church or State, thanks to the education they had received. All schools were either directly or indirectly supported and supervised by the Church, and their history shows us a perfect agreement between Church and civil authorities in matters of education. This remarkable school system was a part, and not a minor one, of the rich legacy of the Middle Ages to modern times.

The Renaissance of the fourteenth and fifteenth centuries had very little, if any, influence on the elementary schools, but it was responsible for some important changes in secondary and higher education. Chairs of rhetoric and literature took their place in the university faculty of arts by the side of the old foundations. The intensive study of the classics was substituted for that of formal grammar in the schools below the university. The medieval liberal arts course, with philosophy as a capstone leading to the degree of master or licentiate in arts, gradually ceased to be the common superstructure of a liberal education. In its place there was established a course of study including some religious instruction, much Latin, less Greek, and sometimes a little mathematics. With the completion of this course, the school life of most young men came to an end. Those who wished to prepare for the professions had first to complete the arts course at some university, then matriculate in one of the higher faculties. The most conspicuous exception to this arrangement was the Jesuit secondary school course of studies which, whenever offered in full, included language and literature, science and philosophy. Everywhere, however, the ability to use classical Latin in speech and writing became and remained for centuries the touchstone of a gentleman's education.

The religious revolution of the sixteenth century opened the way for three modern innovations in school curricula and administration: state control, compulsory elementary education, and a more widespread use of the vernacular in the schools. The Church property, upon which the maintenance of most schools depended, was confiscated by the State in all lands adopting the Reformation. If schools were to continue their work, funds must be supplied by the State or local community, and civil support evidently carried with it civil control of the schools. In point of fact, however, what actually took place at first was a kind of joint control by the civil and ecclesiastical authorities, and it was only gradually that this control of the schools entirely passed to the former. Compulsory elementary school education, with the teaching of the national religious tenets as one of its purposes, was a matter of necessity for any sect, if it would retain its hold upon its members. As to the use of the vernacular in the elementary school, it logically followed from the Protestant appeal to private judgment in matters of religion, that the individual must work out his own salvation through a free interpretation of the Scriptures. Appeal to the Scriptures evidently implies the ability to read, but since there could be no question for the masses of reading the Bible in Latin, Greek, or Hebrew, they must be taught the art of reading in the vernacular.

As a consequence of the early scientific movement of the

sixteenth and seventeenth centuries, there appeared a number of new sciences: algebra, trigonometry, analytic geometry, and the calculus, which gradually found their way into the schools. The same movement was also partly responsible for the foundation of two new types of schools, the academy, and the real school (*Realschule*) in which there was much stressing of knowledge, especially of a scientific character, as a preparation for the business of life. It was also during this period that the modern languages, more particularly the vernacular, began to appear in the school curriculum. In Protestant countries this innovation, as we have just seen, arose chiefly from the Reformation. In Catholic countries the Jesuits were the pioneers of the movement in secondary education, as were the Brothers of the Christian Schools in elementary education.

The history of the school in the last 150 years is one of far-reaching changes affecting the spirit, scope, and technique of its work; its relations to the Church, the State, and society; and the preparation and social status of the teacher. These changes were the consequence in the field of education of the three great eighteenth-century revolutions: the Enlightenment, the political, and the industrial revolutions. To the Enlightenment must be traced, among other educational changes, what is called today non-sectarian education, that is, the elimination of religion from the school. The political and industrial revolutions broke down the historical barriers between the social classes—the political revolution, by displacing political power from a privileged hereditary class to the masses, and the industrial revolution, by displacing the seat of economic power from land ownership to trade and industry.

Both revolutions had a deep and far-reaching influence

upon the schools. Secondary and higher education, which in the centuries following the Renaissance had become a sort of privilege of the upper classes, is now, in theory at least, open to all. To meet the demands of the applications of scientific discoveries to domestic and industrial life, new subjects were introduced into the curriculum, technical schools of every description were founded, and departments of scientific research established at the universities. Elementary school education was made compulsory because the school, it was believed, is the only institution that can give the minimum of education required in a democratic, scientific society. Schools were placed everywhere partially, if not entirely, under government control because the State saw in the supervision of education one of the best means of social control.

Teacher Training

The preparation of prospective teachers in professional institutions is of comparatively recent origin. In earlier times the candidate for the teaching profession would receive his preparation in the common elementary or secondary or higher institutions. Aside from the moral and sometimes religious qualification, the common standard for judging the teacher's fitness was his knowledge of the subject or subjects to be taught, with the practical skill going with that knowledge. Mastery of the three "R's" was thought sufficient qualification for teaching in the elementary schools; mastery of the Latin or Greek grammar, with a good Latin or Greek writing style, would qualify one for teaching the classical languages in a secondary school. The methods of teaching were transmitted with the content of school education from generation to generation. Under the supervision of the head master and with the advice of his seniors, the young novice would teach a subject as he had seen it taught in his student days and would gradually develop his particular technique along traditional lines.

The first normal schools, though not appearing under that name, date from the sixteenth century. They were the new Catholic congregations of men and women devoted to teaching, some in secondary schools or higher institutions, most of them in elementary schools. More than a score of those teaching congregations had been established before the close of the seventeenth century, every one of them an institution for the preparation of teachers or, let us say rather, educators in the best sense of the term.

To St. Jean Baptiste de LaSalle belongs the honor of founding, in 1684, the first normal school for lay teachers in elementary schools. In 1697 August H. Francke founded a similar institution at Halle, the first one of its kind in Protestant Germany. A few other normal schools were founded during the eighteenth century in both Prussia and the other German states. A normal school was established in Denmark in 1789, and the National Convention in France decreed the foundation of a Superior Normal School, which was reorganized by Napoleon a few years later. On the whole, however, the elementary school teacher training movement was contemporary with, and the consequence of, the spread of Pestalozzianism in the first decades of the nineteenth century.

Pestalozzian instruction called for a serious preparation of the prospective teacher: he must possess an extensive knowledge of the subjects to be taught; he must be able to interest the class and hold it under control; he must be able to keep in mind the essential points in the lesson, to raise questions and elicit answers in their proper sequence, thus leading the class along to the desired conclusions; in short, he must be able to stand on his own feet and teach, and that, aside from native ability, called for a serious preparation.

The first European state to take up in earnest the question of the elementary school teacher training was Prussia; by 1840 it possessed thirty-eight Teachers' Seminaries, as normal schools are commonly called by the Germans; the other German states quickly followed the lead of Prussia. In France, normal schools for the training of lay teachers were comparatively few until 1870, but after the Franco-Prussian War, their number grew rapidly; today there is a normal school for men and one for women in each one of the departments into which the country is divided for administrative purposes. In the United States the normal school idea did not make any headway worth mentioning until after 1870, though a few State normal schools had been founded before that time, the first one at Lexington, Massachusetts, in 1839.

In England, during the first decades of the nineteenth century, the only training prospective teachers received was that given by the Bell and Lancastrian Societies to their monitors, the pupils who were to assist the actual teacher in the conduct of classroom work. Later on, the country came to depend upon the pupil-teacher system, an arrangement by which promising pupils were apprenticed for a number of years to a master who agreed to give them instruction in secondary school subjects and the art of teaching, in return for their help in the classroom. A few training colleges were established to which prospective teachers might go after completing their period of apprenticeship. Further progress has been made in England in recent years chiefly as a consequence of the World War. During the last two generations the normal school movement has spread through the world and it is an integral part of the state school system in practically every civilized country.

Success in teaching, it seems to be fully realized at last, like success in any profession, is contingent upon a combination of at least three factors: natural talent, knowledge, and practice. The talent to teach is commonly presupposed in its students by the normal school, but because of the long course in theoretical preparation, unfitness is not detected until the teacher is actually at work in the classroom. It has been suggested that a practical test of a candidate's professional fitness be included among the requirements for admission into the normal school. Such a test would certainly reduce the number of misfits, but it would also bar from the profession candidates who might through training develop remarkable teaching ability. Besides, the natural talent for teaching is usually more or less one-sided; a teacher will show remarkable skill in the handling of a certain subject or the use of a certain method and will be merely normal or even fall under the average in the teaching of other subjects and the use of other methods. Would a practical entrance test detect every candidate's forte which might more than outweigh possible deficiency along some lines?

Efficient instruction and classroom management call for skill in the art of teaching, the result of natural talent and experience; the prospective teacher should first get the benefit of the experience of others by observing the work of trained teachers and then practice the art of teaching under the guidance of tried masters. But much more is required from the teacher than the skilfull application of the rules of his art; intelligent teaching presupposes a knowledge of the laws and principles upon which the art of teaching ultimately rest; and in the process of teacher training, theory and practice should be closely related and supplement each other.

Besides this knowledge, theoretical and practical, of methodology which is the technical part of his professional training, the teacher should be acquainted with the system of education in general, as well as with the special kind of school in which he intends to teach; he should know something of the system of education in the past and of its relation to other social forces; he should have a clear conception of the end of education, its agencies, its forms, its content; he should study their relation to ethics, psychology, logic, sociology. Back of this all there should be a solid academic preparation. No less than the lawyer, the physician, the engineer, in short, all who occupy positions of trust and responsibility in the community, the teacher needs breadth of culture to enrich his own life and that of those who will be committed to his charge, to be a credit to the profession, to feel at ease and exert his own due share of influence in society.

But academic preparation means much more for the teacher than breadth of culture. All teachers, including even those in the kindergarten, are concerned with instruction of some kind; they have to impart at least some of the knowledge they have acquired, and they should know much more than they have to teach. Thus, for example, a mastery of elementary school arithmetic implies some knowledge of the theory of numbers and the elements of algebra and geometry. It is not requiring too much of the elementary school teacher that he should hold the four-year high school diploma, and that high school teachers should have grad-

uated from a college of good standing. Even then it will
require on the part of teachers much diligent study in the
preparation of daily lessons before they can feel perfectly
at home in the subject they have to teach.

To all this an important element is added in the preparation of religious teachers. As novices, the members of religious congregations have to go through a period of at least
one year (often two) of spiritual preparation, through
prayer, self-control, and self-denial; and after the completion
of the noviceship not a day passes in the life of the religious
without a few hours given to spiritual exercises. Aside
from the deep influence these exercises must have upon the
character of the teacher, such work cannot fail to vitalize
what knowledge he may have acquired of psychology
through experience and book learning, and it must constantly keep before his mind the real purpose of education to
uplift the individual, to raise him above the world of sense,
to bring him nearer and nearer to his Lord and Maker.[1]

The Church and the State

Of the óther three formal educative agencies the first one,
the apprenticeship system, is today practically a thing of the
past as an agency for moral or vocational education and
therefore need not detain us here.[2] On the educative
function of the Church and the State no better nor more
authoritative statement can be made than that contained in
the Encyclical of Pope Pius XI on Christian education, extracts from which are given here.

---

[1] See Marique, P. J., *History of Christian Education*, Fordham University Press,
1932, Vol. III, pp. 257ff.

[2] See Marique, P. J., *History of Christian Education*, Vol. I; also *Catholic Encyclopedia*, article on "Guilds."

And first of all education belongs pre-eminently to the Church, by reason of a double title in the supernatural order, conferred exclusively upon her by God Himself; absolutely superior therefore to any other title in the natural order.

The first title is founded upon the express mission and supreme authority to teach given her by her Divine Founder: "All power is given to me in heaven and in earth. Going therefore, teach ye all nations, baptizing them in the name of the Father, and of the Son, and of the Holy Ghost, teaching them to observe all things whatsoever I have commanded you, and behold, I am with you all days, even to the consummation of the world." [3] Upon this magisterial office Christ conferred infallibility, together with the command to teach His doctrine. Hence the Church "was set by her Divine Author as the pillar and ground of truth, in order to teach the Divine Faith to men, and keep whole and inviolate the deposit confided to her; to direct and fashion men, in all their actions individually and socially, to purity of morals and integrity of life, in accordance with revealed doctrine." [4]

The second title is the supernatural motherhood, in virtue of which the Church, spotless spouse of Christ, generates, nurtures and educates souls in the Divine life of grace, with her Sacraments and her doctrine. With good reason then does St. Augustine maintain: "He has not God for father who refuses to have the Church as mother." [5] . . .

Therefore with full right the Church promotes letters, science, art, insofar as necessary or helpful to Christian education, in addition to her work for the salvation of souls; founding and maintaining schools and institutions adapted to every branch of learning and degree of culture. [6] Nor may even physical culture, as it is called, be considered outside the range of her maternal supervision, for the reason that it also is a means which may help or harm Christian education. . . .

Again it is the inalienable right as well as the indispensable

[3] *Matt.* xxviii, 18–20.
[4] Pius IX, Ep. *"Quum non sine,"* July 14, 1864.
[5] De Symbolo ad Catech., XIII.
[6] Cod. Jur. Can., c. 1375.

duty of the Church, to watch over the entire education of her children, in all institutions, public or private, not merely in regard to the religious instruction there given, but in regard to every other branch of learning and every regulation insofar as religion and morality are concerned.

Nor should the exercise of this right be considered undue interference, but rather maternal care on the part of the Church in protecting her children from the grave danger of all kinds of doctrinal and moral evil. Moreover, this watchfulness of the Church not merely can create no real inconvenience, but must on the contrary confer valuable assistance in the right ordering and well-being of families and of civil society; for it keeps far away from youth the moral poison which at that inexperienced and changeable age, more easily penetrates the mind and more rapidly spreads its baneful effects. For it is true, as Leo XIII has wisely pointed out, that without proper religious and moral instruction "every form of intellectual culture will be injurious; for young people not accustomed to respect God, will be unable to bear the restraint of a virtuous life, and never having learned to deny themselves anything, they will easily be incited to disturb the public order." [7] . . .

In general then it is the right and duty of the State to protect, according to the rules of right reason and faith, the moral and religious education of youth, by removing public impediments that stand in the way.[8]

Informal Education

Over against the formal educative agencies there is the vast field of informal education, the first and never exhausted source of knowledge and discipline. Foremost among informal educative agencies is conversation. It is through this medium that the child acquires in the home his first knowledge of the native idiom and the community's outlook

---

[7] Ep. Encyc., "Nobilissima Gallorum Gens.," February 8, 1884.
[8] See Chapter II, *Nationalism*.

upon life. It is through the same medium that he comes to learn much that is good or bad from his playmates, and all through life conversation remains an important means of increasing one's store of knowledge and source of inspiration for intellectual and moral improvement.

Conversation is the basis of the dialogue and epistolary style and it is one of the essential elements in dramatic literature. Among the ancient Greeks the free exchange of views through conversation on questions of literature, art, and philosophy was an integral part of their symposia and the practice was revived during the Renaissance. "If we are to take the writers of dialogue literally," says Burckhardt, "the loftiest problems of human existence were not excluded from the conversation of thinking men, and the product of noble thoughts was not, as was commonly the case in the North, the work of solitude but of society." [9]

More than one of our modern academies owes its origin to one of the learned circles. The French Academy, for instance, began as a private literary club which Cardinal Richelieu transformed into a national institution. The vogue of the modern counterpart of the Greek symposium reached its height with the eighteenth century French salons which became centers of "philosophical" propaganda for the leaders of the Enlightenment. "Philosophical inquiry was the centre of interest in the salon, and all that met there wished to arrive, by means of public and many sided discussion, at clear views. Moral and aesthetical questions were always popular but in the early fifties, philosophy commanded the greatest interest, and in the sixties, this gave way

---

[9] Burckhardt, J. J., *The Civilization of the Renaissance in Italy*, S. J. C. Middlemore, London, 1898, p. 383.

to political economy and in the seventies, to questions of government." [10]

Conversation and social intercourse at once suggest traveling as another educational agency. Its educative value has ever been recognized. Among the ancient Greeks and Romans it was a common practice to travel, seeing the world as a means of completing one's education. Sometimes the practice had for its purpose to study at some famous centers of learning; thus, for instance, we read of Caesar and Cicero going to Rhodes and Athens to attend the lectures of celebrated rhetors and philosophers. During the Middle Ages the more common purpose of traveling was religious, to go and pray at the Holy Sepulchre or at the tomb of some famous Saint. The Universities were also objective points for traveling and there was for the prospective master in a craft what came to be known among the French as the "tour de France," going around the country, from city to city, for at least a year in order to become acquainted with all the secrets of one's handicraft. The ancient practice of traveling as an integral part of one's education became a fashion with the Renaissance, though some educators of the times, as for instance Ascham, were strongly opposed to it on moral grounds.

Architecture, sculpture, painting, music, poetry and particularly the drama are educative for both young and old. They formed a potent educative agency in the ancient Greek city states and they have ever been one in Christian education. The Church has called into her service all the fine arts, not only to enhance the beauty and dignity of her ritual and thus increase its educative influence, but also to convey her teach-

---

[10] Rosenkranz, J., *Diderot* II, p. 83. Cf. Willmann-Kirsch, *op. cit.*, Vol. I, p. 302.

ings to the unlettered. "What the book does for the reader,"
says Gregory the Great, "that the picture does for the unlettered, for in the picture they can see what they are to do,
and from the picture they read what they cannot read from
books." [11]

The educative influence of the fine arts is felt mostly in our
leisure hours, but in the routine of our daily life we come
across the thousand and one things with which industry has
surrounded us and which cannot fail to prove of educative
value if carefully examined. Important today as sources of
informal education are the museums and the libraries, but
the most important for good or evil are probably the novel,
the newspaper, the radio, and the motion pictures.

Informal education possesses obvious advantages over
formal, regular education. Its process is more spontaneous,
more elastic, and it is richer in opportunities for self-development along some specific line. Those opportunities, however, will avail only the highly gifted few who have "eyes
to see and ears to hear," with a will to conquer besides. But
even those privileged few cannot expect to reap the full
benefits of their informal education without the discipline
of a complete, regular course of studies. For the vast
majority of average men and women who lack any strong
particular incentives and the capacity to forge ahead unaided,
informal education will remain what it has ever been: a
sort of supplement to the formal, regular educative process.

Topics for Further Study

1. Discuss the educative value of the press.
2. Discuss the educative value of the library.
3. Discuss the educative value of the motion picture.

---

[11] Gregory, M., Ep. ix, 9.

4. Discuss the educative value of the radio.

5. Discuss the educative value of travel.

6. Discuss the indebtedness to the past of our system of education.

7. Discuss the relation of educational progress to tradition.

8. Discuss the relative importance of method and ideal in any system of education.

9. State and comment on the danger of specialization in the science of education.

10. State and comment on the consequences for education of too much reliance on book learning.

11. State and criticize the biological conception of education.

12. State and comment on what you consider the proper psychological knowledge in a teacher.

13. Show the psychological value of the religious teacher's spiritual life.

14. State and comment on what you consider the minimum professional preparation for the prospective elementary school teacher.

15. State and comment on what you consider the minimum professional preparation for the prospective high school teacher.

16. State and comment on what you consider the minimum professional preparation for the prospective college teacher.

17. Selecting any ancient educational system, state and comment on its relation to national ideals in life and culture.

18. Selecting any modern educational system, state and comment on its relation to national ideals in life and culture.

19. Show the importance of a knowledge of history as a prerequisite for the study of educational science.

20. Show the importance of philosophy as a prerequisite for the study of educational science.

Suggestions for Reading

De Hovre, F., *Le Catholicisme, ses Pédagogues, sa Pédagogie* (Bruxelles, 1930).

Demiashkevich, M., *An Introduction to the Philosophy of Education* (New York, 1935).

Foerster, F., *Christentum und Paedagogik* (Munchen, 1920).

Marique, P., *History of Christian Education,* Vol. III (New York, 1932).

Martin, E., *The Meaning of a Liberal Education* (New York, 1926).

Pius XI, *Encyclical on the Christian Education of Youth* (tr.) (New York, 1930).

Rusk, R., *The Philosophical Bases of Education* (Boston, 1928).

Shields, Th., *Philosophy of Education* (Washington, 1917).

Spalding, J., *Education and the Higher Life* (Chicago, 1928).

Willmann-Kirsch, *The Science of Education* (Beatty, 1921).

Index